W.C. FIELDS

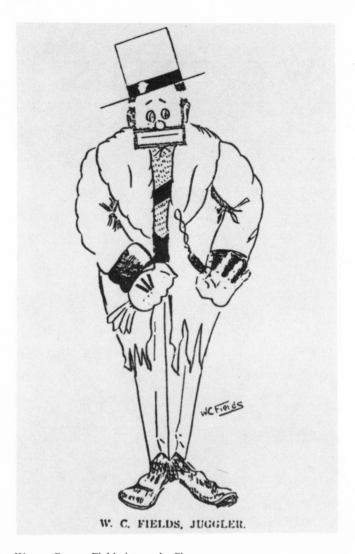

W. C. FIELDS, JUGGLER.

W.——C.—— Fields is rough, Sir;
Old Bill is tough, but he's slick, Sir;
Slick is Bill.
As the Prince of Wales said when he shook my hand,
"Fields is rough, and he's tough,
But he's dev-ilish slick."

With Apologies to Joe Bagstock

A W.C. Fields self-caricature and poem which originally appeared in a December 1907 issue of *Variety*. Fields's art work/advertising frequently was showcased in various publications during his early career. (From the author's collection.)

W.C. FIELDS,
A Bio-Bibliography

Wes D. Gehring

ADULT
92
Fields
(W.C.)

Popular Culture Bio-Bibliographies

Greenwood Press
Westport, Connecticut • London, England

Acknowledgments

The frontispiece and all stills, with the exception of Fig. 3, were provided by the Museum of Modern Art/Film Stills Archive and the author's own collection. Fig. 3 came courtesy of the Metro-Goldwyn-Mayer Corporation. The Charles Bruno caricatures (Figs. 4, 8, 9) originally appeared in Charles Darnton's November 1937 *Screen Book Magazine* article, "Mr. Fields Wins By a NOSE!" Paul Montgomery's group caricature (Fig. 5) was drawn for this book. The *W.C. Fields* cartoon strip (Fig. 7) came courtesy of the *Los Angeles Times* Syndicate. All art work, except Montgomery's, was photographed for reproduction in this volume by Frank Foster.

Library of Congress Cataloging in Publication Data

Gehring, Wes D.
  W.C. Fields, a bio-bibliography.

  (Popular culture bio-bibliographies, ISSN 0193-6891)
  Bibliography: p.
  Filmography: p.
  Discography: p.
  Includes Index.
  1. Fields, W. C., 1879-1946. 2. Fields, W. C.,
1879-1946—Bibliography. 3. Comedians—United States—
Biography. 4. Moving-picture actors and actresses—
United States—Biography. I. Title. II. Series.
PN2287.F45G43 1984   791.43'028'0924 [B] 84-4454
ISBN 0-313-23875-8 (lib. bdg.)

Library of Congress Catalog Card Number: 84-4454
ISBN: 0-313-23875-8
ISSN: 0193-6891

First published in 1984

Greenwood Press
A division of Congressional Information Service, Inc.
88 Post Road West
Westport, Connecticut 06881

Printed in the United States of America

10 9 8 7 6 5 4 3 2 1

To Eileen and Sarah and my
grandparents, the McIntyres
and the Gehrings

IN MEMORY OF
CUTHBERT J. TWILLIE
by
Wes D. Gehring

In an era that gave us little
Shirley, Asta, and Toto, too,
Fields inspired the claim that
Anyone who disliked children
And dogs couldn't be all bad.

While Capra celebrated small-town
America Fields was busy deflating
Big wheels on Main Street,
Making W.C. a red-nosed hero
To all blue-nose victims.

And as if to protect himself during
Such "blasphemous" undertakings he
Covered his tracks with such calling
Cards as—Egbert Sousé, Larson E.
Whipsnade, and Cuthbert J. Twillie.

His humor was often huckster,
As was the Fields motto that
Eventually graced one of his films—
Never Give A Sucker An Even Break,
A fitting refrain for a Scrooge fan.

And while his con-man cracks were
Always timely, his comedy costume
Was often 19th century camp, from
An eleven-gallon stovepipe hat, to a
Cutaway coat and cane—the perfect
    wolf in gentleman's clothing.

Like *Little Chickadee* co-star Mae West,
Who also gave herself to period costume,
He was the master of the double entendre,
But unlike Mae, it was not limited to
Sexual parody (Godfrey Daniel, no).

His comedy reflections, whether double
Entendres, or double takes, were always
Double-cross attacks on the pestilence

Of day-to-day living, from *Twilight
Zone* landladies to food broadcasting kids.

Fields was an everyman cynic for a
Depression age, and he's been treating
Various forms of depression ever since,
Though, unlike Chaplin's tramp, he
Was never romantic about anything,
   save maybe his liquor.

CONTENTS

ILLUSTRATIONS

PREFACE

The goal of this work is to present a combined biographical, critical, and bibliographical estimate of the life and times of W.C. Fields in the areas of cinema and the popular arts. Consequently, the book is divided into five chapters. Chapter 1 is a biography of Fields which examines both his on-screen personae and the man behind the screen—two worlds whose line of demarcation is often more than merely fuzzy. However, three key reasons make the emphasis of Chapter 1 Fields's career and his growth as a performer. First, from the beginning he put his career ahead of everything else. Second, what private life he had was recycled frequently in his comedy sketches. And third, because Fields's career began so early (in his teens) and often necessitated constant travel, much of a traditional life-style was both sacrificed and minimally documented.

Chapter 2 is a critique of the impact of his career upon American comedy and American popular culture in general. To understand Fields's ongoing influence adequately, it is necessary to examine his work—and the Fields-as-icon phenomenon which accompanies it—in relation to important literary figures of the past (particularly Falstaff), the development of the American comic antihero, and the movement literary criticism calls "the revolt from the village."

Because no examination of an artist would be complete without including some of his own observations, Chapter 3 is composed of excerpted reprintings from six interview/articles with the comedian: Sara Redway's "W.C. FIELDS Pleads for Rough HUMOR" (1925), Ruth Waterbury's "The Old Army Game" (1925), Helen Hanemann's "He Hated Alarm-Clocks" (1926), Jack Grant's "THAT NOSE of W.C. Fields" (1935), Maude Cheatham's "Juggler of Laughs" (1935, reprinted in its entirety), and James Reid's "Nobody's Dummy" (1937). These particular interview/articles were chosen because they richly showcase many basic characteristics of Fields and the world around him and because they cover a time span which encompasses most of his film career.

Chapter 4 is a Fields bibliographic essay that assesses key published reference materials and locates research collections open to the student and/or scholar. The majority of the chapter is allocated to reference works and is divided into two sections. The first is devoted to book-length sources written about and/or by Fields. These materials are then subdivided into four categories: Fields viewed by insiders, Fields on Fields, Fields critical biographies, and Fields references. The second section of Chapter 4 is comprised of shorter works and includes articles, interviews, book chapters, and monographs. It is subdivided into three parts: Fields critical film analysis, Fields on Fields, and Fields's world view. To facilitate the use of both sections as a reference guide, Chapter 5 is a bibliographic checklist of all sources recommended in Chapter 4, as well as of copyrighted writing (primarily stage routines—several of which were later adapted, at least in part, for the screen). The checklist is meant to be a research guide, not an all-encompassing bibliography on the comedian (although it is more detailed than any other such listing encountered in the preparation of this book).

The pivotal research collections examined in Chapter 4 are found in the Library of Congress (particularly the Manuscript Division; the Motion Picture, Broadcasting and Recorded Sound Division; the Copyright Office; the Library Reading Room; and the Harry Houdini Collection) and the New York Public Library system, especially the Lincoln Center branch which houses the Billy Rose Theatre Collection.

The appendices contain a chronological biography, a filmography, and a discography.

As any student of comedy would assume, writing this book has been a special joy, especially for an author whose earliest film comedy memory (by way of a 1950s television set) is that of Fields, as the always resourceful Professor Eustace McGargle, selling a talking dog in *Poppy* (1936).

Few books, however, are solely the result of one person, and special thank-yous are in order for a number of individuals: Catherine M. Hensley, Library of Congress copyright certifications specialist; Emily Sieger, film reference librarian, Motion Picture Division of the Library of Congress; Elizabeth Burdick, reference librarian, International Theatre Institute of the United States (New York City); Dorothy L. Swerdlove, curator, the Billy Rose Theatre Collection; Mary Corliss, who heads the stills division of the Museum of Modern Art (New York City); and Kathleen M. Cabana, Library of Congress bibliographer, Reference and Bibliography Section.

Closer to home, additional thank-yous are in order for Janet Warrner, my typist; Veva McCoskey, interlibrary loan librarian, Ball State University Bracken Library; David Webb, a 1982-1983 Ball State Honors college senior, who provided research assistance during winter quarter; Frank Foster, Ball State assistant professor of art, who photographed several drawings for reproduction in the book; and cartoonist Paul Montgomery, who provided an original drawing.

I also wish to acknowledge the support and suggestions of friends, colleagues, and students (especially members of my recent 1930s film comedy seminar) for their contributions to this volume. And I would particularly like to recognize the support my past comedy writing has received from Professor Larry Mintz, editor of *American Humor* (University of Maryland); Professor Jacqueline Tavernia-Courbin, editor of *Thalia: Studies in Literary Humor* (University of Ottawa, Canada); Professor and Chairperson Timothy J. Lyons, Department of Cinema and Photography (Southern Illinois University at Carbondale), and Professor and Chairperson John Raeburn, Department of American Civilizations (University of Iowa).

Finally, I would like to thank both Dr. M. Thomas Inge and Greenwood Press for encouraging me to undertake the project; my department chairperson, John Kurtz, for lightening the author's teaching load while the work was being finished; and my family's patience and understanding through all the minidramas that constitute writing a book.

I hope this study represents not only further insight into the subject at hand but also one more evidence of comedy's equality with the "more serious" arts.

W.C. FIELDS

1.

W.C. FIELDS'S BIOGRAPHY

I was the oldest child. We were all very poor, but I was poor
first.[1]

— W.C. Fields on his early childhood

America's greatest native-born comedian died on Christmas Day 1946. His
most celebrated biographer described a passing away which included a wink
to those around him.[2] But his last mistress chronicled an ending with curses
on his lips.[3] In death as in life, mystery surrounds the man born William
Claude Dukenfield, who became better known to the world as W.C. Fields.

It is ironic that such an acclaimed misanthrope should die on Christmas,
a day he always claimed to hate;[4] it is equally paradoxical that he should be
born in Philadelphia, the city of brotherly love. But such was the case.

Fields was the first child born to James and Kate Dukenfield. And while
there has always been some question as to the exact date of William Claude's
birth (many texts avoid the subject), January 29, 1880, has found the widest
acceptance in recent years.

James immigrated from England to the United States before the Civil
War (in which he was wounded) and never lost his Cockney accent. Kate,
whose maiden name was Felton, was a housewife and native Philadelphian.
Fields, like comedy contemporary Charlie Chaplin, seems to have been
profoundly influenced by his mother's sense of humor. But whereas
Hannah Chaplin taught her boy mime and mimicry, Kate Dukenfield
enjoyed greeting passersby from her doorway and then zinging them with
caustic under-her-breath asides. For example, "Her front-door act would

run like this: 'How do, Mr. Flinders. You're looking mighty happy today.' (Aside to family: 'He always looks happy when he's been beating his wife.')''[5]

The apparently congenial address followed by the cutting aside is the cornerstone of Fields's comedy. In fact, years later, after Kate had seen her very successful son on Broadway, he asked her opinion of his work. Her simple reply was, "I didn't know you had such a good memory."[6]

While there seems little doubt that Mrs. Dukenfield was entertaining, Fields's childhood was decidedly not. The family was poor ("poor but dishonest" was how Fields sometimes described it)[7] and much of his time was consumed with odd jobs. The most influential was probably helping his father sell vegetables from a cart in the streets of Philadelphia. Fields's nasal drawl is sometimes said to have originated as a parody of his father's vegetable-hawking voice; his interest in unusual words was even then showcased when he was moved to announce, "Pomegranates, rutabagas, calabashes"—whether his father had the produce or not.[8] Such things did not endear him to Mr. Dukenfield, nor did the boy's propensity to bruise the produce with his early attempts at juggling. Indeed, *the* event of his childhood (one might mark it as the close of his childhood) was the result of a conflict arising from personality differences between the two. Though many variations of the event exist, the following story is at its heart.

An eleven-year-old Fields had left a small shovel in the yard. His father stepped on it, causing the handle to strike James in the shin. Young Fields found this funny, and father promptly bounced said shovel off the boy's head. Fields, no doubt one of the first proponents of the "do not get mad, get even" school of thought, considered an appropriate revenge for days. He eventually decided upon, and successfully executed, the dropping of a wooden crate on his father's head. Feeling that it would now be difficult to maintain any working rapport with Mr. Dukenfield, not to mention the inherent dangers of such one-upmanship, Fields ran away from home. And "for four years Fields was a big-city version of Huck Finn"[9]—an iconoclastic hero to his boyhood friends.

Fields himself described this latter period as a "glorious adventure," although it seems to have had initial drawbacks:

> At that time . . . we boys [the Orland Social Club—a euphemism for the gang in which Fields ran and who helped take care of him after his revolt] had dug a big hole, which we called "the bunk." It was covered with some old planks and there were a few boards on the dirt floor inside. When I fled from my father's wrath I took refuge in the bunk, sleeping there at night with only the boards as a bed. . . . As a permanent bedroom, however, the bunk had two drawbacks: it was so short that I

couldn't stretch out full length; and when it rained the water came through the cracks overhead. I would climb out in the morning, wet through and covered with mud. . . . [Eventually] I moved out and went to live at the [Orland Social] Club.[10]

For years this was the accepted story on Fields's relationship with his family. But with the publication in 1973 of *W.C. Fields by Himself: His Intended Autobiography* (a massive collection of Fields papers compiled by his grandson, Ronald J. Fields), the family has strongly contested that view because of its derogatory portrayal of the Dukenfields. Yet they offer little conflicting evidence. In fact, they even include a Fields letter which would seem to negate their own position. Written in 1938 to a boyhood friend from the Orland Social Club, it reads in part:

I have never forgotten the old days at the Orland Social Club, over Mr. Wright's wheelwright shop . . . when I slept on an improvised bed made . . . of hay. . . .

Sincerely, your old tramp friend,

Whitey

[Fields's boyhood nickname][11]

Moreover, like Chaplin, forever thankful in later years for clean sheets and a bed after the street existence of his youth, Fields was equally appreciative: "To this day, when I climb in between clean sheets, I *smile*. When I get into bed and stretch out—god damn, that's a sensation!"[12] And in his last years, mistress Carlotta Monti remembers Fields saying, "I don't want any funeral. Just cremate me. I had enough of the cold ground in my youth."[13]

There is no denying Fields later reconciled with his family (the grandson's book includes part of a 1901 interview with Fields which has him back home at fourteen; there is also evidence that later, when Fields was a famous juggler, he took his father on tour).[14] Yet it seems difficult to negate all the references to Fields being on his own at an early age. The truth, no doubt, lies somewhere in between.

At a time when even family members term the father-son relationship "strained," Fields dedicated much of his time to juggling whatever he could find.[15] But it was a difficult period—an apprenticeship in survival. In a series of *New Yorker* articles, which Fields considered the best biography of his life,[16] author Alva Johnston claimed, "The foundation for the comedian's career was laid in those days."[17] Johnston meant Fields had to do whatever was necessary, including cheating and stealing, to survive; such traits later would be pivotal to his comedy personae. *W.C. Fields by Himself: His Intended Autobiography* also includes tales of cheating (the shell game, often referred to as the old army game) and stealing.[18]

It's the Old Army Game (1926) would later be the title of a Fields film, as well as generally representing a philosophy of life for both himself and his comedy characters. Certainly the young Fields had been exposed to a number of "army games." For example, when he was a child and hay wagons came to market, it was his job to gather stray bits of hay for his father's horse. "'Of course you must not steal it,' said the father, 'but if you can grab a few hands full from the wagons it will be all right.'"[19] This same sneaky rule of thumb applied to most of his early jobs. For instance, as a pre-teen he worked in a cigar store which carried only one brand. Yet if someone asked for a more expensive cigar, he was sold the store's sole brand at an elevated price.[20] An early teenage booking as a juggler at Fortescue's Pier in Atlantic City also required that he pretend to drown when concession business was slow:

> He would get into a bathing suit, wade out till the water was neck deep, and cry for help. Saved, he would be carried to Fortescue's and rolled on a barrel. Barkers urged beer and sandwiches on the excited people who had seen the rescue and had come in to watch the resuscitation act. Fields sometimes drowned three or four times a day. . . .[21]

This latter sham frequently is said to have contributed to his dislike for water.

If these job-related bits of chicanery encouraged his later con-man image, another early position inspired him to continue his long hours of juggling practice, even after he had succeeded in vaudeville. As a teen he once worked on an ice wagon and had to rise every morning at four o'clock. Later, whenever he wanted to dodge his juggling practice, he threatened himself with "Screw back to Philadelphia and get on that ice wagon."[22] In fact, Fields also credited his early morning ice wagon phobia for generally getting him into the late-rising entertainment profession (see the appropriately titled 1926 essay, "He Hated Alarm-Clocks").[23]

Fields's hard work paid off—with more hard work! After Fortescue's Pier, he managed to join a modest New York-based road company which toured backwater America with acts and dramatic sketches, not unlike the troupe parodied in Fields's later film, *The Old-Fashioned Way* (1934). Experience was the troupers' real pay, for as Fields observed: "In that kind of company, salaries were only polite fictions."[24]

Another "polite fiction" was that the manager of the company would not leave them stranded anywhere. But in Kent, Ohio, despite the promise of forthcoming money from New York, to which the manager had returned, Fields—still only in his mid-teens—found himself stranded. In a difficult situation, he managed to obtain enough money to limp back to New York.

For a time he even worked in a cheap circus at a number of lowly positions. But any illusions he might have had of the entertainment medium which inspired James Whitcomb Riley's popular 1880s poem, "The Circus-Day Parade," quickly soured. Eventually he was back with the same agency which had launched his previous ill-fated troupe. Unfortunately, history tends to repeat itself in show business, and Fields again found himself stranded.

This time, after returning to New York, the teenager obtained booking in a dime museum—an exhibition house of performers with a ten-cent admission price. Though the acts often leaned toward the eccentric (such as a bearded lady and a fire-eater) and "it seemed as if I did my act every five minutes all through the day and half the night," he was actually getting both pay and further experience.[25] After a few months during the mid-1890s he moved to cheap vaudeville; he was now on his way:

> For a couple years after I made my start, I was dead broke
> practically all the time. Then the work and the study I had put
> into my act began to yield a better harvest.[26]

By the late 1890s Fields was playing on the prestigious Orpheum vaudeville circuit. He was saving a sizable amount of his pay, just as Chaplin later did when his career began to flouish. One is also reminded of Chaplin because Fields, nearly from the beginning, billed himself as the "Tramp Juggler."[27] To cut costume costs, he had decided upon this title and hobo attire after his first juggling engagement. The decision also allowed him to capitalize on an even-then popular figure in American vaudeville humor—the tramp. The later addition of a beard probably indicated he was not adverse to disguising his extreme youth. (Chaplin would later add a mustache to his character to quiet the qualms Mack Sennett had about his youthfulness.) In addition, the costume differentiated him from a popular contemporary juggler appearing in a tuxedo and tails.

Fields's initial act had been largely an imitation of the Byrne Brothers, the team which had inspired his career. Thus, besides other items, "he juggled five tennis balls, periodically pretending that one was getting away from him, and catching it, with comic gestures, as it flew off at an angle."[28] Because of his dedication—and his initial need to economize—Fields was able to create some extraordinary, unique routines, using some of the most unusual items. This is best exemplified by his juggling a stack of cigar boxes, which he much later preserved on film in *The Old-Fashioned Way*.

From early on he realized the comic importance of human vulnerability:

> You see, although my speciality was juggling, I used it only as a
> means to an end. I didn't just stand up and toss balls, knives,

plates, and clubs. I invented little acts, which would seem like episodes out of real life; and I used my juggling to furnish the comedy element.[29]

The comedy of human vulnerability is at the center of Fields's art. Years later he described humor as simply the exaggeration of everyday human incidents.[30] Thus the previously described routines go beyond mere juggling when they capture the audience member on an individual basis; the observer falls victim to an apparently wayward tennis ball or some independent-minded hats. Fields's routines are nothing more than early commentaries on twentieth-century man's ongoing battle with the inanimate object. His understanding of this relationship also helps explain how he later was able to move so easily from comic juggling to sketch comedy.

Fields's success was so great that by the turn of the century (fewer than ten years from his career's inception), he was a world-acclaimed performer. Press clippings and program notes all support this, but the most impressive documentation comes from the inclusion of two Fields essays in Percy Thomas Tibbles's authoritative British publication, *The Magician's Handbook: A Complete Encyclopedia of the Magic Art for Professional and Amateur Entertainers* (1901). The book's title page contains the additional description, "Including valuable contributions from those magicians who have made their names famous during the past and present centuries."[31] The Fields essays—"A New Hat and Cigar Effect" and "The Great Cigar-Box Trick"—are straightforward descriptions of two routines then used in his act. The routines required both a juggler with outstanding skill and a comedian with timing to match. Fields had truly arrived. (For a detailed examination of the essays, see "Fields on Fields," section 2 of Chapter 4.)

Fields, whose skill came from long and frequently painful hours of practice (such as catching a thrown ruler on his face and then balancing it), attained international fame by frequently taking his act abroad. There was probably a natural inclination of a formerly deprived child to see the world. Moreover, Fields, like his screen character, had a propensity for flight. In fact, he was said to have approached his first foreign tour with the relaxed "feeling that I was leaving my troubles behind."[32] But Fields also had a goal of making one thousand dollars a week.[33] And he was well aware of the monetary incentive for European bookings: he could avoid the summer declines of American vaudeville resulting from closings because of the heat (air-conditioned theaters were still years into the future). Hence Fields could work continuously by obtaining bookings outside the United States. The comedian suggests just that in a 1910 letter included in *W.C. Fields by Himself: His Intended Autobiography.*[34]

This was also a period when many of the top-paid acts playing American vaudeville were from abroad. And while the previously mentioned letter states Fields took a foreign pay cut, the general consensus was that American acts could duplicate European financial success when playing overseas. (Fields was also not hurt by the apparent absence of European comedians, an area few of these performers seemed to enter.)[35] In addition, international bookings enhanced a performer's reputation when he or she played again in this country. And Fields would strike press agent gold when he gave a command performance at Buckingham Palace (October 11, 1913) before King Edward VII and the Queen of England. No other American performer had been so honored on this particular occasion. Appearing with Fields was the great Sarah Bernhardt, who had shared the bill with Fields before.

Testimony to the charisma of Fields can be drawn from the comedian's relationship with Bernhardt. The first time they were to share billing, the actress let it be known she did not like appearing with magic and animal acts or with jugglers. Fields disappeared from the program. Yet not long after this (but well before their command performance) they did appear together. When questioned about this, Bernhardt replied that in her earlier remarks she had not been alluding to the "wonderful W.C. Fields, whom I admire and consider a rare artist."[36]

Unfortunately for Fields, his relationship with another woman was not quite laudatory. In 1900 Fields had married Harriet Hughes, a chorus girl from one of the acts appearing with him. For a time she traveled with him as an assistant, but pregnancy necessitated her retirement. William Claude Fields, Jr., was born on July 28, 1904.[37]

The natural separation from family with which all vaudevillians had to live soon became the norm. For the rest of his life Fields would support his wife and son with weekly checks, but their relationship became a permanent separation. The family attempts to suggest in *W.C. Fields by Himself: His Intended Autobiography* that Fields and Harriet's was merely a long-distance marriage. But again family members undercut their own argument (as they did when they included an aforementioned letter from Fields to a boyhood friend) by the inclusion of a number of extremely cutting letters from Fields to his estranged wife, written over a period of years. The following are excerpts from several of these letters:

> I do not want to hear how hard you are going to be pressed any more. [19??]

> You have been a lazy, bad-tempered, arguing troubling [sic] making female all your life. . . I havent [sic] one good thought or memory of you, and the very thought of an interview with you fills me with rage. [1920]

> For twenty-nine years now, I have never missed sending you an

amount of money each week plus lump sums. . . . Now what have you done in all these years outside of complacently accepting the money and writing me letters . . . [on] the high cost of living. . . . I hope to Christ the next cold I get knocks me off and then you will know what real hardship is. [1933]

Can you imagine my surprise when I read your letter and you said we had gone through life doing nothing for each other? Sixty smackers a week, year in and year out, for forty years ($124,800.00) you consider nothing. Heigh-ho-lackady. Surprises never cease. [1944][38]

These are hardly the feelings of a close relationship. Yet, like everything else in his life, they seem to have provided at least part of the inspiration for his later characterization of the henpecked American male.

Despite personal tensions, Fields's career continued to be a nonstop success. A 1903 advertisement stated that during his previous European tour he had played the Winter Garden (Berlin) twice, Folies Bergères (Paris), the Palace (London), Hippodrome (London), Orpheum (Vienna), Victoria Salon (Dresden), Theatre Varite (Prague), Palace (Manchester), and "the best houses in Birmingham, Leeds and Blackpool."[39] The same advertisement equated his success with "his constant efforts to improve his act and originate new material."[40] Thus the obsessional juggling dedication of Fields's boyhood—"Hour after hour the damned thing [juggled object] would bang against my shinbones. I'd work until tears were streaming down my face. But I kept on practicing, and bleeding, until I perfected the trick."[41]—continued unabated.

Beyond his dedication, a great deal of his international success was no doubt attributable to the pantomime base of his act. While several sources suggest his decision to go silent (he had begun to emphasize some parts of his juggling verbally) was in anticipation of lucrative foreign bookings, a 1901 interview finds Fields admitting: "You may notice that I stutter badly when I talk, and I therefore concluded that I would go through my act without saying a word."[42] However, as Fields goes on to say in the same interview, he soon realized the advantage that would give him abroad—the universality of pantomime. And though the comedian seems to have given no consideration at that time to a new medium called moving pictures, his pantomime base would eventually lead to a modestly successful *silent* comedy film career.

After years of success in big-time vaudeville, Fields's next major career move came when he was signed for the *Ziegfeld Follies* in 1914. Starting in 1915, he would be with the next seven editions of the *Follies*. (Fields also appeared in the spring and summer *Follies* of 1925). Now he would be able to showcase his talents among the greatest comedians of the day: Will Rogers, Ed Wynn, Fanny Brice, Bert Williams, and Eddie Cantor. While he still juggled, Fields had also developed through the years a number of other routines which he utilized in the *Follies*. The most famous of these, the pool routine, would be recorded on film in 1915 as the one-reel *Pool Sharks*, Fields's first movie.

Pool Sharks was quickly followed by the one-reel *His Lordship's Dilemma,* but it was a premature start to his film career. Not until 1925, when he costarred in the feature film *Sally of the Sawdust,* from the Broadway play *Poppy* (in which he also starred), was Fields's movie career established.

While the rest of the teens and the early 1920s would be dedicated to stage work (his only film appearance between *His Lordship's Dilemma* and *Sally* was a small but impressive supporting role in the 1924 feature *Janice Meredith*), *Pool Sharks* remains a fascinating first film because so much of the Fields comedy persona is already firmly established. Besides his pool table antics, variations of which would continue to appear in a number of his future films, *Pool Sharks* features everything from the patented Fields bit of trying to place his hat on his head—only to get it caught on an upturned cane—to a finale with a bottle of stolen liquor.

Fields was only thirty-five at the time of these two Gaumont films (shot in New York by a British company), but he had been performing professionally for over one-half of his life. They did not launch his film career, but *Pool Sharks* remains an invaluable entertainment time capsule of America's greatest native-born comedian; tragically, *His Lordship's Dilemma* has been lost.

Both films were made after Fields had signed with Ziegfeld, but the *Follies* producer received a great deal of positive publicity by his "gracious waiving of contractual exclusivity" to allow the comedian to try films.[43] Years later, upon hearing of the death of Ziegfeld (July 23, 1932), Fields would declare:

> Nothing or any one could compare with him. My seven years with him were the finest I ever enjoyed in the show business anywhere in the world. Ziegfeld was a wonderful man and a genius. He was a bit eccentric, but never in a mean way.[44]

The reference to Ziegfeld's eccentricity was no doubt a diplomatic comment on a man who had severely tried Fields. At best, Ziegfeld tolerated comedians for the sake of the *Follies*; he could coldly cut a Fields sketch from twenty-eight to seven minutes—the costume-changing time of his showgirls for the next scene. Yet, Fields garnered increased recognition from the *Follies,* as well as an ever-enlarging salary—always an important consideration, especially if a major personal goal is earning one thousand dollars a week. Under Ziegfeld his weekly salary would climb from two hundred dollars to several thousand.[45]

Fields's memory of Ziegfeld probably was also softened by his appreciation of the beauties the producer assembled year after year. The comedian once observed to a friend that "'the 1921 Follies was my happiest year with Ziegfeld and the best revue I ever saw in my life.'"[46] While the *New York Times* called the 1921 *Follies* the "best of them all," biographer Taylor later described them as:

> probably as naked a public spectacle as America has ever enjoyed. . . . All the reviewers mentioned the tall, ripe maidens with especial relish; the consensus was that Ziegfeld . . . had risen up in a distinguished spasm of sexuality.[47]

A popular syndicated humorist of the day, Frank "Kin" Hubbard, creator of comedy character Abe Martin, probably best summarized the respect many men, no doubt including Fields, had for Ziegfeld's greatest talent: "One don't have t' loaf around Miammy Beach very long t' appreciate what an awful time Flo Ziegfeld must have in findin' material t' glorify."[48]

Fields's Ziegfeld years were also the beginning of a time (lasting through the 1920s) when the comedian would copyright much of his stage material. Without listing everything still on file at the Library of Congress (see Chapter 5), much of his writing is immediately recognizable to the student of Fields.

There are three copyrighted variations (dated February 1919; July 12 and November 2, 1928) of the sketch "An Episode at the Dentist's"; these were the foundation for a later film, 1932's *The Dentist*. "An Espisode on the Links" (August 30, 1918) would later be translated into the short subject *The Golf Specialist* (1930), Fields's first sound film. While golfing material would frequently turn up in the comedian's longer films, the best utilization occurs in *So's Your Old Man* (1926) and its remake, *You're Telling Me* (1934).

"The Sleeping Porch" (February 6, 1925), later to be possibly his most celebrated film routine, was in the unsuccessful comedy stage revue, *The Comic Supplement*. But variations upon this routine were showcased in both *It's the Old Army Game* (1926) and the remake, *It's a Gift* (1934). "Stolen Bonds" (July 12, 1928) would later become the black comedy short subject *The Fatal Glass of Beer* (1933), a film classic not fully appreciated until years after its initial release. And "Pullman Sleeper" (February 26, 1921) would later be the premise for a train skit in *The Old-Fashioned Way* (1934) and a plane routine in *Never Give a Sucker an Even Break* (1941).

There were also a number of other key copyrighted sketches which, although not translated as closely as the previous examples, contributed to the spirit of his later films. For instance, there are three copyrighted versions of "The Family Ford" (October 16, 1919; September 3 and October 9, 1920). The sketch finds a family and friends attempting a motor outing. The occupants of the Ford are George and Mrs. Fliverton, Baby Rose Fliverton, Mrs. Fliverton's father, and friends Elsie May and Adel Smith. Predictably, the car serves as the comedy focus, from engine trouble to a flat tire. And appropriately for a skit which plays upon the victimization of twentieth-century man—frequently at the hands of machines—at one point the car "engine starts of its own accord."[49]

The sketch anticipates the attempted exit and eventual travel of the Harold Bissonette (W.C. Fields) family in *It's a Gift*. The routine's use of a blind character is also reminiscent of *It's a Gift*'s more famous inclusion of the blind hotel detective, who nearly destroys the Bissonette drugstore. And there are small bits in "The Family Ford" which appear with only slight variation in later films. For example, Elsie May drops her hat while George (Fields) is pumping up an inner tube. He pushes the hat away, but it makes a complete circle and returns exactly where it started. This is repeated several times; in each case the hat is pushed in a different direction by George. Eventually, he picks up the hat and throws it away. In *Poppy* (1936) Fields suffers from another returning hat, though he now is trying to play a small bass fiddle instead of change a tire.

Fields also focused on domestic comedy (in a more intensified fashion) in his three later copyrighted versions of "Off to the Country" (May 25 and June 29, 1921; April 3, 1922). This sketch finds Fields trying to get his family onto a busy subway train for a trip to the peace of a rural setting. The family is composed of Baby Sammy, "Sap"; daughter Ray, "Tut"; a nagging wife, Mrs. Fliverton; and Emmeline Fliverton, apparently Mr. Fliverton's (Fields's) mother. Besides the difficulty Fields's character has in directing this crew, they are weighed down by a massive collection of vacation items, including a mandolin in a case, a tennis racket, a parrot cage, a suitcase, balloons, an all-day sucker, a can of worms, folding fishing rods, a gun, various bundles, a big doll, a teddy bear, an umbrella, a ukelele in a case, a small phonograph, a baseball mask, a bat, and a hatbox.[50]

"Off to the Country" is full of missed trains, troublesome children, a bothersome wife, a surly ticket taker, a sneaky revenue officer ("Pussyfoot Anderson"), and loads of slapstick—largely due to that warehouse of props. The Flivertons never do get their trip; instead, Papa is arrested for violation of the Volstead Act—he is found to have a bottle of brandy, although it was used only "for medicinal purposes."[51] And the family follows in tears as Mr. Fliverton is dragged off to jail.

A misunderstood radio broadcast is the basis of an important routine in Fields's *Tillie and Gus* (1933). Augustus Winterbottom (Fields) is mixing paint according to instructions being dictated on the "Handy Andy" radio show, and Baby LeRoy switches the dial to an exercise program.

Still more domestic comedy is to be found in the two copyrighted versions of "10,000 People Killed" (May 29 and October 10, 1922). The sketch finds Mr. and Mrs. Shugg and their baby Oliotha around the radio. They are soon to be shocked with the statement "10,000 killed," but the radio cuts out before the rest of the facts are announced.[52] Eventually they discover it is only a commercial: "10,000 people in San Francisco killed 10,000,000 flies with the Cadula fly swatter last year. Price: 10 cents all fall."[53]

Yet "10,000 People Killed" offers more than just a misunderstood radio announcement premise for future Fields film comedy. First, it demonstrates author Fields articulating a nicely comic look at the problems and contradictions of another form of twentieth-century mechanization, the radio, and its greatest comedy victim, the male. Thus Mrs. Shugg says of the radio: "I don't know why they call it wireless. They ought to call it 'nothing but wires' and he [Mr. Shugg] doesn't know how to work it anyhow."[54]

"10,000 People Killed" also provides two delightfully bizarre comic bits on domestic middle-class life—both of which will later surface in the short film subject *The Pharmacist* (1933). In the first, a cocktail shaker is affixed to a pogo stick for mixing purposes. In the second, Baby, anticipating Sylvester the Cat by years, eats the family canary. Like Tweetie Pie, however, the bird is recovered.

Other copyrighted material of special interest with relation to Fields's future films include: "An Episode of Lawn Tennis" (October 28, 1918, a nearly all-pantomime routine which incorporates many of his juggling tricks), "The Sport Model" (May 22, 1922, examining the difficulties in both packing a small car and keeping it running), "The Caledonian Express or An American Abroad" (July 31, 1922, an American's refusal to give up a British railroad compartment reserved for a lord), and "Midget Car" (November 25, 1930).

"Midget Car," the last of his somewhat familiar copyrighted material, draws from several sources. It utilizes earlier sketches, many of which eventually would be filmed by Fields, if they had not been already. These include traveling with a large number of items, packing everything in a small car, mechanization problems, domestic frustrations, and comic use of a blind character. "Midget Car" also introduces a character name that would become very familiar to future students of Fields—Charlie Bogle. (Fields would later use the pseudonym Charles Bogle on several original film stories).

Besides these sketches, the comedian copyrighted four other properties, none of which is easily discernible as Fields material: "The Mountain Sweep Stakes" (March 21, 1919, a movie script parody of stage melodrama and silent film stars), "Just Before Dawn" (April 7, 1919, an army farce in three acts, at the time of our entry into World War I), "What a Night" (May 25, 1921, a farcical murder mystery sketch with surreal overtones), and "My School Days Are Over" (July 12, 1928, a short routine of sexual innuendo).

Of the four, "The Mountain Sweep Stakes" most merits further attention. It shows Fields to be a much more avid film fan than has been suggested previously, and it reveals very sympathetic feelings toward Chaplin
and the Tramp. First, to best demonstrate the script as an example of a
product from a 1919 student of cinema, the cast of characters must be
presented:

Jack Cass Fairbanks	An Aviator
Anna Polly Pickford	A Country Girl
Lew 'Left-foot' Chaplin	A wag
Martin Fetlock Keanan [sic]	An Adventurer
Molta Zitkrantz Barra	A Vampire
Bohunk Rogers Hart	A Cowboy
Rollo Bushman	A Sweet Chap
Roughneckington Oldfield	An Auto Race Driver
Takeitaway Itscold	A Greek Waiter
Blaha Dressler	Still in the Ring[55]

The plot is a parody of the standard melodrama, anticipating Fields's
later parody of the play-within-a-play *The Drunkard* in the film *The Old-
Fashioned Way* (1934). In "The Mountain Sweep Stakes," Pickford must
marry Keanan, or he will take over the mortgage on the farm. Pickford, of
course, is in love with Fairbanks ("Dug is my sweet Patootie"), and all will
be saved if he can win the prize money for the big car race ("Good luck
Dug, win the race Baby").[56] The rest of the cast are integrated according to
their stereotyped images, from the picaresque comings and goings of Chaplin to Barra's vamping of him. Fields at all times demonstrated an excellent
understanding of these characters.

Second, to find Chaplin the real hero of the script is even more surprising
than discovering the film-fan nature of Fields. Fields's view of the creator
of Charlie is usually equated with his review of Chaplin's performance in
Easy Street (1917): "He's the world's greatest ballet dancer, and if I ever
meet the son of a bitch I'll murder him!"[57] Even Fields's last mistress
observed: "To his [comedy] contemporaries he was fairly charitable, with
the one notable exception of Charlie Chaplin. He referred to him as a
'goddamned ballet dancer.' It had to be pure jealousy."[58] Yet in "The
Mountain Sweep Stakes," Fields makes the Chaplin character the winner,
literally and metaphorically; he wins the big car race (on foot!) and is
allowed to maintain more of his screen uniqueness. For example, unlike the
other silent film stars parodied in the script, the Chaplin figure maintains
the universality of his silence. He does not fall comic victim to lines like
"Dug is my sweet Patootie."

Fields also pays Chaplin a rather unusual compliment by including a
scene in "The Moutain Sweep Stakes" (and thus copyrighting it) which had
already appeared in the 1917 Charlie film *The Adventurer*. (One is
reminded of the Fields commandment: "Thou shalt not steal—only from

other comedians."')⁵⁹ The Fields scene in question has ice cream being
delivered to Charlie and Barra, with the former spilling some into his
trousers. But in trying to shake it down his pant leg without distracting
Barra, the ice cream drops through both his pants and the floor grating
underneath, ending up on the back of Dressler, who is seated below them.⁶⁰
Interestingly enough, in a later interview Fields acknowledges the source of
the scene (though not in connection with his script), as well as the uniqueness
of Chaplin:

> Chaplin [is] the greatest of all comedians. . . . I think the
> funniest scene I almost ever saw was in one of Chaplin's old pic-
> tures. He is eating some ice-cream and it falls down his trousers.
> You remember that one [*The Adventurer*].⁶¹

All in all, Fields's copyrighted material, begun during the Ziegfeld years,
offers seven unique insights into the evolution of the comedian's career.
First, it documents more fully than ever before the carryover of Fields
material from stage to screen (some of which was repeated more than once
on film). Second, it confirms Fields's authorship of a great deal of his key
routines. Third, while all the sketch material is strongly visual, the inclusion
of dialogue and various supporting players more completely showcases the
evolving nature of Fields's comedy during the Ziegfeld years. He moves
from the juggling, solo pantomimist of the pre-*Follies* days to the speaking
musical comedy star of the Broadway hit show *Poppy* (1923-1924) which
followed the Ziegfeld period. Fourth, the copyrighted sketches, though
frequently more ambitious than earlier Fields material, still do not neglect
the often props-oriented nature (see the aforementioned traveling items
included in "Off to the Country") of a comedian who began as, and never
completely forgot about being, a juggler. Fifth, the very act of copyrighting
more than suggests that Fields had come to recognize the growing importance of his work—a foundation he would utilize for the rest of his career.
Sixth, "The Mountain Sweep Stakes" revealed Fields to be both a keen student of film and—surprise of surprises—a fan of Chaplin (at least in 1919,
the year the script was copyrighted). Finally, Fields's sketch concept of the
victimized central male—his leisure time usurped by females, machines
(especially cars), and the city in general—places Fields's work in the
vanguard of the evolution of the comic antihero in American humor.

The individual who tries to create order in a world where order is
impossible is not new to American comedy. He existed in earlier American
forms but generally not in the spotlight, which was reserved for the seemingly
rational world of the capable hero. This is best exemplified by the early
nineteenth-century geography of the inventive Yankee. Credit for the key
breakthrough of the antihero as a dominant force in American humor is
generally accredited to the *New Yorker* magazine, "which was more

responsible than any other medium for the rise of a new type of humor."[62] More specifically, this meant four writers: Clarence Day, Robert Benchley, James Thurber, and S.J. Perelman.

While these and other artists created an army of antiheroes, today Fields's sketches might best be equated with the writing of Thurber, though the Fields male seldom reached the Milquetoast extremes of Walter Mitty. However, in the mid-1920s Fields's vision of an antiheroic world greatly expanded when he worked with kindred spirit J.P. (Joseph Patrick) McEvoy (1894-1958), an important but neglected American humorist of the 1920s and 1930s. But before expanding upon the Fields-McEvoy antihero connection, which is as ignored today as the memory of McEvoy, Fields's next major career move (after the *Ziegfeld Follies*) should be explored.

The play was called *Poppy*, a musical comedy by actress and author Dorothy Donnelly (1880-1928). It made, or actually remade, Fields's career, presenting him with a new character and feature film opportunites. Celebrated critic Heywood Broun said of Fields's performance in *Poppy*: "We can't remember anybody who ever made us laugh more."[63] Fields played Professor Eustace McGargle, a small-time 1870s con man who attempts to utilize his daugher in a definitely big-time swindle—passing her off as the heir to a fortune. Film historian William K. Everson observes: "McGargle had not been written with Fields in mind, but he well could have been."[64]

Fields would recreate the role twice for film (*Sally of the Sawdust* and *Poppy*), as well as frequently playing variations of McGargle for the rest of his career. And today, of course, Fields is most closely identified with the carnival huckster, always on the lookout for suckers. *But* it is unfortunate to suggest, as so many authors have, that Fields seldom strayed from this trickster character in his future work.[65]

The role of the antihero would continue to be very important to Fields. Granted, a bit of larceny is generally to be found in most of Fields's characterizations, even those more in the antiheroic camp. For example, the picnic scene in *It's a Gift* finds the comedian cheating on splitting his sandwich— he bends all the meat onto his side before dividing it. But even here Fields is the antiheroic husband, traveling cross-country with his family, and at this precise moment is forced by his wife to share a sandwich with a son of whom he is none too fond.

Fields had constantly been exposed to shell-game types of situations throughout his life, and he undoubtedly contributed to the characterization of McGargle.[66] But his own writing, both before and after, most frequently fits in the antiheroic camp. This might best and most simply be illustrated by the names given to his focus families. In the copyrighted sketches, the surname Fliverton appears frequently and is unquestionably a thinly veiled reference to the most antiheroic of machines, the Model-T Ford, then frequently called the flivver. The flivver was so associated with comic frustrations that countless jokes circulated on the subject. For example, "The guy who owns a secondhand flivver may not have a quarrelsome disposition, but he's always trying to start something."[67] And several comedy careers are closely identified with the car, including that of Laurel & Hardy. Thus, to name a comedy family (actually several of them) Fliverton is strongly to suggest antiheroic tendencies (which a reading of the sketches bears out).

Fields's most famous later christening of a comedy clan would be the Sousé family of *The Bank Dick* (1940, original story and script by Mahatma Kane Jeeves, a Fields pseudonym). The name Sousé, like the more recent comedy shtick of stand-up Rodney Dangerfield, never got any respect. Egbert Sousé would patiently explain how his name was to be pronounced: "Soo-zay—accent grave over the 'e.'"[68] But people generally pronounced it without the accent, which resulted in the more alcoholic-sounding rendition—Souse. Thus once again Fields suggests future frustrations for a character by giving him an antiheroic name. After *Poppy*, the comedian's roles would fluctuate between nineteenth-century con man and twentieth-century comic antihero.

Fields's acclaim in *Poppy* continued to grow even after opening night's critical hosannas. This is best demonstrated by comparing program billing at different times during the play's run. The program for the week beginning September 24, 1923 (three weeks after the opening), had Madge Kennedy (who played the title role) billed over *Poppy*, with dark lettering in larger type than the title.[69] Fields was billed under the title in dark, though smaller, type. The program for the week of February 11, 1924, had Fields joining Kennedy in name above the title billing. Kennedy's name still came first, but Fields's lettering was the same size. Fields eventually won star billing, and by September 29, 1924 (on the road program), both performers were equally billed, side by side, over the title.

Fields's Broadway success in *Poppy* gave him the day's ultimate entertainment credentials, not unlike the impact felt by the Marx Brothers with their first success on the Great White Way (in *I'll Say She Is,* 1924). Moreover, it allowed Fields to showcase adequately for the first time another comedy weapon (some would say his ultimate one) in the Fields arsenal of humor—the spoken word. In his *Follies* material, so often drawn from his copyrighted sketches, Fields had been working toward just such an opportunity as the part of McGargle provided. The *New York Times* reviewer said it best when he praised both the old and the new W.C. Fields:

> And then there is Mr. Fields, veteran of many "Follies," and more cigar boxes [his best-known juggling prop] than there are cigars. He has never been quite so amusing as he is in "Poppy"— nor so versatile. His comicalities range from his accustomed juggling to untold difficulties with some bits of tissue paper. But

added to all of these not unfamiliar manoeuvres [*sic*] is a hitherto unrevealed facility with the spoken word. Mr. Fields creates comedy where certainly none existed in the libretto—for it can never be claimed that Dorothy Donnelly's book is funny per se.[70]

In 1924 Fields would have a small but important role as a comic, drunken British sergeant in a prestigious historical epic of the American Revolution entitled *Janice Meredith*. The next year he would costar in the critically and commercially successful screen adaptation of *Poppy* (though retitled *Sally of the Sawdust*), under the direction of no less than D.W. Griffith. At this time, Fields spoke with comic irony on these film developments, courtesy of his Broadway success in *Poppy*: "I couldn't get a straight offer for the silent drama until I got a speaking part on the stage."[71]

The same article, appearing in *Colliers,* suggests Fields as the student of film (as was implied earlier in "The Mountain Sweep Stakes"):

I did everything I could think of [to get into the movies]. I wrote them letters; I applied on beautiful application blanks; I pulled enough wires to make a telephone system for a city of thirty thousand people; I made a million faces for them at which they laughed happily. Yet they wouldn't have me because I was a pantomimist.[72]

Fields, who does not mention the two film shorts he made in 1915, has, however, somewhat simplified his reason for neglect at the hands of the cinema. Though his earlier stage routines focused on visual comedy, such as the celebrated pool sketch, in recent years he had also been working with verbal (story-related) sketches, as demonstrated in the copyrighted material.

Fields casually mentions later in the *Colliers* piece, almost in an aside, what must have been an even bigger stumbling block for getting into films—the movie moguls who felt he had no "screen personality."[73] For Fields, who was nothing if not self-centered (as are most great performers), being a mere pantomimist was probably a much more palatable cause of failure than lacking a screen personality. After all, though he was a continual favorite on stage, his two earlier films had been a cinematic dead end, even though one had focused on his most acclaimed stage routine, the pool sketch. Regardless, however, of the specific "why" behind his neglect, *Poppy* remains the magic vehicle that propelled him into cinema credibility.

Between Fields's 1923 stage success in *Poppy* and his repeat triumph in the 1925 film adaptation, the comedian had still another professional experience of career-changing magnitude—J.P. McEvoy's *The Comic Supplement*. Whereas the Donnelly play had served up a nearly complete comedy character (McGargle), which Fields immediately and wisely recognized as a perfect vehicle for many of his undirected comedy tendencies, *The Comic Supplement* was the proverbial college degree for the comedian's proven antiheroic inclinations.

Ironically, this pivotal revue closed on the road, although its best routines (and Fields's) reached Broadway in the 1925 spring and summer editions of the *Ziegfeld Follies*.[74] Thus little is written about *The Comic Supplement,* both in terms of literature on Fields or the theater in general. Yet it is the basis for the comedian's excellent silent film *It's the Old Army Game,* which was remade as *It's a Gift* (1934) and is sometimes considered Fields's greatest film. *The Comic Supplement* origins for these films are frequently obscured by filmographies which merely credit *It's the Old Army Game* to an unnamed play of McEvoy and Fields or just to Fields.[75]

McEvoy was a prolific humorist who wore a number of writing hats: Broadway playwright, novelist, creator of the syndicated comic strip *Dixie Dugan* (from his 1928 novel *Show Girl*, which was also adapted to the stage and made into a film), poet, radio-television scriptwriter, and film sketch and dialogue author. Besides his Fields connection on *It's the Old Army Game* and *It's a Gift,* McEvoy's 1923 hit Broadway play *The Potters* was the basis of Fields's equally successful 1927 film of the same name (often considered his best silent film).[76] McEvoy also provided dialogue for the comedian's excellent though underrated *You're Telling Me* (1934).

That Fields had found a kindred comedy spirit in McEvoy is also demonstrated by a broader survey of the author's work beyond the material which was adapted to the screen for Fields. This is best displayed in McEvoy's first book, a 1919 collection of verse with the title *Slams of Life: With Malice for All, and Charity toward None*.[77] Beyond that Fieldsian-sounding title, the book offers several poems in the same spirit: "A Plea for Chicago Husbands," "Getting Even," "The High Cost of Licker," "Never Argue with a Woman," "The Cure," and "There Ain't No Cure for Golf."[78] In a later McEvoy book, *Denny and the Dumb Cluck* (1930), the aphorisms have an even more pointedly familiar ring. For example, "If I hadn't wanted to do a good turn, I'd have been all right. It's always that way, Al, when you go against nature. The wages of virtue is a kick in the pants."[79]

Of course, the spirit of many of these McEvoy pieces can be applied to the antiheroic figure in general (after all, the 1920s was the pivotal period in American humor for the switch from a capable to a frustrated character). But a closer look at the evolution of *The Comic Supplement* would seem to suggest uncanny parallels in the comedy thinking of McEvoy and Fields.

McEvoy, and only McEvoy, copyrighted *The Comic Supplement* in 1924.[80] It contained the foundation for two sketches which are now considered classic Fields—"The Drug Store" and "The House by the Side of the Road" (the lawn-destroying picnic). Both scenes, of course, appear in *It's the Old Army Game* and the *It's a Gift* remake, and a variation of "The Drug Store" is the basis of the film short *The Pharmacist*. Since Fields was tied up with *Poppy* for most of 1924, both on Broadway and on tour, it seems unlikely he was involved with the writing of the initial *Comic Supplement* (especially since the antiheroic family opening also parallels the beginning of McEvoy's *The Potters*). Moreover, the fact that only McEvoy copyrighted it, in a period when Fields was especially sensitive about owning his material (see the aforementioned body of writing Fields had already copyrighted by 1924), seems to support McEvoy as the sole author of the initial revue script. And when it is compared to a January 1925 dress rehearsal copy,[81] with a cast headed by Fields, McEvoy's case is made stronger; the second rendition shows the unquestioned influence of Fields.

Most obviously, the revised revue had a billiards routine, which included Fields's standard cue-through-the-table finale. Second, his celebrated "Sleeping Porch" sketch (which he would copyright the following month) first appears in this rewritten *Comic Supplement*. Third, the picnic scene, though strong in the original, is now bolstered by such seemingly Fieldsian antics as opening a can with a hatchet and talking with a full mouth (both of which survived into the later film renditions). Fourth, the sketch "Joyride" (a flivver trip with a couple and their troublesome daughter) anticipates the sequence just prior to the picnic fiasco in both the later films. (The initial *Comic Supplement* had an antiheroic family on a motor excursion in the country, but the comedy did not take the same direction.)

Interestingly, there is little change in "The Drug Store" sketch between the two *Comic Supplements*. Comic bits, or variations of them, made famous by the later film adaptations include: the haughty rich woman, the individual with a large bill wanting change, the patron wanting a two-cent stamp, customer fascination with the correct time, and a telephone order for a box of cough drops.

It is impossible to know how large a part Fields played in the changes. Material like the pool sketch obviously seems to point to him. (While variations on this routine would occur in several of his films, it would not appear in *It's the Old Army Game* and *It's a Gift*—both based upon *The Comic Supplement*.) Fields individually copyrighted only one of the sketches, "The Sleeping Porch." But by the time of *It's a Gift,* screen credit was being given to both McEvoy's *Comic Supplement* and Fields's original story. Regardless of how credit is divided, there is no denying that a McEvoy story or premise seemed to bring out the best in Fields. And while Donnelly's *Poppy* gave Fields a nineteenth-century character to expand upon, McEvoy's *Comic Supplement* (and other McEvoy material used by Fields) gave the comedian situation outlets for a twentieth-century antihero on which he had already been working.

That Fields was never easy to work with is no secret. But besides a display of similar senses of humor, Fields-McEvoy sessions were probably assisted by the latter's unrufflable nature. This later inspired the 1930s headline "A Man [McEvoy] Who Can Laugh at His Own Gags Isn't Upset by Hollywood's Delirious Ways."[82] Credit ambiguities also did not seem to create grudges, at least judging from McEvoy's later delightfully authored Fields piece in the July 26, 1942, *This Week* magazine section of the *New York Herald Tribune* entitled "W.C.Fields' Best Friend."[83] However, the article was not without a certain tongue-in-cheek dig at the comedian, for Fields's best friend turns out to be himself.

Now that general attention has been addressed to both the neglected *Comic Supplement* and J.P. McEvoy, it is equally important to examine the classic antihero comedy traits of the production.

While the 1920s are the focus decade for the full blossoming of the comic antihero in American humor, there had been numerous foreshadowings, especially in the comic strips. Examples include Rudolph Dirks's "Katzenjammer Kids" (1887), Fred Opper's "Happy Hooligan" (1900), H.C. "Bud" Fisher's "Mutt and Jeff" (1907), George Herriman's "Krazy Kat" (1913; also see Herriman's earlier "Dingbat Family"), George McMannus's "Bringing Up Father" (1913; see also McMannus's later "The Whole Blooming Family"), and Billy De Beck's "Take Barney Google" (1919). And the comic strip is the ongoing focus of McEvoy's *The Comic Supplement,* which is, after all, what the title is taken from.

The revue opens with two less-than-pleasant children, Johnny and Gertie (the later name being reminiscent of Winsor McCay's pioneer animated cartoon *Gertie, the Trained Dinosaur,* 1914) who are pestering their father to read them their favorite comic strips:

> *Gertie:* Oh, look where the littlest boy is hitting the man on the head with an ax. Isn't that funny?
>
> *Johnny:* No, you gotta read mine first. Right here where they are building the fire under the cow.[84]

The strip settled on itself contains a father reading to less-than-pleasant children:

> This is the first picture. It shows a father reading a nice story to his children and the little boy says: "Let's hit the old man on the head with a brick." And his sister says: "No, let's hit him on the head with a hammer. It will make more noise."[85]

Thus far, the family members of *The Comic Supplement* have been fascinated by the comic strips, which reflect their violent physical values. But then McEvoy literally has them and their surroundings become a comic strip, with all its fierce (though harmless) slapstick:

> Light changes as swiftly as possible, changing room to violently colored representation of comic supplement interior. . . . The father, mother and two children are also dressed in red, yellow

and green clothes . . . they have typical comic supplement masks. . . . Music begins and a regular comic supplement scenario of brutal comedy is done in pantomime, interrupted only by "Zowie's", "Ook's", "Pow's", etc. as various members of family are hit by bricks, clubs, etc. . . . Furniture broken, window smashed, general pandemonium, during which Radio Sermon [on how civilized—nonviolent—American society has become] proceeds with unctuous deliberation.[86]

In the revised *Comic Supplement* of 1925, which seems strongly to exhibit Fields's influence, the antiheroic characters are accented even more. While the light-show transition of the family to cartoonland is retained, the revue opening (instead of an immediate meeting of the family) is a dancing chorus in brilliant comic strip colors. A fast likeable dance is performed "and suddenly turning their backs to the audience are discovered to be a chorus of well known comic supplement characters, Mutt and Jeff, Barney Google, Jiggs [of "Bringing Up Father"], etc."[87]

Besides literally footnoting the production with some of the comic strip characters which seemingly inspired it, the revised revue further emphasizes the battle of the sexes (a pivotal element of the antiheroic world). For example, the comic strip which Pa reads to his children now includes: "Paps comes home and says Hello, sweetheart and mama says, Take that, you big bum and hits him over the head with the rolling pin [strong shades of "Bringing Up Father" characters Jiggs and Maggie]."[88] Mother soon adds: "I just love the Sunday papers. They're so instructive, don't you think."[89]

The "Alley Scene" of *The Comic Supplement,* which Fields would soon copyright in a slightly different form as "The Sleeping Porch," is a cartoon compendium of antiheroic frustrations (women receive a special noise-making focus), often utilizing the unlimited potential of off-stage sound effects to heighten the absurdity of the modern world. (Fields utilized sound on radio in a similar manner during the 1930s and 1940s.) The fate of the sleeping porch victim, who has everything happen to him except sleep, was Fields as his checkmated best. Appropriately, the sketch, as presented in the 1925 *Comic Supplement,* closes when a Dada newspaper curtain is drawn.[90] Like the Krazy of Krazy Kat, a Dada curtain nicely underlines the irrational nature of the antiheroic world.

Not surprisingly, in a later interview that year, Fields stated he would like to play film roles of the "American husband"—the "pathetic" figure of the "newspaper cartoons."[91] While the cartoonlike physical persona of Fields (who frequently drew comic caricatures of himself in his early entertainment years) will be examined further in Chapter 2, it is paramount to be cognizant of the visual nature of the antihero, regardless of the medium. Even with the *New Yorker* camp, the trials of the antihero are constantly expressed through physical imagery. Just a glance at some titles demonstrates this: "The Day the Dam Broke," "The Night the Bed Fell," "A Box to Hide In," "Exercise for Those at Sea," "Penguin Psychology," and so on.[92] Moreover, cartoons do literally complement the *New Yorker* group, from the celebrated drawings of Thurber and Day to the delightful caricatures by Gluyas Williams which grace the Benchley books.

For Fields, accenting the visual was now of supreme importance; he was on the verge of a real silent-film career after the aborted beginnings of 1915. His success on stage in *Poppy* introduced the opportunity; his success in the film adaptation made possible a multiple-picture contract with Paramount. That he was signed for the adaptation, *Sally of the Sawdust,* was a major accomplishment because, as Everson has suggested, Broadway stars, then and now, frequently are overlooked when the film adaptation is cast.[93]

There were, however, other possible factors for Fields again playing McGargle. Director D.W. Griffith was possibly not unimpressed with Fields's small but well-received role in *Janice Meredith* which, though directed by E. Mason Hopper of a rival studio, was of the epic scale akin to Griffith's own movies. And Fields later suggested that his selection was assisted by Griffith seeing him in the *Ziegfeld Follies* earlier in 1925.[94]

There are some noticeable differences between the stage and first screen versions of *Poppy*, something which has been almost totally ignored since the adaptation took place.[95] In fact, this probably explains a frequently asked question since then—why did Griffith call the film version *Sally of the Sawdust*? No doubt, as *Variety* would seem to suggest, because "Griffith . . . followed the stage story but sparsely. His picturization is nearly an original other than characters."[96]

The most surprising difference is that Fields, as carnival huckster Professor McGargle, is not quite the con man of the play, where he manages to install his adopted daughter as the heir to a fortune, *unaware* she is the rightful descendant. In the film Fields not only knows the girl's true parentage all along, he does not even attempt to use it (misuse it?) until it is necessary to save her from a possible jail term.

Another major difference finds Griffith's screen production taking place in the present (1925), while the Donnelly play is set in 1874. If for no other reason, this allows the inclusion of bootleggers (a contemporary issue and a liquor tie-in with Fields), car chases, and a brief insert of an overhead airplane—which McGargle uses as a distraction when he pickpockets someone.

Fields, however, in top hat, checkered pants, and a small, repulsive, clip-on mustache (which he wore throughout his silent-film career), is still a huckster of whom to be wary—the circus sharper forever ready to play "the old army game." In fact, his definition/defense of the shell game as a pastime far removed from gambling turned up on more than one occasion: a game of science and skill—"the old army game."

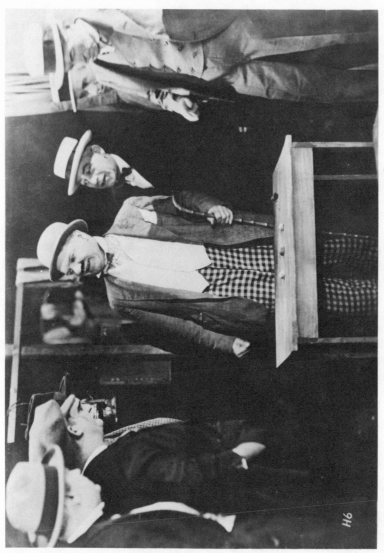

1. W.C. Fields busy at "The Old Army Game" in *Sally of the Sawdust*, 1925. (Courtesy Museum of Modern Art/Film Stills Archive.)

His direct-address smile at the camera during a flight scene, the later wiping of an eye, and the nearly solo (strolling down a road) film close are reminiscent of Chaplin's tramp, though not so strongly as the opening moments of *Pool Sharks* (ten years earlier), where his twirling cane seemed very derivative. Otherwise, he is the Fields one knows from sound films. And when a Fields title card describes Judge Foster (Erville Alderson) as having "a face that looks like he wore out four bodies," it is difficult not to "hear" Fields.

Ironically, Griffith's forte—editing, especially his propensity for cross-cutting between events occurring simultaneously at two locations—frequently distracted from Fields's physical humor. Like most silent comedians, Fields needed his classic routines such as juggling to be filmed in long take and long shot; this could allow the comedy to build as his antics became more complex and would provide the added comic intensity forever present when the clown is really performing the stunt. Editing breaks the rhythm and makes one question authenticity.

Strangely enough, the film's best comic routine is now flawed more by an act of history than Griffith's editing. McGargle and Sally (Carol Dempster) have become soaked while riding the rails. A kind baker offers them a chance to warm themselves if they will fire his nearly walk-in-sized ovens while he is gone. Fields, true to form, climbs in one for a nap. But Dempster, as conscientious as any of his future film daughters, soon goes to work with the coals, and Fields quickly becomes more than uncomfortable. His hopping antics are comic, as is Dempster's spatulalike rescue with a long ladle after Fields passes out. Today, however, thoughts of the Holocaust keep this from becoming the large belly-laugh routine it must have been to a world which did not yet know of Nazism.

The boy from Philadelphia was a hit:

> Mr. Fields has put in bits of business and gags that will make the Chaplins and the Lloyds bawl out their gag writers. And Fields plays them as well as though on the stage. He gives a smoothness to his comedy stuff and his playing that can not be missed.[97]

In the next four years he would make eight more silent features: *That Royle Girl* (1926), *It's the Old Army Game* (1926), *So's Your Old Man* (1926), *Running Wild* (1927), *Two Flaming Youths* (1927), *The Potters* (1927), *Tillie's Punctured Romance* (1928), and *Fools for Luck* (1928). While miscast in Griffith's *That Royle Girl,* which was essentially a murder melodrama, Fields scored strongly in *It's the Old Army Game,* the film drawn from *The Comic Supplement.* The movie uses the revue's "Druggist" routine for the general setting, and an early title card establishes a lengthy tongue-in-cheek premise:

This is the epic of the American druggist—a community bene-
factor. His shop is at once the social center, the place of countless conveniences and the forum of public thought. It is the druggist we seek in hours of suffering and adversity, and day and
night he is often the agency between life and death.

But what sounds like the wise, traditional crackerbarrel figure, dispensing
practical goods and practical advice from his store, becomes parody when
the viewer meets druggist Elmer Prettywillie (Fields). Fields has returned to
an antiheroic posture that features most of the characteristics (save his
voice) now associated with his stories of frustration. For example, the
introductory card for Fields's bothersome wifelike sister (Mary Foy) reads:
"Elmer's sister, who nagged at him all day and even talked in her sleep."
Naturally, her child (Mickey Bennett) receives a similar introduction:
"Prettywillie's nephew was a combination Peck's Bad Boy and Jessie
James."

The film opens with a car speeding through the night on an apparently
desperate mission. The driver awakens druggist Fields with the night
bell—or almost awakens him, since Fields puts the only available slipper on
the wrong foot, pulls a coat over his jammies, and completes his wardrobe
with a top hat. On the way to the door, Fields's pace is accelerated by
accidently stepping on some roller skates. But the desperate need of the
woman whose wild drive had barely beaten a train through an intersection is
merely for a postage stamp. She then uses Fields's tongue for a blotter with
which to moisten the stamp, as he is distracted by a yawn. Moreover,
Fields is not paid for the single stamp, and his "customer" contemplates
suing him when she misses the mail train. This might not be a typical
beginning to a Prettywillie day, but it is certainly typical of the rest of this
day's events, which include his attempt to take a nap (Fields's "Sleeping
Porch" routine) and a customer who wants a half-box of cough drops
delivered.

But in time a holiday arrives—April Fool's Day, "a legal holiday in the
Prettywillie household." This allows the film to slip into the "By the Side of
the Road" (picnic) routine where comic disorder continues as the family has
the messiest of picnics on a private estate. After April Fool's Day, when the
legality of stock Fields is selling on the side is questioned (it will prove
valuable at the film's close), he goes on a fact-finding trip by flivver. This
allows Fields to utilize the comic spirit of "The Joyride" routine, as well as
his own stage material on cars. His driving frustrations in the film are best
summarized by the title: "Prettywille was just one more Ford in the
labyrinth of New York's traffic."

It's the Old Army Game is a very funny film, full of a comedy of
frustration consistent with his 1930s antihero sound films. But as theater

and film critic Walter Kerr has observed: "the comedian [Fields] could not become whole—or a star of the first magnitude—until the visual and the verbal in him stopped interrupting each other, ceased occupying separate frames."[98] Moreover, unless the action of a silent film was constantly interrupted with titles, some excellent stage lines were always going to be dropped. Thus the *Comic Supplement* had numerous superb bits of dialogue which did not surface in *It's the Old Army Game*. One example is Pa Jones's comment to Ma after an especially trying time with their daughter: "I'm beginning to understand those animals you read about where the mother has got to hide the young so the father won't eat 'em."[99]

The film is also somewhat flawed by fluctuations in the nature of Fields's comedy character. Generally, Prettywillie is antiheroic, as previous examples have demonstrated. Yet glimpses of Fields as trickster occasionally slip in. For instance, Prettywillie wins at a shell game by outconning the game's con man. Knowing that in such contests the pea usually finds its way into the huckster's pocket, Fields "proves" his shell selection by lifting up the other two empty shells. Thus the con man must declare Fields a winner or risk being certified a cheat. The routine is in the same take-a-chance comedy tradition as Fields's later draw-poker bit: he states his winning card to be an ace but never shows it—only to fish it out, when all hands are back in the deck, after being questioned.

The shell game is funny, even giving the film its name, but it showcases a trickster Fields who would not have suffered the comedy indignities of druggist Prettywillie. Since it was produced early in the comedian's film career, there was probably a natural tendency to want to draw from both the spirit of *Poppy*'s McGargle and the *Comic Supplement*'s Pa Jones (as well as Fields's Fliverton father). In time, Fields's characterizations of huckster or antihero would be much more pronounced, with much less flip-flopping in a single film.

After *It's the Old Army Game* Fields made another strong film—*So's Your Old Man* (1926), which would later be redone in the sound era as *You're Telling Me* (1934). The movie was an adaptation of Julian Street's "Mr. Bisbee's Princess," which had won the O. Henry Memorial Award as the best short story of 1925. The work owes more than a little to the spirit of Sinclair Lewis's *Babbitt* (1922).

While Fields's comedy-satire connections with the world of Sinclair Lewis will be examined at greater length in Chapter 2, parallels in their work, at least when Fields is pursuing his antiheroic character, should be realized. (The ongoing influence of McEvoy—"an apt pupil of Sinclair Lewis's Babbitt-baiting school"[100]—did not hurt this tie.) Both Lewis and Fields attack Main Street hypocrisy, and while Babbitt is more a part of the estab-lishment than Fields's screen antihero will ever be, both suffer under many of the same antiheroic frustrations. In fact, Fields's celebrated "Sleeping

Porch" routine quite possibly owes more than a little to the 1922 publication of *Babbitt*. The novel, one of the greatest international publishing successes of all time, first introduces George F. Babbitt as a sleeping porch victim of noise:

> Rumble and bang of the milk-truck.
>
> Babbitt moaned, turned over. . . . The furnace-man slammed the basement door. A dog barked in the next yard . . . the paper-carrier went by whistling, and the rolled-up *Advocate* thumped the front door. Babbitt roused, his stomach constricted with alarm. As he relaxed, he was pierced by the familiar and irritating rattle of some one cranking a Ford. . . . Not till the rising voice of the motor told him that the Ford was moving was he released from the panting tension.[101]

Although the interruptions to sleep encountered by Fields in his "Porch" routine are sometimes more than auditory (his baby nephew hits him over the head with first a mallet and then a milk bottle in the *It's the Old Army Game* adaptation), the same helpless leisure-time frustration is at the center of both. Moreover, Lewis's very description of Babbitt paints a portrait of Fields:

> His large head was pink, his brown hair thin and dry. His face was babyish in slumber. . . . His was not fat but he was exceedingly well fed; his cheeks were pads, and the unroughened hand which lay helpless upon the khaki colored blanket was slightly puffy. He seemed . . . extremely married and unromantic.[102]

In *So's Your Old Man* Fields plays inventor Samuel Bisbee, whose latest creation is the nonbreakable windshield. His testing method maximizes car comedy: he drives into a tree eight to ten times, with everything *but* the windshield suffering because if it. Eventually, the invention will make Bisbee's fortune, but as the film begins the Murchison family is the group with whom to reckon. Indeed, the opening title states: "When distinguished strangers came to Waukeagus, N.J., they were shown the Shoe Factory, Riverside Park and the home of the Murchisons, on the upper West Side." The Bisbees, however, live on the proverbial wrong side of the tracks. This quickly becomes an issue when Mrs. Murchison (Julia Ralph) comes for a visit, concerned about the romance between their children.

Mrs. Murchison is, however, in a position to be won over—until Fields arrives, casual in undershirt, work pants, and with cigar. While Mrs. Bisbee (Marcia Harris) had been making points with Mrs. Murchison on her own family background, Fields scuttles everything with the Bisbee photo album, complete with pictures of Fields in prison stripes and of Cousin Sadie, the "best dancer in burlesque, until she lost her voice." (All the while he has a mouth full of crackers, a carryover from the picnic scene of *It's the Old Army Game*.) The best impression has not been made.

Bisbee's next undertaking, his big business trip to Washington, D.C., where he had planned to sell his nonbreakable windshield to a gathering of car manufacturers, is also a failure. Having installed the windshield in his own car for demonstration purposes, he makes the mistake of leaving the automobile in a no-parking zone while meeting with conference members. Naturally, it is towed away by the police—figures of anxiety for countless Everyman figures, from the world of comic antiheroes to that of Alfred Hitchcock. (Fields will expand greatly on this comic antagonist in the future.)

Predictably, Bisbee (armed with a hammer and bricks) returns with some conference members and tries to conduct a demonstration on one very breakable flivver windshield and then on another thinking each is his own car. While the automobile people are hardly impressed, the owners of the unvolunteered test cars are more than anxious to make contact with Fields. But the frustrated inventor escapes and travels home by train.

On board, he decides upon suicide by iodine. But in true antihero tradition, he is a failure here, too. (More recently, Burt Reynolds devoted an entire movie, *The End* [1978], to an antihero repeatedly failing at suicide.) But Fields goes from victim to rescuer, or so he thinks, when the movement of the train throws him into the compartment of Princess Lescaboura (Alice Joyce). Seeing a bottle of iodine, he assumes the worst.

He attempts to dissuade her from "suicide" by describing someone who really has it bad—himself. The two part company as friends, with Fields thinking he has saved her; never does he realize she is a princess. But then, he has a lot on his mind, and he goes on an alcoholic bender to prepare: "It was three days before Sam Bisbee felt sufficiently braced to go home and meet the missus" (title card).

By the time he resurfaces, the princess has returned to help "Old Sam," claiming a long friendship with this "great man." The Bisbee social position is made. In fact, Mrs. Murchison tells Fields's wife, "My dear Mrs. Bisbee—you're the luckiest woman in Waukeagus." And Mrs. Bisbee answers in the best tradition of the antiheroic wife: "Is my husband dead?"

Position has its advantages, and Fields is asked to drive the first ball at the new country club. He alibies: "I don't know anything about golf. I wouldn't know which end of the caddy to use." But the viewer has little opportunity to judge his skills because Fields will be too frustrated by his caddy and a number of inanimate objects (a pie, some sticky paper, a trick club) actually to play golf. The comedian borrows freely from his stage routine "An Episode on the Links." His attempts at golf end suddenly when the princess's jealous husband arrives and pulls a gun. But the princess deflects his gun hand up, and all he bags is a duck—which falls on Fields.[103]

The film's close has one of the Washington car magnates arriving (Fields's real car has been found and tested), and after some confusion over just what he wants (Fields initially thinks one more person is out to get him), inventor Bisbee receives a million-dollar check.

So's Your Old Man is an outstanding comedy, with all of Fields's actions consistent with the character of Mr. Bisbee. He also proves adept at pathos both in the frustrated suicide scene and in his "rescue" of the princess. In addition, the film provides him with a less-than-happy marriage, though Marcia Harris's Mrs. Bisbee has nowhere near the witch-of-the-week abilities of later movie wife Kathleen Howard. In Fields's future antihero roles he will consistently have a frustrating nemesis of a wife.

At the same time, *So's Your Old Man* continues several general traditions firmly established in *Sally of the Sawdust*. First, there is a happy and prosperous surprise ending, with the way now clear for Bisbee's daughter to marry into the story's wealthy family. Second, the storyline makes room for some Fields stage material. Third, small-town gossips, busybodies, snobs, and hypocrites in general are under attack.[104] Finally, a beautiful young woman (generally a daughter but in *So's Your Old Man,* a princess) helps make Fields's prosperous conclusion possible. Despite his reputation as a misogynist, a sympathetic daughter or a daughter figure is seldom missing from his best films.

The 1927 reviews of Fields's next movie, *The Potters: An American Comedy,* suggest it was his best-received silent vehicle. Based upon McEvoy's successful play of the same name, which was on Broadway while Fields was appearing in *Poppy,* it is about the rollercoaster relationships of an average American family. In other words, it was another tale of the Everyman antiheroic male. Heywood Broun describes it best in his 1924 foreword to the play:

> Mr. Potter's home is ugly, and a little messy. He is crowded and jostled on his way to work. His work is without any vestige of dignity or importance. But Mr. Potter's life has this, also, in common with all other lives—it has to be lived.[105]

While no prints of *The Potters* are now known to exist, McEvoy's original play is still extant, and it reads as if it were tailor-made for both Fields's public (antiheroic) persona, as well as his private one. His character has two quarrelsome children and a faultfinding wife. Early in the play, Pa observes: "All right, all right, I wish you'd quit naggin' me about money."[106] (Interestingly enough, *W.C. Fields by Himself: His Intended*

Autobiography includes numerous Fields letters to his estranged wife on money matters during the late 1920s, as well as both before and after this time. And his often ironic tone sketches Mrs. Fields as the most nagging of wives. See early Chapter 1 and Chapter 4 for examples.) Later in the play Ma exclaims: "We're headed there [to the poorhouse] right now. (Her anger rises.) What did I ever do to have such a boob of a husband?"[107]

Ma Potter frequently nags her husband during the play, but there is more justification in the latter example. She has just learned he has made a large and seemingly foolish investment. And Pa, even during the original transaction, was frightfully aware he had usurped his *wife's* position:

> Not a word to the wife about the investment. She-uh, women don't understand such matters. . . . You know if she found out I invested that four thousand dollars in oil [wells] she-she-well she wouldn't understand it, that's all. She'd ask a lot of questions. . . . Mrs. Potter asks questions that nobody can answer.[108]

Pa has, in fact, been swindled, which is later spelled out in the most Fieldsian manner by one of the confidence men: "If we didn't take him somebody else would. You know the old saying—there's a sucker born every minute."[109] Unlike Fields's participation in a con in *It's the Old Army Game* (winning at a shell game), where it was not appropriate for his anti-heroic character, its use in *The Potters* (with Fields as victim) is consistent with his role as another incompetent. Though it might seem like comedy blasphemy to suggest, Fields characters, at least the antiheroic ones, were more likely to be suckers than to cast that aspersion upon others. Later classic examples include Harold Bissonette's (Fields's) purchase of a seemingly worthless orange grove in *It's a Gift* (the remake of *It's the Old Army Game,* where the questionable items were stocks) and Egbert Sousé's purchase of some uncertain beefsteak mine shares in *The Bank Dick* (1940).

Surprise of surprises, however, is that Fields's antiheroic character somehow emerges winner at the close of these films based in comic frustration. Dry oil wells turn out to have oil, property takes on value, bonds become precious. (In this type of fantasy-world conclusion, the princess of *So's Your Old Man* and the remake, *You're Telling Me,* is hardly out of place.)

Among Fields's film comedy contemporaries, the fairytale reversal is most reminiscent of Harry Langdon. Frank Capra, who was largely responsible for molding Langdon's screen persona, described it thus: "'If there was a rule for writing Langdon material it was this: his only ally was God. Langdon might be saved by the brick falling on the cop, but it was *verboten* that he in any way motivate the brick's fall.'"[110] For example, in *All Night*

Long (1924), Langdon is a cowardly World War I soldier retreating from the bombardment of the enemy by climbing farther and farther up a pole. The shells inch closer, taking bites out of the wood as they climb with him. He suffers a direct hit and is blown away into the darkness. However, his unscheduled flight ends with a touchdown on an Allied general, saving not only Langdon's life but that of the endangered officer. And, through a further whim of the god of comedy, Langdon is given a promotion.

More recently, this kind of charmed-life comedy persona could be applied to Peter Sellers's Inspector Clouseau. For instance, in the Pink Panther films made during Seller's lifetime, Clouseau survived what seemed like a million-and-one assassination attempts, generally without even being aware of them.[111]

Unlike Langdon and Seller's Clouseau, however, Fields's character received the grace of God only at the conclusion of much comedy turmoil. Thus the general tone of Fields's films anticipates the total frustration which soon would be showcased in the short subjects of Laurel & Hardy. But Laurel & Hardy seldom received a film-closing reprieve. They seemed forever fated to do antiheroic penance, like a comedy monument to Sisyphus, whose tale could have inspired their most celebrated work—the repeated carrying of a crated piano up an endless flight of steps in *The Music Box* (1932).[112]

Because a happy ending is affixed to a story of continued comic frustration, one might read the tale as unrealistic and therefore not appropriate. But such a position should be avoided. As this author noted in his *Charlie Chaplin: A Bio-Bibliography* (Westport, Conn.: Greenwood Press, 1983), it ignores the basic pattern of the comedy genre itself, which moves toward the happy ending after overcoming some initial problems, just the opposite of the tragedy. Northrop Frye suggested in his pivotal *Anatomy of Criticism* (Princeton, N.J.: Princeton University Press, 1957) that the comedy happy ending is not there to impress the audience with truth or reality but rather to give them what is desirable—a happy ending.

A consideration of the typical Fields film conclusion does grant, however, that his happy endings are more ironic (often coming in a deus ex machina manner, after little demonstration of capableness by Fields) than any companion happy endings by Chaplin. With Chaplin, no matter what the comic dilemma, his screen persona Charlie has a uniqueness which belies any suggestion of impossibility. (For more on the neglected capableness of Chaplin see the author's *Charlie Chaplin: A Bio-Bibliography*.)[113]

Fields's next film after *The Potters* was *Running Wild* (1927), which again suffered from unevenness. But once the rather drawn out premise is established—that Fields is by far the most Milquetoast of husbands and business clerks—the film becomes a delightfully uproarious comedy. The original story, by Gregory LaCava, was something of a comic variation of *Dr. Jekyll and Mr. Hyde.* That is, Fields goes from milquetoast to he-man when he accidently is hypnotized into thinking he is a lion.

Like Chaplin's accidental shot of dope in the earlier *Easy Street,* which turns him into a he-man also, or Jerry Lewis's deliberate mixing of the potents which transform him into the dominant Buddy Love of *The Nutty Professor* (1963), Fields's change is immediate and comically extreme. In what no doubt is his most physical role, the hypnotized Fields jumps, yells, hits, chases, and just generally asserts himself against the former forces of restraint. This involves his most frightful film wife to date (Marie Shotwell), a repugnant stepson who sics the dog on him (Barney Raskle), and a dominating boss (Frederick Burton).

Fields's physical retaliation, from the destruction of the giant picture of her first husband his wife keeps to the strapping of the boy behind the closed door of a closet that quivers and shakes, is a delightful cartoon catharsis which would rival Wile E. Coyote finally catching the Road Runner. Moreover, title card room is also saved for some verbal revenge. For example, Fields tells the boss, "Listen cripple brains—keep your mouth shut and give your ears some exercise." And the film frequently is punctuated with Fields's battle cry, "I'm a lion."

The cartoonlike nature of the film was unquestionably aided by the fact that LaCava (who also directed *Running Wild*, as well as *So's Your Old Man*) was a former newspaper cartoonist. More specifically, LaCava produced the first animated cartoon series of Dirk's antiheroic "The Katzenjammer Kids."[114] In fact, Fields's position in *Running Wild* was not unlike the role of Der Captain in "The Katzenjammer Kids" in that he had to play surrogate father to an unruly youngster as well as avoid the rolling pin philosophy of a wife not far removed from Die Mama.

Other story sources involving LaCava also lurk in the film's background. As suggested in the examination of *The Potters,* Fields's antiheroic screen persona often suffers from frustrations that afflicted the private man. This has special significance in the production of *Running Wild* due to the working methods of LaCava. LaCava's later producer, the award-winning Pandro S. Berman, has described LaCava's need to get his key actors on the set:

> He would go into action and as he would talk to these people and get to know them and let them talk to each other—he would learn what their real personalities were. This was the secret of everything LaCava ever did—to capture on film the basic personality of the person he was using, and that's when he could function, and when he could crystalize on what he wanted to do and when he would create.[115]

LaCava, who would become one of Fields's closest friends, had in *Running Wild* a story about a henpecking wife and a bothersome son called Junior. In real life, though long separated from his wife, Fields saw her as an ongoing nag (see previously noted letter excerpts). And he felt his son, William Claude, *Junior,* had long ago been turned against him by the mother.

When Fields remade *Running Wild* in 1935 as *The Man on the Flying Trapeze,* the alienated mama's boy has been changed into an adult named *Claude,* who was suggested to be lazy. A letter written to Fields's estranged wife before this second production was undertaken suggests more than a little similarity between film and real world: "why should a man [Fields's son Claude] twenty-eight years old with the advantage of a college and musical education not contribute to the upkeep of his home?"[116]

Running Wild also features certain givens which invariably turn up in Fields's antiheroic comedies. First, he had a loyal daughter from a previous marriage who helps him to change. Second, he comes into wealth—a $15,000 commission—at the film's close. And third, the happy ending which is normally associated with sudden riches is here more a product of Fields's ability to learn from his accidental hypnosis. (This difference is underlined when a mere $15,000 is compared to the oil well conclusion of *The Potters* or the million-dollar contract which closes *So's Your Old Man.*)

As if reflecting the energetic acting and the ultimate revenge allowed Fields's character in *Running Wild,* the comedian's next three films find him returning to his con-man role. First he plays carnival showman Gabby Gilfoil in *Two Flaming Youths* (1927), then the ringmaster in the 1928 remake of *Tillie's Punctured Romance,* and finally the shifty oil man of *Fools for Luck* (1928).

Two Flaming Youths was a generally well-received production which teamed Fields with veteran silent comedy star Chester Conklin, with whom he would again be paired in *Fools for Luck. Two Flaming Youths,* remade as *The Old-Fashioned Way* (1934), finds both Fields and Conklin courting the wealthy Madge Malarkey (Cissy Fitzgerald). But Fields's interests are purely monetary, anticipating the cause of Groucho Marx's periodic screen interest in Margaret Dumont during the 1930s and early 1940s.

Though neither man ends up with Malarkey (a name descriptive of Fields's general view of women), the comedian often manages to make town sheriff Conklin look foolish. Moreover, Fields reserves some time for juggling. *New York Times* film reviewer Mordaunt Hall described Fields as a "resourceful performer . . . [and] a good pantomimist, one who does not have to pretend that the rest of the world is deaf because he is acting for the 'silent screen.'"[117]

While *Two Flaming Youths* ushered in 1928 with some good reviews, the rest of the year was frequently trying for Fields. Neither *Tillie's Punctured*

Romance nor *Fools for Luck* was well received, and Paramount did not renew his contract. But Fields, never one to panic, played golf and waited for something to develop. Something did.

Earl Carroll wanted Fields for his *Vanities,* and he was willing to meet the comedian's unbelievable demand for $6500 a week, as well as replace his name with Fields's on the marquee. However, Fields's salary demands and general egomaniac behavior during the negotiations caused the resignation of longtime agent and friend Bill Grady. Though they would maintain personal contact, their professional ties were permanently broken.

Fields's Broadway return in the *Vanities* was an event—a movie star's return (until 1928 his film performances had generally won critical praise, though he had never done big box office). After describing the production as "the best *Vanities* of them all," the *New York Times* stated: "the funniest single items in the show [are in] *At the Dentist's.*"[118] (The complete program title was *An Episode at the Dentists's.*) However, his *Vanities* reception was not a full embrace:

> Where ideas are concerned [as opposed to beautiful girls], the best it [Earl Carroll's *Vanities*] can do is a series of playlets by W.C. Fields. Fields is one of our favorites, and when he appears our mouth is almost half open ready to laugh. But we didn't laugh very much this time. Most of his playlets are off color stories we've heard before, turned into *Vanity* acts and not very good ones at that.[119]

(Interestingly enough, the 1932 film adaptation of the *Dentists's* routine had a scene censored.) That things were less than perfect is suggested in a December 1928 Fields letter to his estranged wife, which suggests he would soon be dropped from the *Vanities.*[120] But since his wife was again requesting more money, this might have been merely a ploy upon Fields's part.

William Everson's book on Fields credits the *Vanities* as the revue in which the comedian used his golf routine *despite* Earl Carroll's attempt to have him change it to a fishing sketch in order to better showcase his girls.[121] But the earlier Robert Lewis Taylor volume attributes the battle over the sketch to a previous *Follies,* with Ziegfeld pushing for a fishing routine.[122]

A copy of the *Vanities* program of August 27, 1928 (shortly after its opening), would support the Taylor position, as there is no golf routine listed.[123] According to this program Fields appeared in the following routines: "Stolen Bonds" (previously copyrighted by Fields), "Mrs. Hubbard's Cupboard" (no writing credit), "The Caledonian Express"—with Fields playing four of seven parts (previously copyrighted by Fields), "All Aboard" (written by Thomas R. Tarrant), "School Days" (presumably Fields's previously copyrighted "My School Days Are Over"), "The Mormon's Prayer"—with Fields playing Brigham Young (written by Herman Meyer), and "An Episode at the Dentist's" (previously copyrighted by Fields).

The most famous anecdotes born of Fields's involvement in the *Vanities* gather around his ad-libbing abilities, which were only then being fully utilized by the comedian. For example, a deafening off-stage noise produced an effective Fields reference to mice; the falling of some prop house scenery had him observing they didn't build houses the way they used to.

Approximately six weeks after the *Vanities* opened, Fields was involved in a minor romantic scandal. Onetime mistress and former *Follies* girl Bessie Poole died on October 8 of myocarditis (inflamation of the heart muscle) and complications, a few days after she had received a fractured nose (she claimed to have been hit) in Tommy Guinan's Chez Florence nightclub. (Poole had told her attending physician, "I guess I forgot to duck.")[124] When her will was filed, one clause bequeathed a diamond ring to Fields. Newspapers made much of the former romance between the two, with the suggestion (due to the bequest) that she loved him still. Fields was not available for comment (earlier he had denied knowing her), but friends stated they had once been married, later agreeing upon an amicable divorce (as well as making arrangements for a son, William Rexford Fields Morris, born in 1917). However, since Fields never divorced his first wife, it is unlikely the comedian and Poole were ever formally married, since such a union would have been illegal. It is more probable that the marriage was "created" for the benefit of a more orthodox public. Taylor's biography of Fields later undercut (without directly referring to it) the suggestion of lingering romance by observing, "A relative of Fields believes . . . that the gifts [Poole received from Fields] . . . were handed over with the stipulation that if she died, they should all come bouncing back to the comedian."[125]

Fields was absent from the screen in 1929 for the first time since 1924. But the following year he made his sound film debut in the short subject *The Golf Specialist*. This two-reeler is important for several reasons beyond being his first sound film. First, it includes more of the end of *So's Your Old Man*. Second, it not only preserves much of the sketch, its canned theater presentation (no prize here for cinematic adaptation) gives the viewer an excellent documentarylike sense of how the sketch appeared on stage. It was not unlike the equally canned theater filming of the Marx Brothers' *Cocoanuts* the previous year, 1929.

Third, *The Golf Specialist* was a comedy compendium of nearly everything one wanted to know about Fields's personae—condensed into two reels. Before he reaches the golfing segment, Fields plays huckster. He is wanted by a dangerous-looking sailor (the Slaughterhouse Kid) for an unpaid bill. He tries to steal a little girl's piggybank. And when a very real-looking toy dog appears to have wet on Fields's feet, he kicks the innocent pooch into the next county.

Once on the tee, he is subject to nearly every antiheroic frustration known to golf—generally at the hands of his caddy. As noted earlier, inanimate objects—a pie (a snack for the caddy), a trick club, sticky paper—give Fields comic fits. And now with sound, many of the objects are aurally distracting, too, such as the papers the caddy seems obsessed to straighten and fold.

Beyond the dichotomy of personae, *The Golf Specialist* is peppered with references to, or example of, much of Fields's comedy philosophy. For example, he manages to footnote his interest in alcohol when he ponders how strange it is for someone to take a pie to the links: "Imagine bringing a pie to the golf course. A pint, yes, but never a pie, never!" His flexible club nicely demonstrates his long-standing rule that the maximum comedy mileage is exacted from props which bend but do not break. He manages to include a "Godfrey Daniel" in his dialogue and get his hat planted upon an upturned cane instead of his head.

More thorough, however, than anything else is the film's secondary but nonstop essay upon women—W.C. Fields-style. First, the film starts in a hotel lobby, where the house detective's wife flirts with anything in pants. Yet when her husband beats someone who has reciprocated those advances, she mechanically says, at a conversational level, "murder, murder" (it evidently happens frequently) while calmly applying lipstick. The inference is clear; women enjoy creating problems for males. Or as Fields later observed (possibly borrowing from humorist Kin Hubbard) in his most sexist manner: "Women are like elephants to me; they're nice to look at but I wouldn't want to own one."[126]

His interaction with the little girl and the piggybank, still in the lobby, continues his antifemale diatribe along a more subliminal line. The pushy girl shakes her bank at Fields, implying he should make a contribution. He ignores this and innocently asks her age while encouraging her to sing. She replies she is five and that a song will cost a dollar. To this Fields grumbles, "You're more than five!" She then provokes a comedy attack by sneering back at him, "I've got more than fifty dollars in here."

On the course Fields addresses what he might have called the screwball nature of women. He is distracted when a woman in a riding costume walks by, stopping to observe, "I forgot something." Fields promptly counters with, "Probably her horse." But before he can recover from this intrusion she starts to wander back, stops, and reverses her course again. She is then followed by a second woman with a huge Afghan hound on a leash.

All his uses of the female in *The Golf Specialist* do not, however, support a misogynist position. As suggested earlier, Fields films frequently utilize an idealized young woman as a loyal daughter figure. And *The Golf Specialist* seems to make an attempt even at this. After the flirtatious wife of the hotel detective accompanies Fields to the tee, she assumes many of the more innocent characteristics of a Fields screen daughter. As the comedy shifts to a golf focus (and its accompanying frustrations), her flirting ways are dropped and she simply becomes a young woman learning golf from an ever more flustered master. And since everything possible keeps Fields from demonstrating point one—merely hitting the ball—the viewer admires her patience. Moreover, Fields himself comically defines her as innocent when, after the pie and paper have created a sticky mess, he soberly tells her, "I'm sorry you had to see this."

Despite this essence of Fields air, *The Golf Specialist* was not a catalyst into sound films. Thus late in 1930 Fields opened on Broadway in *Ballyhoo,* a satire on promoter C.C. Pyle's across-the-continent footrace a few years earlier. Fields's sketches included: "Poker Game," "Austin Car," "Billiard Table," "Drug Store," and comic juggling.[127] A variation of "Austin Car" had been copyrighted shortly before this as "The Midget Car," a title which makes more obvious to today's reader a key focus of the sketch—the comic frustrations of packing and riding in a small car. And "The Midget Car" routine is based upon Fields's even earlier "The Family Ford" and "The Sport Model" sketches.

Ballyhoo's loose plotline connected some of Fields's material by making him "the harrassed manager of a bankrupt transcontinental footrace, fleeing creditors and fleecing poker partners by the blandest sort of chicanery with the cards."[128] It was W.C. Fields as con-man. *Ballyhoo* reviews generally praised Fields but found the overall production mediocre.[129] However, that recycled Fields could be a problem (earlier suggested in Francis R. Bellamy's review of the 1928 *Vanities*) was noted in Heywood Broun's somewhat later review (January 7, 1931) of *Ballyhoo* (though Broun, a fervent Fields fan, was not bothered by it):

> Much is made of the fact that Mr. Fields does things now which he has shown us previously. This seems to me an ungrateful form of criticism. The fact that he can produce endless fun by capers in an Austin car should not be minimized simply because some seasons ago he did tricks with a Ford. And I feel that one of the high spots in the present theatrical year has been underlined in red because W.C. Fields is juggling again.[130]

Ballyhoo producer Arthur Hammerstein dropped the production after approximately two weeks (December 22, 1930-January 7, 1931) ironically paralleling Broun's supportive review of Fields. But the show was continued for another seven weeks (through February 21, 1931) as a cooperative effort between the actors and the labor unions.[131] Interestingly, Fields behaved contrary to his thrifty personal nature with the venture: while *Ballyhoo* "principals got 84.2 per cent of their regular salaries . . . Fields, show's star . . . refused to take any money unless the show climbs to a paying basis."[132]

The comedian's kind gesture probably was assisted by the fact that Hammerstein (according to a Fields letter of January 12, 1931) was "condemning everyone for the closing . . . [including] your friend Fields."[133] Moreover, an earlier letter, written while Hammerstein was still producing, noted Fields's salary was late even then.[134] Regardless, however, of the "why" behind the action, Fields and the cooperative received support from the entertainment community. For example, a January 21, 1931, *Variety* article listed such comedy talent as Eddie Cantor and the team of Moran and Mack as already having volunteered time to the show, while Will Rogers wired "he would like to participate."[135]

While never known to be a fan of Horace Greeley, Fields decided to go west permanently in 1931. He actually had established California residency in 1927, but stage commitments kept him in the East for much of the time between. Most of Fields's previous film work had been shot there. But this phase of Fields's career was over. With the coming of sound, Hollywood was more than ever the movie capital of the world. By returning to the west the comedian hoped to resume his film career.

Fields's biographer Nicholas Yanni has stated what many authors have implied—that the comedian was taking a risk in leaving New York and the stage.[136] Certainly this is true to a point, but Fields authors have almost completely ignored the commercial failure of *Ballyhoo*, as well as the general box-office toll the depression was taking on Broadway. Thus the west coast decision seems a logical move (especially with critical comments about recycled material), not some Kiplingesque homage to "If" or risk on a throw of the dice.

Fields's western venture was more brave than risky, for at fifty-one he had saved enough never to need work again. Despite stories of having lost his fortune in the stock market crash or through a dishonest investment broker (the latter suggested by the film *W.C. Fields and Me*, 1976), Fields headed west in a new Lincoln, weighed down with a fortune in currency.

It has not been recorded how long the trip took, but no doubt it was lengthy. Besides facing a less than promising highway system, and being a less than promising driver (Fields once put friend and passenger Will Rogers in the hospital while racing late at night), the comedian loved both motor sightseeing trips and roadside picnics—facts already well documented in his stage and screen work.

Later in 1931, after his celebrated arrival at a Hollywood hotel (surrounded by a sea of luggage, he demanded the bridal suite), Fields appeared in his first sound feature, *Her Majesty Love*. Though in support of Marilyn Miller and Ben Lyon, Fields's role seemed hand-tailored. He played Miller's father, an out-of-work vaudevillian with juggling abilities and drinking interests. And the dialogue for his first appearance is vintage Fields. Miller has called him about her engagement to Lyon, not making much sense over the telephone, and Fields replies, "I think you're a little bit tipsy." But then, so she will not get the wrong impression, he adds, "Never mind. It's a very good omen for marriage. I was half-stewed when I proposed to your mother."

Also in true Fields tradition is the fact that Miller plays a loyal daughter in love with a wealthy young man, which allows Fields to take his standard pot shots at high society. The formal dinner where the families meet is the comic highlight of the film. Besides juggling plates and flipping chocolate eclairs the length of the table, he proposes the most Fieldsian toast, "Here's to your liver!" and innocently reveals his daughter is a barmaid (how appropriate!).

The film, moreover, is frequently peppered with Fields's references to vaudeville. For example, when he leaves on a drive with his daughter and prospective son-in-law, he must ride in the rumble seat. And when Lyon asks if he could help, Fields replies, "No, I used to be in vaudeville." Later, when Miller and Lyon have had a falling out and she is being courted by the Baron (Leon Errol), Fields observes, "I haven't seen such lovely roses since I was in vaudeville. My public used to send them to me. I shall put them in water. Not my public, the roses."

Miller, undecided about her rebound relationship with the much older Errol, receives fatherly advice best given by the huckster in Fields:

He's a great catch. He's rich. He's old. What more do you want?
A rich old man is worth two rich young men and they're less
bother. And you can always look forward to a happy widowhood.

For a supporting role in a musical comedy, Fields could not have been better showcased. Warner Brothers released *Her Majesty Love* to good reviews late in 1931.

Fields was soon back in the Paramount camp, appearing as a featured star in *Million Dollar Legs* and *If I Had A Million* (both 1932). In the former film he plays the president of a mythological country named Klopstokia, where all women are named Angela and all men George. Not surprisingly, there is government instability, heightened by a presidential "election" system based upon Indian wrestling.

Anticipating the absurdist world of the Marx Brothers' *Duck Soup* (1933) by over a year, where Groucho is prime minister of a mythological country named Freedonia, *Million Dollar Legs* parodies not only politics but athletics. (*Time* described it as a "Marx Brothers comedy.")[137] Klopstokia needs eight million dollars, and a victory at the Los Angeles Olympics will assure this. "Coincidentally," the 1932 Olympics were also in Los Angeles, with the film going into general release that summer.

In addition, *Million Dollar Legs* is a parody-salute to the movies themselves, from Major-Domo's (Andy Clyde's) ability to outrun a horse, car, and speedboat (à la the chases of Mack Sennett) to the seductive Mata Machree's (Lyda Roberti's) more pointed takeoff on Greta Garbo's *Mata Hari* (1932), which had opened at the beginning of the year. In fact, Roberti's special dance to fortify Hugh Herbert (Fields's political rival) during the weight lifting competition plays upon Garbo's celebrated dance in Mata Hari.

While Fields is not on the screen as much as Migg Tweeny (top-billed Jack Oakie), the former brush salesman who organizes the Klopstokian Olympic team, his actions are standard Fields. As president he assumes his huckster persona (how appropriate for politics), to the point of telling his daughter (Susam Fleming) at the beginning, "Let's take it on the lam," when there is clearly no need to do so. His physical presence, necessary to maintain the presidency, is reminiscent of his "lionized" behavior in the latter half of *Running Wild*.

The self-importance one associates with Fields as huckster is nicely parodied when early in the film he is announced as president, the soundtrack blaring the pageantry of horn and drum. Upon his arrival he is literally seen to be blowing his own horn and pounding his own drum. Also interspersed in the film's first half are bits of Fields juggling (his hat, Hugh Herbert's hat . . .).

The film even manages cameo references to such key Fields shticks as problem children and alcohol. When the train transporting Klopstokia's athletes misses Los Angeles and ends up in San Francisco, it is discovered that a bratty kid has been at the throttle since Kansas City. And at the film's close, Fields alibies his weakened condition (despite having just thrown a thousand-pound weight far enough to win both the shot put and the weight lifting medals) with: "It's the [California] climate. I've been drinking too much orange juice." (Fields frequently touted alcohol by knocking healthy beverages).

While the story for *Million Dollar Legs* was by Joseph L. Mankiewicz, the film bears certain parallels with Fields's copyrighted script "The Mountain Sweep Stakes." The latter work also satirized Hollywood, especially specific stars. The film's send-up of Garbo's Mata Hari can be compared with Fields's parody of Theda Bara as Moltz Zitkrantz Barra. And Andy Clyde's ability to outrun cars was a key component of Fields's employment of the Charlie Chaplin screen persona in "The Mountain Sweep Stakes." Both works also allow one player to maintain his silent comedy persona throughout (the film uses Ben Turpin, Fields's script has Charlie), and both end in a competition.

The movie was a hit and is still considered a classic by many today. (For example, see Chapter 4's reference to Pauline Kael and the film.) Interestingly enough, the similar *Duck Soup* (even Fields's monologue ability to build anger against an absent general anticipates Groucho's topsy-turvy soliloquy on Ambassador Trentino) was a box-office failure the following year. Sociological film historian Andrew Bergman has convincingly suggested that *Duck Soup*'s flop was the result of political timing—the nation was not receptive to a movie which attacked everything political at a time when the New Deal was trying to get off the ground.[138]

If that was the cause of *Duck Soup*'s initial failure (a film now considered the Marxes's best), it would suggest that part of *Million Dollar Legs*'s opening success was based on a public more receptive to political satire at the close of an administration perceived as having done very little. In addition, *Million Dollar Legs* utilized a more broad-based satire, comically sideswiping films and athletics as much as politics. Fields's return to Paramount was a hit, flawed only for his fans by a limited screen time.

His next film, *If I Had a Million,* found him starring with Alison Skipworth in one of several stories focused on the title's premise. More specifically, the wealthy but dying John Glidden (Richard Bennett) decides to give away his millions at random by picking names from the telephone book rather than have the money fall into the hands of his undeserving relatives (a premise which has Fields written all over it).

The Fields-Skipworth episode might best be labeled "The Revenge of the Antihero," for they play a gentle older couple whose new Ford, purchased with their life's savings, is wrecked by a roadhog seconds after they leave the showroom. Their sudden wealth allows them to hire a fleet of cars and drivers to search out and attack all roadhogs. Though this becomes a one-joke episode (various wrecks), there is an ongoing antihero catharsis for the viewer who also has suffered at the hands of the roadhog.

Besides the car premise, which brings to mind Fields's earlier automobile sketches and flivver humor in general, the *If I Had a Million* episode contains a collection of other Fieldsian touches. For example, the initial wreck is caused by a milk truck; in fact, Fields spits milk out of his mouth after the accident. In the years to come milk would be an ever-greater comic nemesis to the hard-drinking comedian. The sketch also finds room, amid crashing cars, for a brief homage to the comedian's love of language. Thus Fields and Skipworth are Rollo and Emily LaRue, a last name which would, no doubt, if the sketch were longer, cause pronunciation problems, as happens in later films for other of Fields's antiheroic couples. Fields also manages to include a reference to Emily as "my little chickadee."

The year 1932 was significant for two other reasons—one private, one public. First, Fields met Carlotta Monti, who would soon become his longtime companion. They met on the Paramount lot after the beautiful Monti (then under contract to RKO) was borrowed to appear in some publicity stills. Their relationship, while sometimes stormy, would prove unique for both. Monti would be privy to the private side of a celebrated American clown, and Fields would enjoy a sustained relationship with a woman capable of weathering his frequent changes of mood. Even though Monti was only twenty-four, and there is a tendency today to visualize the comedian as he would become in his wasted later years, one should not preclude the mutually romantic tendencies of the couple. Monti has described the then fifty-two-year-old Fields as "blond, trim-figured, and handsome, with an unblemished complexion and bright blue eyes . . . the omnipresent martini had not as yet exacted its toll on his physiognomy."[139] Moreover, he had a personality which attracted both genders, as Sara Hamilton's 1934 article, "A Red-Nosed Romeo," demonstrated.[140]

A second key Fields event of 1932 was the completion of the Mack Sennett-produced, Paramount-distributed short subject *The Dentist*. This was to be followed by three additional two-reelers in 1933: *The Fatal Glass of Beer, The Pharmacist,* and *The Barber Shop*. The success of these films (only *The Fatal Glass of Beer* was poorly received) is now generally believed to have encouraged Paramount to give Fields more creative freedom in his subsequent feature appearances.

Fields wrote the screenplay for each of the four, drawing heavily from his previously copyrighted stage material. *The Dentist* had three earlier versions of the stage routine "An Episode at the Dentist's" from which to draw; the film's funniest line—"Your doctor is off his nut"—had appeared only in the first copyrighted version (1919).

These films allowed Fields to showcase some of his strongest stage material for a screen public to whom the routines were largely new, although some material from *The Pharmacist* had already appeared in *It's the Old Army Game*. Moreover, though it was possibly not a conscious decision, three of the four films represented marked contrasts in their humor presentations, as if they were a comedy laboratory for the feature films to follow.

In *The Dentist* he was comically ruthless, a thirties Don Rickles who showed consideration for no one, from the patient on whom he uses his "404 circular buzz-saw" to the golfer he knocks cold with a tee shot. And while "this made it hardly less funny,"[141] as William Everson has suggested, it would have been a one-note character—both difficult to sustain over an extended period of time and comically shallow, especially for someone who appreciated Charles Dickens as much as Fields. Moreover, the extreme nature of Fields's character in *The Dentist* (in the original copyrighted sketch he was called Dr. O. Hugh Hurt, shortened to Dr. Payne in subsequent versions) had already created a censorship problem, which only would have become worse. That is, an extended sequence from one Fields extraction of a tooth was cut because patient Elise Cavanna had her legs wrapped around the doctor (Fields was moving around the room), very much as if they were copulating. And after the implementation of the Motion Picture Code in 1934, even a mild obscenity like "hell," which Fields used in *The Dentist,* would no longer be permissible. In fact, to demonstrate how excessive censorship concerns would become, one has only to read a January 1935 *Variety* review of *The Gift,* possibly Fields's greatest but in no way controversial film: "Not for polite houses because of the doubtfulness of several spots in the dialogue, such as when Fields, in the bathroom, tells his daughter to come on in; he's just shaving."[142]

The aforementioned scene of sexual suggestion had been copyrighted in the third version of "An Episode at the Dentist's"—no doubt one of the routines which had prompted critic Francis R. Bellamy's earlier comment about Fields's "off color stories" in the *Vanities,* in which the sketch was included. Censorship is more likely to become an issue, however, when the medium serves a mass market (where mores must be more homogeneous), as did film in the 1930s. If Fields were filming today, or even utilizing original, uncensored material like "An Episode at the Dentist's," his comedy reputation would certainly have a bluer tint to it.

His next short subject, *The Fatal Glass of Beer,* did poorly in 1933 but is now often considered the best of the four Sennett-produced films. Fields drew the story from his copyrighted sketch "Stolen Bonds," which, like the third version of "An Espisode at the Dentist's," had been included in the 1928 *Vanities.* (Both routines were copyrighted in July 1928, shortly before the *Vanities* opened.) In addition, "Stolen Bonds" was part of his act when he played vaudeville's famous Palace in early 1930.[143]

The Fatal Glass of Beer takes place somewhere in the frozen north, with Fields and Rosemary Theby playing the Snavely couple, whose son Chester (George Chandler) has succumbed to the evils of the big city, all because of a fatal glass of beer. There is little physical action in the film, which is largely dominated with Fields's antimusical ballad of Chester (ostensibly sung for a passing mountie [Dick Cramer] and Chester's postprison return).

The only discernible structure in this story, which wanders almost as much as *The Dentist,* is Fields's recurring line, spoken after staring out the door at a presumably winter wasteland: "And it ain't a fit night out for man nor beast!" Fields is then immediately hit in the face with a handful of fake snow. Besides being progressively funnier, the predictable falseness of the scene is the capsulized message of the film.

The Fatal Glass of Beer is a broad satire on sentimentality, the type of melodrama at which Fields was poking fun in his copyrighted script "The Mountain Sweep Stakes" and to which he would return with "The Drunkard" play in *The Old-Fashioned Way* (1934). This was of the stuff which he once had to play straight in grade-Z vaudeville (after a performer's regular routine he might have to double as a character in a Victorian playlet).

The Fatal Glass of Beer also satirizes the capable crackerbarrel figure of American humor, a figure who celebrates rural and small-town America

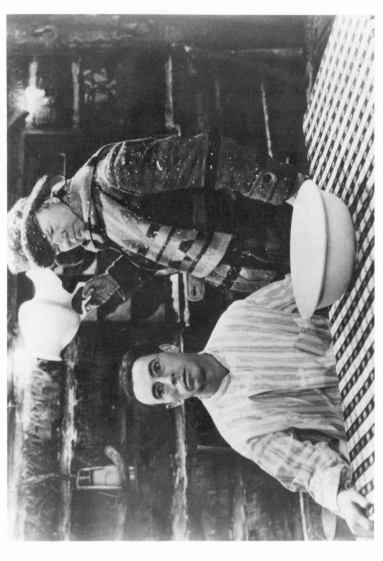

2. W.C. Fields ready to bash his unsuspecting son in *The Fatal Glass of Beer*, 1933. (Courtesy Museum of Modern Art/Film Stills Archive.)

while questioning the values of the large metropolitan area, often in a knee-jerk (city-equals-sin) equation. (The increased visibility of the comic antihero additionally, of course, attacked the crackerbarrel figure because greater prominence implied that modern man identified more with a figure of frustration than with one of capableness.)

The broad-based attack of *The Fatal Glass of Beer* becomes a broadside when one considers its technical whistling in the dark, from the obviously fake snow to the poor back-projection of the only exterior scene—all of which *enhance* the film's attack. That is, the not-to-be-believed production compliments the message: the old melodrama was not to be believed. More recently, Mel Brooks's satire of the movie western, *Blazing Saddles* (1974), works a variation upon this theme when the film eventually breaks out of its historical time and place and enters the present. The implied message is twofold: (1) this satire has become so ambitious that the genre can no longer withstand the attack, and (2) the myths of the Old West are so patently false and dangerous that it is healthiest to escape the genre, even when it is being satirized.

Inexplicably, the satirical nature of *The Fatal Glass of Beer* went over most cinema audiences' heads in 1933, despite using such a celebrated drinker as the spokesperson for its tongue-in-check diatribe against alcohol. Ironically, the viewer who "read" the film on a mere surface level probably was mystified by its comic highlight of an ending: the parents throw Chester out after they discover he has discarded the stolen bonds for which he went to prison. This comic surprise (a device Fields enjoyed using) is perfectly in keeping with the work's attack on melodramatic values, but it would be jarring to anyone immersed in a straight rendition of the story. Paradoxically, earlier stage productions of the routine, in the 1928 *Vanities* and at the Palace in 1930, were critically praised.[144]

After these two somewhat controversial short subjects, Fields firmly returns to his antihero persona in *The Pharmacist* and *The Barber Shop*. In both films he is the perennial victim, an abused doctor in the former and a berated husband in the latter.

While Fields's Dr. Wilweg, the pharmacist, is not quite henpecked at home, he has little more control. For example, when his younger daughter (Babe Kane) is disciplined by losing dinner privileges, she calmly downs first the canary's birdseed and then the canary. While the world of Fields humor is usually grounded in reality, about which he felt strongly, he also realized the importance of exaggeration.[145] Hand in hand with this understanding was his belief that comedy should never be far from a sense of the "vulgar": "Things should be a little rough on the stage or in pictures just to be consistent [with the roughness of life]."[146] The downing of the canary nicely combines those favored elements of exaggeration and vulgarity.

Canary comedy of this sort was a favorite of Fields; he included similar bits in two stage sketches, "What a Night" and "10,000 People Killed" (copyrighted 1921 and 1922 respectively). Other effective illustrations of the absurd in *The Pharmacist* include a cocktail shaker which can be attached to a pogo stick (copyrighted by Fields in the second version of "10,000 People Killed," also in 1922) and a reference to the fictitious book *The Sex Life of the Polyp,* which was really a 1928 film short subject by fellow antiheroic writer/performer Robert Benchley (drawn from earlier Benchley writing).[147]

Via *The Barber Shop,* Fields's final short subject produced by Sennett, there were several more excursions into the absurd, including an extremely obese man shrinking to half his size in the shop's steamroom and Fields's cello giving birth to a brood of little cellos. Such examples reemphasize the frequent cartoon nature of Fields's comedy.

Fields's character in *The Barber Shop,* Cornelius O'Hare, is both the most passive and the most incompetent of the four personae in the Sennett films. A dog waits by the barber chair in case Fields cuts off another patron's ear, said to have happened earlier (before the film opens). And a customer Fields does not recognize explains his face is "all healed up since the last time."

Elise Cavanna (the long-legged patient of *The Dentist* and the wife in *The Pharmacist*) is again Fields's spouse in *The Barber Shop.* This time, however, she is a spouse with a bite, anticipating the comic venom of later screen wife Kathleen Howard. The supportive daughter figure and balance to Howard is the pretty manicurist who listens to such Fieldsian fables as his experiences in the "Bare-Handed Wolf-Choker's Association."

The comedy laboratory nature of the Sennett short subjects seems to have been most instructive for Fields in the last two vehicles. (They also received the best critical response.)[148] While none of his later features will demonstrate anything quite like the comic meanness of *The Dentist* or the all-encompassing satire of *The Fatal Glass of Beer,* several will continue in the comic antihero nature of *The Pharmacist* and *The Barber Shop.* This will include his two greatest films, *It's a Gift* and *The Bank Dick.* In fact, *The Bank Dick* concludes with the same perfect antiheroic capsulization which closes *The Pharmacist* and *The Barber Shop*—Fields's little-man persona comes in conflict with a gun-toting crook.

In each case, Fields the artist is able to juxtapose a world of action with the uneventful little world of the antihero (who frequently imagines what he would do in a high-adventure setting for example, Cornelius O'Hare's "Bare-Handed Wolf-Choker" yarns or Walter Mitty's secret mission for mankind). And as transitional crackerbarrel to antihero humorist Kin Hubbard observed during the period, "The first thing a feller does when he's held up is change his mind about what he used to think he'd do."[149] Thus in each case the bravery of the antiheroic Fields is found comically wanting, although by the time of *The Bank Dick,* more circumstances outside his control allow him to become a hero.

Fields appeared in one additional short subject during 1933, a Warner Brothers film entitled *Hip Action*. This one-reeler was the third lesson in a *How to Break 90* collection of the *Bobby Jones Golf Series*. Now the comic frustrations (golfing) of Fields are juxtaposed (for teaching purposes) with the championship form of celebrated golfer Bobby Jones. *Hip Action,* which was directed by George Marshall and also featured Warner Oland and William Davidson, is frequently absent from Fields filmographies, no doubt because of its unique status among the comedian's films.[150] Fields's only appearance in a "how to" film was probably a tribute to his fascination for golf, footnoted in so many films and in his stage routine "An Episode on the Links." *Hip Action* and the Sennett films are the last short subjects Fields made, although espisodes from later features continue to be released in abridged versions.

Besides making the shorts in 1933, Fields appeared in three features: *International House, Tillie and Gus,* and *Alice in Wonderland*. The verb *appeared* is well chosen because full use was made of Fields only in *Tillie and Gus*. However, in all fairness to Paramount, the box-office message of 1932 was that studios needed to bring former "big-draw names together . . . [because] the day of the so-called single star power had faded."[151] Yet while Fields had to compete with a raft of *International House* comedians for both screen time and laughs, *Time* magazine correctly labeled this "a private spree for W.C. Fields."[152]

The film itself is *Grand Hotel* (1932) run amuck—Paramount's comic takeoff of MGM's famous drama from the previous year. Set in Wu Hu, China, the modest plotline is about Doctor Wong's (Edmund Breese's) invention of a television (called a "radioscope" in the film) and the international collection of eccentrics gathered to buy the rights, from the nebbish American Tommy Nash (Stuart Erwin) to the aggressive, pompous Russian General Petronovich (Bela Lugosi). Additional characters are provided both by the hotel staff—George Burns and Gracie Allen are doctor and nurse, Franklin Pangborn is the manager—and the radioscope itself (numerous performers, including Fields, are introduced via the small screen).

The radioscope, in fact, is an apt metaphor for the generally antihero nature of the film because the device constantly frustrates its inventor. While Doctor Wong patiently tries to tune in the telecast of a six-day bicycle race, everything but the race appears, including the alcoholic takeoff by an autogiro (helicopter) of Professor Quail (Fields).

Fields's role has the cynical directness of *The Dentist*, yet unlike the character in that short subject, he is here humanized by frequent comic frustrations. For example, his original flight destination was Kansas City, not China, but like most people in the wrong he denies it: "I'm here, Kansas City is lost." Also, his character can never get enough alcohol, something with which his immediate American audience could strongly identify, since the Eighteenth Amendment to the Constitution establishing Prohibition had not yet been fully repealed. There are countless other Fields frustrations, including losing an oddball conversation with Gracie Allen (are there ever winners?) and entangling himself in the lines of the hotel switchboard, which he calls a "Chinese noodle-swamp."

Fields does manage, however, to make his escape from an ever more turbulent *International House,* towing none other than Peggy Hopkins Joyce, the real-life gold digger who plays herself in the film. The escape is made possible by the comedian's undersized car (it must be able to fit inside the autogiro), drawing its general compact-car humor from the premise of two copyrighted Fields stage routines, "The Sport Model" and "The Midget Car." As might be expected, the car produces frustrations as well: the ceiling is so low that Fields "wears" his hat on the roof approximately over his head, only eventually to have his head go through the ceiling. (Fields utilized another variation of the routine in *Sally of the Sawdust.*)

With *Tillie and Gus,* Paramount again draws comic inspiration from Metro-Goldwyn-Mayer with the teaming of Alison Skipworth and Fields (the Tillie and Gus of the title), no doubt inspired by the earlier pairing of Marie Dressler and Wallace Beery in *Min and Bill* (1930) and the later *Tugboat Annie* (released in summer 1933, while *Tillie and Gus* appeared in late fall of 1933).[153] Fields and Skipworth had been teamed previously in their *If I Had a Million* vignette and would later appear together in *Alice in Wonderland* and *Six of a Kind* (1934), but *Tillie and Gus* is easily their best joint offering.

In this film Fields moves from con man to antihero. As Augustus Winterbottom, Fields is first seen as a cardshark on trial in Alaska for the sins of his profession. "Requested" to leave town promptly, he receives a telegraph message promising a possible inheritance back in the States. Skipworth, as Tillie Winterbottom, Fields's estranged wife, receives a similar telegram in China, where she runs a gambling house. These two old crooks accidently meet on the way back and after a near shootout decide to rejoin forces, starting with a little scam at a nearby poker game. But when they realize the town lawyer (Clarence Wilson) has almost completely robbed their niece (Jacqueline Wells) of her inheritance, they decide to help.

All the girl and her husband have is their child (Baby LeRoy) and a decrepit steamship on which they live. Once aboard, Fields slips more and more into his antiheroic persona—a reflection of his now-domestic surroundings. This transition is best exemplified by his attmept to mix paint via the 'Handy Andy" radio show. Fields cannot keep up with the various ingredients being listed, even when he attempts to save time by not removing products from their containers. Then, unbeknown to Fields, Baby Leroy switches the radio dial to an exercise program. And Fields is immediately hopping about in a radio physical fitness routine, not unlike the opening of *Running Wild* where the meek Elmer Finch (Fields) exercises wearing his crystal set (radio) headphones.

Fields's radio frustrations in *Tillie and Gus* are also reminiscent of the basic comedy premise of his copyrighted stage routine "10,000 People Killed": how easy it is for the radio to create misunderstandings. And the stage sketch also included a distracting baby who would provoke Fields's character to say: "Will baby sit down before papa knocks her for a home run."[154] However, the domesticated Fields of the second half of *Tillie and Gus* is so far from "sporting" threats he actually gives Baby Leroy a ride on his back at the film's close.

Before this happy conclusion, though, Fields has suffered several other antiheroic frustrations. He gives a comic but very unimpressive demonstration of the old ship's soundness (even a life preserver sinks) and bumblingly releases the fuel logs into the river during the climactic riverboat race. The antiheroic developments soften a character who might again have succumbed to the comic harshness of *The Dentist*. *New York Times* film critic Mordaunt Hall nicely capsulizes the result: "It is the sort of thing [role] admirably suited to Mr. Field's [*sic*] peculiar genius."[155]

The following month—December—Hall described Fields's portrayal of Humpty Dumpty in *Alice in Wonderland* as "downright good," where he "gets everything out of the part."[156] Reviewers consistently singled out Fields for praise in Paramount's all-star Christmas release-salute to Lewis Carroll. In fact, *The Literary Digest* was so taken with his verbal characterization (almost all the *Alice* stars lost their personal identities because of the ambitious costuming and makeup), its March 24, 1934, review of another Fields film, *Six of a Kind,* continues to expound upon Fields's Humpty Dumpty, considering him the most unique of all players concerned.[157] Paramount had filled the film with excellent performers, especially major star Gary Cooper (White Knight) and soon-to-be major star Cary Grant (Mock Turtle). Yet here again, in a film where Fields is just one of several stars, he manages to be singled out. There are two distinctive reasons.

First, the importance of his voice cannot be overemphasized. (His later entry into radio was an immediate success.) As film historian Gerald Mast has suggested, Fields often used his grandiose language just as he used his grandiose clothing (when playing the con man) to disguise his crooked intentions.[158]

Second, Fields was uniquely suited to play the part of Humpty Dumpty. As suggested by an unidentified article in the Fields files at the Billy Rose Theatre Collection (New York Public Library), both the literary character and the comic performer have a way of making words mean what they want. More precisely, Lewis Carroll's character describes the phenomenon this way: "When I use a word," Humpty Dumpty said, in rather a scornful tone, "It means just what I choose it to mean—neither more nor less."[159]

Fields, besides giving the world endearments like "my little chickadee" and such pseudonyms as Mahatma Kane Jeeves, also coined several new words. For example:

> Squeemudgeon: Director who calls an actor down to the
>   studio at 8 A.M., and doesn't use him till 11.
> Obstructroid: Male camera hog.
> Obstructrix: Female ditto.
> Philanthroac: One whose mission in life seems to be taking care
>   of drunks who don't want to be taken care of.[160]

All in all, Fields's success in *Alice in Wonderland* was a unique coup; he had stolen the show in a production which had generated such great print-medium attention that it was showcased on the cover of *Time* magazine.[161]

In December of 1933 the world's newest Humpty Dumpty announced he had been appointed official Santa Claus for Hollywood[162] and proposed several gag gifts for his fellow performers. Charlotte Henry (who played the title role in *Alice*) was to receive a copy of the book *Alice in Wonderland* because "She's been a busy girl all her life, and I'll bet she'll have a swell time sitting up reading."[163] (Despite Fields's insinuations, Henry's *Alice* reviews were generally good.) Other gift suggestions included water wings for champion swimmer-turned-actor Larry (Buster) Crabbe and a fashion book for Mae West "telling how the slim figure is coming back, and how women shouldn't wear diamonds. Mae should be pleased with that."[164] It seems that the man who frequently claimed to dislike Christmas could enjoy the holiday, too, if certain black-comedy adjustments were made.

The frantic film pace of 1933 continued through 1934, a year in which there were five Fields features: *Six of a Kind, You're Telling Me, The Old-Fashioned Way, Mrs. Wiggs of the Cabbage Patch,* and *It's a Gift.* The Fields appearances can be broken into two categories: guest-star-type roles late in the story (*Six of a Kind* and *Mrs. Wiggs*) and top-billed remakes of silent Fields features (*You're Telling Me* of *So's Your Old Man, The Old-Fashioned Way* of *Two Flaming Youths,* and *It's a Gift* of *It's the Old Army Game*).

In *Six of a Kind,* Fields plays Sheriff John Hoxley, a position as seemingly incongruous as Chaplin's portraying a cop in *Easy Street.* But it allows Fields to dust off his pool routine one more time, as well as comically elaborating on how he received the nickname "Honest John." Even in his abridged screen time, he easily steals the show.

With *You're Telling Me,* an excellent silent feature improves in the retelling, especially with the addition of the Fields voice and dialogue by the neglected J.P. McEvoy. Fields again plays underdog inventor Sam Bisbee, whose fortune changes after meeting a princess (this time played by Adrienne Ames). *You're Telling Me* follows *So's Your Old Man* so closely that several silent titles are incorporated into the sound dialogue of the remake, such as Mrs. Bisbee's (Louise Carter's) response to being called the "luckiest woman": "Is my husband dead?"

There are, however, some differences which accent basic Fields trends of the 1930s. For example, his antiheroic character is more pronounced here than in *So's Your Old Man.* In the earlier film, when several town gossips walk around him on the sidewalk, he threatens to hit them with his cane (though he does save this action until they are safely past). In *You're Telling Me,* when another gossipy type scoops up her child so she will not be scandalized by association with the infamous Bisbee, the comedian checks one of his shoes for dog droppings and then smells his cigar. His actions acknowledge a certain level of inadequacy—"something must be wrong with me"—as opposed to the proud but repressed anger of the raised cane in *So's Your Old Man.*

You're Telling Me also accents the increased importance of the loyal daughter figure in a Fields film. And while Bisbee's daughter Pauline (Joan Marsh) fulfills one's expectations (she is even the one to whom Father Fields writes his suicide note), the role of the princess assumes an even more daughterly posture than it did in *So's Your Old Man.* This is best demonstrated by a variation in the close of the later film. The earlier work had Fields being offered a million dollars outright for his invention; in the latter film the princess makes a similar price possible by instituting a bidding war with the prospective buyer. (The following year, 1935, Fields will assign a similar bartering scene to his daughter in *The Man on the Flying Trapeze.*)

Quite possibly the increased importance of the 1930s daughter figure for the screen Fields was in response to the equally increased frustration caused him by most other females in the story. While this reflects Fields's more antiheroic tendencies in the thirties, it also showcased a basic technological development—a portrait of a nag is much more effectively drawn with the use of sound. And *You're Telling Me* is rich in female nemeses for Fields, from Louise Carter's Mrs. Bisbee to the town's stuffy matron of high society, Mrs. Murchison (Kathleen Howard, who will play Fields's screen wife twice in the future). Even Elise Cavanna, who caused Fields so much comic frustration in the Sennett films, is given a small supporting role as a gossip.

Besides these three general developments, which can be equated with basic 1930s transitions taking place in his comedy, there are some other changes specific to the remake. For instance, *the* invention of the earlier film, Fields's unbreakable windshield, became a puncture-proof tire in *You're Telling Me.* In addition to being more humorous (flattening a tire versus breaking a window), it seemed to inspire increased comic action in

Fields. Thus when he tests his tires by shooting them with a pistol, he wears a baseball glove with which to catch the ricocheting bullets. And the sight of a boy rolling a hoop with a stick encourages him to chase his tire in like manner—leading him onto train tracks and some predictable yet funny thrill comedy. As with the dogsled scene in *The Fatal Glass of Beer*, the use of obvious back projection on the tracks—an approaching train—actually adds to the humor. Fields almost seems to be parodying the extreme frustrations to which an antihero is vulnerable, while once again drawing parallels with the anything-goes world of the cartoon strip.

The release of *You're Telling Me* was followed by *The Old-Fashioned Way,* which provided Fields with a strong starring role as the Great McGonigle, manager (and contributing performer) of a very modest collection of late nineteenth-century traveling thespians. Moreover, as *You're Telling Me* had finally given Fields the opportunity to devote an entire sound feature to his antihero persona (with top billing and nearly continuous on-screen role), *The Old Fashioned Way* supplied that chance for his con-man persona, though there are still some moments of defused antiheroic humor. For example, a boardinghouse child (Baby LeRoy) dips Fields's watch into a jar of molasses during dinner. The scene obviously suggests the domestic frustrations of the comedian's antihero movies, though the child is not his. Yet even here, Fields's forceful but sneaky revenge accents the central con-man thrust of the film: when no one is watching he nearly punts Baby LeRoy out of the room. (The film also allows Fields safely to bean someone with a revenging croquet mallet.) The comedian's antihero movies seldom allow his frustrated character such satisfaction (other than in frequent miracle conclusions). For instance, in Fields's antiheroic *It's a Gift*, which soon followed *The Old-Fashioned Way,* Baby LeRoy again creates a molasses mess by draining a barrel of the sticky stuff onto the floor of Fields's store. Yet despite this even greater inconvenience (necessitating the posting of the sign "Closed on Account of Molasses"), the comedian is allowed no comic revenge. In fact, the scene becomes more antiheroic because the boy's mother rails against Fields for allowing Baby Leroy to become (sticky) dirty.

The Old-Fashioned Way contains numerous classic scenes, from the comic symmetry of an opening escape from the sheriff to a near closing escape from the landlady. But the most memorable turn is Fields's juggling, especially of the celebrated cigar boxes. Though he originally made his name as a comic juggler, very little of this skill has been recorded on film. And sometimes even that which is preserved, as in *Sally of the Sawdust*, is flawed by a camera which quickly treats the juggling as a backdrop for other narrative action. Consequently, this scene from *The Old-Fashioned Way* presents the best showcase of Fields as juggler. In later years it would become available for rental as part of a short subject excerpt from the feature entitled *The Great McGonigle*.

Once again, Fields received critical hosannas. In fact, *Time* magazine observed: "Although he never seems to suspect that he is funny, he is fast becoming a comedian as valuable to the talkies as Charles Chaplin was to the silent cinema ten years ago."[165] The always insightful 1930s film critic Otis Ferguson suggested in his review of *The Old-Fashioned Way* that Fields was the best comedian then working in motion pictures.[166]

The Old-Fashioned Way was followed by *Mrs. Wiggs of the Cabbage Patch*, the sentimental story of the financially poor Mrs. Wiggs (Pauline Lord) and her five children. Though Fields, as Mr. Stubbins, is given second billing, he does not appear until near the film's close. He is to be the husband of Miss Hazy (Zasu Pitts), close friend of the Wiggs family. Theirs has been a mail-order "romance," under the direction of Mrs. Wiggs. As is normal in an antiheroic situation, Fields frequently plays pawn to a female, or in this case, females: he has consented to marry Miss Hazy if she can cook. She convinces him of "her" culinary skills with dishes prepared by Mrs. Wiggs.

Fields's last 1934 film, *It's a Gift*, is probably his greatest work, rivaled only by the later *Bank Dick* (1940). Film historian William Everson ranks *It's a Gift* "among the finest comedy work from any period and any country."[167] A remake of *It's the Old Army Game,* which in turn was drawn from McEvoy's pivotal *The Comic Supplement,* the film's credits also note the original story contribution of Charles Bogle (Fields). Thus, like most Fields films, *It's a Gift* is largely a collection of earlier routines tied loosely to a slender plotline. But in this case, the sketches are not only superb (including the best rendition of Fields's greatest sketch, "The Sleeping Porch"), they dovetail with little strain. There is also a consistency of comedy character which was sometimes lacking in *It's the Old Army Game.* Consequently, the viewer follows the antiheroic frustrations of Fields at home (including a family "game" called sharing the bathroom mirror), at work in a soon-to-be molasses-covered store, back home trying to sleep on *that* porch, taking the family across country in an overloaded car, and finally the highs and lows of California living.

While Fields was never as big at the box office as Chaplin or the pre-censorship code (1934) Mae West, he had a dedicated and loyal following, not unlike the pre-*Annie Hall* disciples of Woody Allen. Also as with Allen, most critics were more appreciative than the fans of his talents. Thus besides overviews of praise, such as the aforementioned quote from *Time*, critics frequently singled out individual scenes for high marks. Examples would include Fields's ability to make even suicide "hilarious" in *You're Telling Me* and the equally difficult accomplishment of using a blind and deaf detective for comic effect in *It's a Gift*.[168]

This is not to say, however, that critics who favored Fields were oblivious to seeming flaws in his films. For example, in the mid-1930s there was a tendency to rail against studio misuse of this comedian. Ferguson said

Fields "was given a walk-on in *Mrs. Wiggs of the Cabbage Patch* and his name was dishonestly starred on the marquee to float that whole lighter of garbage."[169] And throughout his career, there was a tendency to note his haphazard film narratives; this will be examined later in the chapter. Concerning the film at hand, *It's a Gift,* some initial reviewers were bothered by its low production values.[170] (Ironically, what was once labeled a flaw now seems to enhance the antiheroic world of *It's a Gift,* just as back projection now strengthens the parody slant of *The Fatal Glass of Beer.*)[171]

Field's second use of the pseudonym Charles Bogle (first on *The Old-Fashioned Way* and then on *It's a Gift,* both for original story credit) merits special consideration for three reasons. First, it begins to suggest the affection he had for this pen name. He would use it for original story credit on two additional films: *The Man on the Flying Trapeze* and *You Can't Cheat an Honest Man.*

Second, it illustrates Fields's interest in the comic effect of character names or words in general. *It's a Gift* alone offers numerous examples besides Charles Bogle, including the customer who keeps requesting kumquats and the salesman in search of Karl LaFong (a name which is spelled out by both Fields and the salesman during the "Sleeping Porch" routine). And, of course, there is the frequent antiheroic mispronouncing by others of Fields's character's name in *It's a Gift*—Bissonette.

Third, Fields's reasons for liking the name Bogle also provide basic insights into his views on comedy. The comedian once observed that "'Charley Bogle,' spoken slowly and solemnly with a very long 'o,' is a laugh."[172] This interest in verbal word games is in the tradition of what comedy historian Walter Blair calls the "Literary Comedians," an American humor movement in the second half of the nineteenth century.[173] Literary comedian Charles Farrar Browne, under the celebrated alias Artemus Ward, demonstrates several comedy variations on the letter *o* in an "Interview with President Lincoln": "'Virto,' sed I, holdin' the infatooated man by the coat-collar, 'virtoo, sir, is its own reward. Look at me!'"[174] Moreover, the fact that "nearly all of the names I [Fields] have used on the screen are real people I have met in traveling around this crazy world"[175] underlines his repeated desire to keep at least one comedy foot in reality:

> I once knew a Cleopatra Pepperday and suggested her name for the character Jan Duggan played in *The Old-Fashioned Way.* Baby LeRoy played *Albert Wendeschaffer* [in *The Old Fashioned Way*], who is actually a theatre manager in New Jersey. . . . Charley Bogle and Dr. Beebe are also very near and dear to me. [See also *You're Telling Me.*] They live in a small town in upstate New York.[176]

Fields's interest in comedy names also represents a natural bridge to his next film project—Dickens's *David Copperfield:*

> I can't claim any originality for picking amusing character names. Dickens thought of that a long time ago and has yet to be equaled, let alone surpassed. . . . Reading Dickens was my start in collecting names. I have picked up odd and amusing names from billboards, newspapers, or wherever I found them.[177]

But Fields's interest in the author went beyond character names. The comedian's last mistress described him as "an avid Dickens buff" and portrayed his bedside as something just this side of a Dickens library.[178] Fields was taken by Dickens's dialogue and "character delineations . . . [which] simply walked off the pages into your life, to live on with you until the end of your days."[179]

Fields's view of his childhood as largely outcast in nature, despite later denials by his family, undoubtedly also contributed to his fascination with Dickens. The English author's work is focused almost completely on orphaned or outcast children, with David Copperfield and Oliver Twist merely the most celebrated cases. A difficult childhood is obviously the reason why Fields's comedy contemporary Charlie Chaplin was also greatly taken with Dickens. However, while Chaplin created The Tramp, who was often lovingly parental toward waif figures, Fields's screen personae were frequently rough on the overprivileged child—a favored status he had never known as a youngster. Thus any Fields-equals-child baiter equations do not necessarily apply to Dickens's literary children. Besides, in the novel in question, young David frequently displays devastatingly cutting overstatements (though offered ∖innocently, in a wise-fool manner) which the generally cynical comedian no doubt enjoyed. For example, David described the frequent punishment of schoolmate Tommy Traddles thus: "He was always being caned—I think he was caned every day that half-year, except one holiday Monday when he was only ruled on both hands."[180] And young David characterized his dear nurse Peggotty's new husband's (Mr. Barkis's) attempt at lucidity in the following manner: "I might have stood looking in his face for an hour, and most assuredly should have got as much information out of it as out of the face of a clock that had stopped."[181]

David Copperfield was a Metro-Goldwyn-Mayer production, and Fields was loaned to the studio from Paramount to appear as Micawber, one of the comedian's favorite literary characters.[182] In addition, Fields's screen personae (particularly the huckster) bear strong parallels to Micawber in four ways. First, Fields's verbal-juggling con man is predated by a Micawber who takes language to even further extremes. This quickly becomes a celebration of absurdist style over content and also gives a false

3. W.C. Fields as Micawber, one ot his favorite literary characters. (From the MGM release "DAVID COPPERFIELD" © 1935 Metro-Goldwyn-Mayer, Inc.)

importance to very common activities. For instance, in the first meeting of David and Micawber in the novel (the boy has just arrived in London and will lodge with the Micawber family), Micawber offers the following assistance:

> "Under the impression," said Mr. Micawber, "that your peregrinations in this metropolis have not as yet been extensive, and that you might have some difficulty in penetrating the arana of the Modern Babylon in the direction of the City Road—in short," said Mr. Micawber, in another burst of confidence, "that you might lose yourself—I shall be happy to call this evening, and install you in the knowledge of the nearest way."[183]

Second, the Fields con man is constantly hounded by creditors; this is also the constant fate of Micawber. In fact, as if to accent that parallel, the 1935 adaptation of *David Copperfield* first introduces Fields's Micawber sneaking around some creditors, instead of in the actual aforementioned scene. Thus Fields's initial Micawber speech, spoken to his family and David as he enters the house by way of a skylight: "I have thwarted the malevolent machinations of our enemies [the creditors]. In short, I have arrived."

Third, Fields's personae (both con man and antihero) frequently have a loyal daughter, while the antihero figure is just as frequently buffeted about by a henpecking wife. Dickens's work, particularly *David Copperfield,* is full of idealized young heroines from which Fields might have drawn a model. A particularly strong case could be made for the character of Agnes Wickfield, an extremely loyal daughter to a father being cheated by the infamous Uriah Heep—all three of whom have close narrative ties to Micawber. Interestingly enough, in terms of a Fields connection, Mr. Wickfield has a drinking problem.

David Copperfield also offers several character types from which Fields could have drawn material for the pestering wife of the antihero (if not suitably inspired by the relationship with his own estranged wife). These could vary from the nonstop complaining of the harmless Mrs. Gummidge (whose very name suggests flapping gums) to the sinister Miss Murdstone, who assisted her brother in nearly killing David's once bubbly childhood (just as her name implies a weapon of death). Conversely, one would not initially think of Mrs. Micawber as a "henpecking" wife because she is so very loyal to her husband and forever the good mother to her children. But she does have a way of recapping Micawber's woes which smacks of the complaining wife, something Fields seems to have found entertaining, if not comically instructive. That is, Carlotta Monti observed that the comedian

> loved the lines uttered by Mrs. Micawber before her husband is thrown into a debtors' prison: "I never thought, before I was married, when I lived with Papa and Mamma [*sic*], that I should

ever find it necessary to take a lodger [the boy, David Copper-
field]. . . . If Mr. Micawber's creditors *will not* give him time,
they must take the consequences. Blood cannot be obtained from
a stone, neither can anything on account be obtained at present
from Mr. Micawber."[184]

In the following chapter of *David Copperfield,* from which the Monti
quote is originally drawn, Mrs. Micawber reaches an ever more comically
hysterical recap of her bruised loyalty, forever punctuated by "but I never
will desert Mr. Micawber!":

The pearl necklace and bracelets, which I have inherited from
mama, have been disposed of for less than half their value; and
the set of coral, which was the wedding gift of my papa, has been
actually thrown away for nothing. But I never will desert Mr.
Micawber.[185]

The fourth manner in which Fields's ongoing screen personae seem to be
drawn from the world of Micawber comes in the almost magical turn of
events which inevitably allows happy endings, sudden riches granted the
antiheroes, and perennial escapes of the con men. Dickens, of course,
grants Mr. Micawber a new start in Australia. In fact, the close of *David
Copperfield* has a years-later report from the colony stating that Micawber
is now a prominent district magistrate!

Certainly, the apparent influence of Dickens on Fields was not lessened
by the effect of Dorothy Donnelly's Dickensian *Poppy* on the comedian's
career. But the Dickens presence seemed truly continuous with Fields. His
volatile mood changes were so reminiscent of Micawber's constant flights
from highs to lows; his comically eccentric distrust of servants was so much
like that of Miss Murdstone, who "dived into the coal-cellar at the most
untimely hours, and scarcely ever opened the door of a dark cupboard
without clapping it to again, in the belief that she had got him [an imagined
man she believed the servants to be hiding]."[186]

Lauded Fields biographer Robert Lewis Taylor, who drew so strongly
from the comedian's close friends, observed: "From the moment of their
first acquaintance [when Fields was a youth], Fields had felt an especial
affinity for Dickens, in some of whose characters he saw strong traces of
himself."[187] Taylor suggests the comedian's fascination with Dickens was
also fed by the once popular vaudeville performer Owen McGiveney, "who
specialized in Dickens impersonations."[188] Appropriately, the example of
McGiveney's work which Taylor presents finds him impersonating
Micawber.

Taylor later notes, upon examining the comedian's writing form: "His
style was extravagant, florid, influenced in large measure by Dickens,

whom he knew by heart."[189] Fields's personal secretary, Magda Michael, added: "Despite his love of simplicity, he could never say, 'Hit him on the head,' he always had to make it 'Conk him on the noggin.'"[190]

Naturally, all of these ties to Dickens begin with the aforementioned affinity the comedian no doubt felt between his own difficult childhood and that of the typical Dickens waif, a link which also drew Fields's sometimes model, sometimes nemesis Charlie Chaplin to Dickens.

Fields received top billing in the film adaptation of *David Copperfield,* heading a cast which included Lionel Barrymore (as Dan Peggotty), Maureen O'Sullivan (Dora), Lewis Stone (Mr. Wickfield), Freddie Bartholomew (David, the child), Roland Young (Uriah Heep), and Basil Rathbone (Mr. Murdstone). The comedian more than met the demands of the billing, as he garnered rave reviews. Said the *New York Times:* "the one performance that is able to remain predominant among such splendors of character acting." Added *Newsweek:* "The real hit of the show is W.C. Fields as the longwinded dramatic Micawber. He dominates every scene he is in and reaches perfection in the final show-down with Uriah Heep."[191] Due to the epic scope of the novel and the constraints this places upon any film adaptation of a conventional length, Fields is not on screen for a sustained period, though his important reappearances throughout the story help to unify a plot that covers a number of years, and even more characters.

The production itself also received strong reviews, from *Time* magazine's "an example of the cinema's ability to use one masterpiece to create another" to the *New York Times*'s "the most profoundly satisfying novel that the camera has ever given us."[192] Because Fields received special praise in such a highly lauded film, *David Copperfield* was probably, during Fields's lifetime, his most roundly applauded cinema achievement.

The Dickens adaptation was followed by *Mississippi,* from the Booth Tarkington story "Magnolia." Fields, as the con man, plays the delightful Commodore Jackson, captain of a Mississippi riverboat. While Bing Crosby receives top billing as a singer on the boat, the comedy of Fields makes the film—especially his recurring tall tale about his days as an Indian fighter, when he took down his old Bowie knife and "cut a path through a wall of living flesh."

Fields literature has sometimes suggested Crosby stole the film from the comedian. No doubt much of this stems from biographer Robert Lewis Taylor's statement that Fields "got the uneasy notion . . . none of this [his comedy] was detracting from Crosby."[193] But while there is no denying the singing abilities of Crosby, Fields's concerns were not mirrored in contemporary reviews. For instance, *Variety* stated: "Fields works hard throughout the film and saves it, giving it whatever entertainment value it has"; the *New York Times* printed: Fields "provides the entertainment with its memorable moments."[194] This is especially true for today's viewer, because the down-South plantation romances (and complications) of Crosby have not aged very well. It is particularly difficult to take seriously Crosby's identity as the "Singing Killer." Granted, this is the brainchild of Fields's con-man character, and as long as Fields and Crosby share the screen the viewer can accept this as more comic magic by the master of charlatans. But there are several scenes without Fields where Crosby, as the "Singing Killer," is to be taken soberly; these scenes more than strain the film's credibility. *Variety* indirectly endorsed this when it states: "Paramount obviously couldn't make up its mind what it wanted to do with the film. . . . For a few minutes it's sheer farce, for a few moments it's romance."[195]

The tall-tale nature of Fields's contribution to the film, which would seem to mirror his interest in Mark Twain's humor (as well as the fact that Twain was once captain of a riverboat on the Mississippi and much of his writing involves life along her shores), also allows Fields to attack hypocrisy—a favorite target—in his own con-man persona. Near the film's close, Commodore Jackson is again heroically rambling along about his "path through . . . living flesh." But at this point some wooden Indians are being loaded on board, unbeknown to Fields, and he mistakes them for the real thing as they are pulled past his porthole. His speech quickly flip-flops from boastful courage to imitation compassion, with lines like "some of my best friends are Indians."

The comedian's last 1935 film was *The Man on the Flying Trapeze,* a remake of his silent *Running Wild.* Once again Fields had an excellent antiheroic film, though reviews were mixed. Fields plays Ambrose Wolfinger, a henpecked businessman, who lives unhappily with his second wife (Kathleen Howard), his mother-in-law (Vera Lewis), his brother-in-law (Grady Sutton), and a daughter by his first marriage (Mary Brian). As stated earlier during the examination of *Running Wild,* the film is given a strong biographical stamp; it mirrors something of Fields's real estranged marriage and gives the lazy brother-in-law the same name as his legitimate son, about whom he was then having similar feelings. (Grady Sutton's apparent age, thirtyish, also made him seem more like a stepson to Fields, as well as approximating the age of the real Claude.)

As if to add further comic melodrama for the insider, Fields's mistress Carlotta Monti plays the comedian's loyal secretary. In fact, her defense of Mr. Wolfinger, accused of having been drunk in the gutter, is so strong that Monti deserves listing among the sizable loyal-daughter category in Fields's films. Between Monti's character and that of Mary Brain's, who played the real daughter to Wolfinger (and who negotiates a lucrative new contract for him), Fields's comic antihero once again exits a picture with a monetary miracle.

Fields's transition from weak-kneed husband to lion is much briefer and more realistic than in the original. Whereas *Running Wild* had him hypnotized at a vaudeville show, the remake merely has him become exasperated and start swinging; Claude is K.O.'d, but Wolfinger misses his mother-in-law. And the antihero's new life-with-respect is precipitated more by the success of the new contract won by his daughter than by the continued tough-guy policy suggested at the close of *Running Wild*. These and other changes allowed Fields (as Charles Bogle) and friend Sam Hardy to take original story credit, though *Running Wild* is credited to Fields's friend Gregory LaCava. As a side note, Monti might have done some contributing of her own to *The Man on the Flying Trapeze,* because the remake builds much of its comedy around professional wrestling, and she had ended a serious relationship with a professional wrestler before meeting Fields.

Variety's review of the film suggested the title was an attempt to capitalize on the previous winter's song hit.[196] If that were the case, Fields was in good company, for fellow antihero creator James Thurber published his excellent *Middle-Aged Man on the Flying Trapeze* the same year. But while there were no direct ties between title and tale, Fields had long been associated with carnival or circus settings, and it would seemingly demand no great metaphorical leap of the imagination to see the comic antihero as a twentieth-century trapeze artist, forever trying to tightrope his way through modern life.

In October 1935, after the autumn release of *The Man on the Flying Trapeze,* it was announced that Fields had signed another contract with Paramount (for one year).[197] The comedian planned to do three films in that period and was then resting following a recent illness. Unfortunately, ill health would reduce his 1936 film total to one—*Poppy*—and would keep him entirely out of movies in 1937.

This second film adaptation of *Poppy* is closer to the original play than Griffith's *Sally of the Sawdust,* which means Fields is thankfully showcased as more of a con man. Unfortunately, Fields's poor health, though not apparent on the screen, necessitated the periodic use of a double so the comedian's "strength could be conserved for the dialogue and comedy business that only he could do."[198]

Film authors William Everson and Nicholas Yanni both prefer the more realistic, on-location look of *Sally* versus the studio fantasy of *Poppy*.[199] Yet a fantasy realm is hardly inappropriate for a romanticized, Dickensian look at nineteenth-century America. (Griffith had, as noted earlier, updated the story.) Moreover, a fantasy realm is perfectly in keeping with the comedy highlight of the second adaptation—Fields's alleged sale of a talking dog. Thus the importance of the second adaptation needs to be upgraded considerably.

Fields spent a great deal of time in hospitals and sanitariums during the 1930s, particularly in 1936 and 1937; in fact, mid-1936 found his condition "grave" as he suffered from pneumonia.[200] *Poppy*, which went into general distribution at this time, had been a severe trial for Fields. Producer William LeBaron and director Eddie Sutherland (each rare examples of a Fields friend who could also work professionally with him) even had to do some fancy talking to get the comedian through a Paramount preproduction physical for insurance purposes. This was not simplified by discovering Fields "at one time . . . had tuberculosis in both lungs, very badly."[201] Besides adding more evidence as to the difficulty of his youth, it provoked a reluctant observation (Fields distrusted doctors) that a similar medical diagnosis must have been correct years before. Ever the rebel, he had then refused to give up smoking, drinking, and performing. Yet this time, for a while, things would be different—severe health problems would see to that. There were even questions as to whether he would ever work again.[202]

Besides the natural trial ill health produces for anyone, sickness for Fields meant added stress. As previously stated, he had trouble believing doctors, something frequently suggested in his films. One joke was about the physician who treated a man three years for yellow jaundice before discovering the patient was Japanese. (Fields had difficulties with anyone in a position of authority, from the celebrated "disagreement" with his father to ongoing battles with film directors. The antisocial nature of his personae was very much based in reality.)

Medicine, moreover, or any professional services, meant spending money, and Fields could be very close with his funds. The added medical stress from distrust (as in the bedside manner) and dollars found comic fruitation in a story he told after his 1937 recovery:

> I'm going to call my new picture *The High Cost of Dying*. I'm an expert on that topic. In one scene a doctor will come in and say to me, "Let me see your tongue," and then he'll say, "ummm, five hundred dollars, please," and I'll sink back into my coma. I'll be in a coma through most of the picture, you see.
>
> If I show any signs of coming out of it, some doctor will be there to say, "Five hundred dollars, please," and I'll sink back.[203]

Fields's extended illness and his strong (if temporary) recovery seem to have had a multifaceted impact on the comedian. First, it gave him a completely new outlook:

> "I feel," he said in all seriousness, "that this is my second time on earth. I am starting all over again from scratch. It's all borrowed time I am living on, but I'm certainly enjoying it. . . . What I've gone through and come out of by a narrow squeak has certainly made me appreciate living, something I never did before."[204]

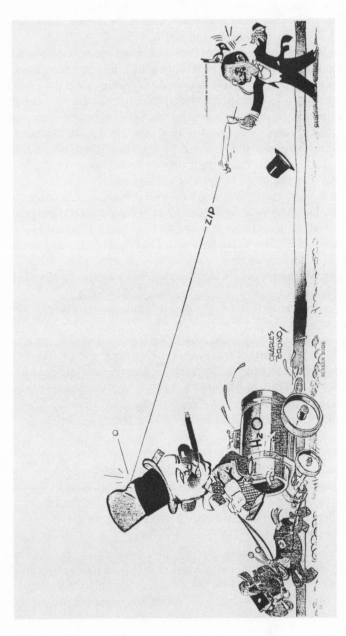

4. A caricature of Charlie McCarthy taking a potshot at W.C. Fields in their ongoing battle. (Done by Charles Bruno for the original Charles Darnton article "W.C. Fields Wins by a NOSE!" *Screen Book* magazine, November 1937.)

Fields had been especially moved by the size and sincerity of the mail he received, particularly from fans who were seriously ill themselves: they "hoped I would soon be back on the screen so that others could enjoy them [Fields's films] . . . they were hopelessly, incurably ill, [yet] they were just sorry for me. Those letters broke me all up."[205]

Interestingly enough, just the opposite of a softening was immediately discernible in his screen characters. This is unlike the more recent easing of Richard Pryor's film anger after his near fatal accident and the great show of public concern it generated. However, part of the reason is based in a second key impact of Fields's extended illness—he became interested in radio, and radio became interested in him. That is, Fields's career took a new twist—an aggressive high—when he started exchanging radio wise-cracks with Edgar Bergen's dummy Charlie McCarthy, whom he less than affectionately referred to as a "termite's flophouse."

Third and finally, his ability not only to recover but to come back as a bigger star than ever in a new (for Fields) medium reinforced an old Darwinian constant in his life—he was a survivor. Journalist Sara Hamilton nicely captured all of this in the title of a Fields piece, "That Man's Here Again."[206] The caption was an unacknowledged triple pun. While hailing his return and yet suggesting its inevitability, this was also to have been the title of a Fields film.

The new, recovered Fields always, of course, reinforced the old norm—that was part of being a survivor. For example, though he was on the wagon, he had told reporter Sara Hamilton: "Best they [the public] think of Bill with his bottle."[207] (Earlier, he had preferred to have friends think an illness-produced difficulty with his balance was merely a state of tipsyness.) And soon he was playing a public game of subterfuge concerning his nondrinking and using his best weapon—comedy. Thus in a later article that year (1937), he confessed to being dry but then added:

> Still, I admit I do enjoy a rum omlet for breakfast, brandied peaches or cherries for lunch, and mince pie with brandy sauce— sometimes I have several helpings—for dinner. But I do not drink. On this point I stand firm. . . . I now find I can get a pleasant glow for far less than it formerly cost me.[208]

While he was not drinking during his convalescing period, he was undoubtedly pursuing another favorite—picnicing, a pastime footnoted in more than one of his films. Fields's fondness for such outings probably represented an attempt, however subliminal, to recapture part of a youth from which he felt cheated. Moreover, these recreations, which also involved long drives, allowed him to pursue several other favored activities. He enjoyed both sightseeing and just observing people from his car, inter- ests which sometimes provided him with comedy material (and reinforced his belief in keeping at least one foot of his humor in reality). He also enjoyed owning large and luxurious automobiles, a fact demonstrated excellently in a short *Los Angeles Times* piece a few years earlier:

> W.C. Fields has bought one of those block-long automobiles as a celebrating gesture over the signing of his new contract with Paramount.
>
> "Yeah," admitted Fields, "It's so darn big I found a couple of stowaways the other day, and I expect to catch a guy riding the rods any minute.!"[209]

Fields's preference for large and expensive automobiles could undoubtedly be traced again to the deprivations of his youth, just as the California houses "he rented were all elaborate and expensive; Fields had a horror of cramped quarters, dating from the time when he lived in caves and barrels, and he left any neighborhood where an influx of population seemed imminent."[210]

Besides uncramped quarters and cars, Fields's long convalescence was no doubt made easier by the reviews he had garnered in his last film, *Poppy*. This second film adaptation of the play which had helped establish him was a personal triumph, though the film itself was rather bandied about. For example, *Variety* observed: "There's one thing that Bill Fields will never be, and that's unfunny. . . . Amidst . . . 19th century melodramatics . . . Fields manages . . . to get his laughs."[211]

Frank S. Nugent's *New York Times* review was a trifle more conciliatory concerning the relative merits of *Poppy*, but he left no doubt that "the real news . . . and the occasion for our rejoicing is this: that man is here again."[212] Nugent's tone was not unlike several earlier reviews that year for Chaplin's *Modern Times,* which had also celebrated more the return of a comedian than the content of a movie. *Poppy* is not in the same league as *Modern Times,* but when Fields is on screen, it is a very entertaining film.

Interestingly, despite having done the original Broadway play and two film adaptations, Fields was not yet finished with *Poppy*. In March 1938 "Lux Radio Theatre" presented still another rendition of the property. And if the other versions had been less than full utilizations of the comedian, the final outing was all Fields, from Program Producer Cecil B. De Mille's opening background notes on him to the comedian's paraphrasing of his ongoing refrain from *Mississippi*—how we "cut a path through this wall of human flesh, dragging our canoes behind us."

Fields's association with radio had begun the previous year when he had honored a Paramount request to take part in a special program honoring Adolph Zukor's (founder of Famous Players in Famous Plays, the fore-runner of Paramount) twenty-fifth anniversary in film. Illness kept him from the actual festivities, but the radio microphone brought to his sickbed produced immediate results—Fields was a hit. From that he received an offer to go on NBC's "The Chase & Sanborn Hour" with Edgar Bergen and Charlie McCarthy.

Guests Bergen and McCarthy had been such a hit on Rudy Vallee's "Royal Gelatin Hour" in late 1936 and early 1937 that Chase & Sanborn decided to create a show for them beginning May 9, 1937.[213] The show would also star Fields, Don Ameche (as master of ceremonies and as referee to Fields and McCarthy),[214] and Dorothy Lamour. While Fields left the program as a regular after "about five months," "much of the credit for the early showing goes to W.C. Fields, who started an immediate feud with Charlie McCarthy and kept the show moving at a fast pace."[215]

"The Chase & Sanborn Hour" was certainly an unlikely radio hit. As 1930s journalist Martin J. Porter observed "Drawing-room humorists used to make their victims howl with the subtle quip: 'You're about as useful as a juggler on the radio.' Sometimes they'd vary the . . . crack by substituting for the juggler—'a ventriloquist's dummy.' "[216] No more.

Of course, there were some surefire comic elements. Fields had a naturally comic voice, one which sponsors had been trying to put on the air for years. But he had never taken the medium seriously until he came to depend upon it for entertainment during his extended illness and found that lucrative salaries were available. (Fields would receive $6500 a week from Chase & Sanborn in 1937 and $7500 the following year, when he moved to Lucky Strike.)[217] Moreover, a key to the success of the Fields-McCarthy rivalry was based in the long-established comic premise (true or not) that Fields hated children. And Charlie McCarthy was just Baby LeRoy grown into a smart aleck kid. In fact, the *New York Times* editorial board observed, "Although Charlie is apparently still in his 'teens, his little voice is aweary of the world. It has the infernal, fatigued assurance of a lad who has been too much in the company of his elders: it is suave, condescending and impertinently familiar."[218]

In this new battle royal, however, Fields was in a more sympathetic position than in his former rivalry with Baby LeRoy. That is, while LeRoy certainly deserved anything he got (such as the boot for dipping Fields's watch in molasses), he was still a cute (seemingly innocent) baby. Such was not the case with Charlie McCarthy. Consequently, Fields had a greater license for revenge. The *New York Times* addressed this issue when it stated Charlie McCarthy "is impudent, lazy, egotistical and artful. A stern parent should have whaled the conceit out of him years ago, and perhaps W.C. Fields . . . will do it yet."[219]

Fields no doubt received additional comic sympathy because, though he was landing verbal punches, McCarthy seemed to be winning the fight. *Life* magazine, in an article entitled "Charlie McCarthy Is the Most Objectionable Young Man in America," baldly states, "Even the great Fields got the worst of it [in their verbal duals]."[220] *Motion Picture* also reflected that sentiment in the title of a Fields article published later in 1937: "Nobody's Dummy."[221]

Obviously, as this chapter has documented, Fields's personae, particularly the antihero, had been losing comedy battles for years. But then, as now, the image most popular with the public was that of the more capable con man, albeit even here Fields sometimes came up short. Fields's losses to a dummy, therefore, were news. (Interestingly enough, Chaplin's tramp figure suffered just the opposite public phenomenon. Charlie was more likely to be a capable winner, yet the public best remembered his scenes of touching pathos.)

While Fields was a regular on "The Chase & Sanborn Hour" only during the first year (1937), he made guest appearances well into the 1940s. And the Fields-McCarthy verbal exchanges are celebrated today as classic examples of American radio comedy during its golden age. Especially memorable lines would include Fields describing McCarthy as a "woodchigger's snack bar" and a "woodpecker's pin-up" or McCarthy's "is it true Mr. Fields that when you stood on the corner of Hollywood and Vine forty-three cars waited for your nose to change to green?"[222]

Fields's inspiration for the rivalry with McCarthy quite possible came from the famous Jack Benny-Fred Allen radio feud, which Allen first instituted in 1936. Moreover, the long-heralded radio showdown of Benny and Allen took place on March 14, 1937, less than two months before the premier of "The Chase & Sanborn Hour."[223]

In October 1938 Fields became a regular on CBS's "Your Hit Parade," a forty-five-minute program which presented the fifteen top songs of the week and a quarter-hour of comedy. The program was sponsored by Lucky Strike cigarettes (upset with Fields for referring to fictitious son *Chester Fields*). The comedian played a man who won a failing department store in a golf match. Christened Larsen E. Whipsnead, the key to Fields's particular character "may be obtained by pronouncing the first name and the initial as one word."[224] Later, when he would star with Bergen and McCarthy in the movie *You Can't Cheat an Honest Man* (1939), Fields would again use Larson E. Whipsnade, with minor spelling alteration, as his con-man character's name, though his failing business would switch from department store to circus. Thus while the film is generally described as capitalizing on the success of Fields's first radio program, it obviously draws a great deal from the second.

Sandwiched between *Poppy* and *You Can't Cheat an Honest Man* was *The Big Broadcast of 1938*, which was Fields's comeback film after his near fatal illness. Like earlier "Big Broadcast" pictures (1932, 1935, 1936), the 1938 edition was a variety-show production glued to the thinnest of plot lines. In this case, two luxury ocean liners are in a transatlantic race from New York to Cherbourg, France, and the viewer is given front row seats to a thousand and one subplots and sketches on board the S.S. *Gigantic*.

Ironically, the best scenes take place on land. S.B. Bellows (Fields) single-handedly destroys a massive gas station, then plays one of the fastest rounds of golf on record (he rides a motor scooter between shots). He then converts his little scooter to an equally dinky airplane and flies to the S.S. *Gigantic*, which has already departed.

The rest of the film never returns to this comic high, possibly because Fields is never allowed as much liberty in later scenes. Of additional interest, however, is the fact that Fields plays dual roles which compliment the con-man versus antihero dichotomy already delineated in this chapter. As T. Frothingell Bellows he is on view briefly as the crafty and wealthy businessman-owner of the S.S *Gigantic*. However, most of Fields's screen time is spent playing T.F. Bellow's brother, S.B. Bellows, a character with antiheroic luck. While S.B. is more abrasive than the average Milquetoast type, T.F. describes his brother as so jinxed that he has "been connected with every major accident since the sinking of the *Merrimac* [an armored warship of the Civil War]."

The trickster in T.F. tells his unlucky brother to land on the competing ship (the S.S. *Colossal*), assuming S.B.'s jinxed state will be more than enough to guarantee the victory of the S.S. *Gigantic*. But S.B. is so hexed that his scooter-turned-plane lands on his brother's ship, and he proceeds to work his unintended hoodoo on things, nearly losing the race.

Fields received top billing, with his name and a caricature above the film's title. The reviews justified the action. *Variety*, which was uniformly impressed by the whole production, opened its review as follows: "With the rejuvenated W.C. Fields at his inimitable best, . . ." *Time* more aptly summarized the thoughts of today's viewer: "Shipshape when Great Man Fields is on deck, it lists badly whenever he goes below."[225]

One year later, upon the completion of *You Can't Cheat an Honest Man,* the Masquers's Club continued the celebration of Fields by holding a banquet and roast in his honor. It was at this event, surrounded by the likes of Groucho Marx, Bob Hope, Jack Benny, Edgar Bergen, Milton Berle, Red Skeleton, and George Burns, among others, that the then largely unknown author and political scientist Dr. Leo Rosten (pseudonym Leonard Q. Ross) made a remark which will live through the ages: "Any man who hates dogs and babies can't be all bad." Unfortunately for Rosten, while the remark lives on, history has usurped credit for it from the insightful doctor, assigning it to Fields.

Rosten later chronicled the background of the event in a *Saturday Review* article entitled "My Most Embarrassing Moment."[226] It won this distinction because his inclusion on the dais was a last minute surprise, and his now famous description of Fields was a complete ad-lib, preceded by several moments of tongue-tied fear. For the record, his complete remark was: "The only thing I can say about W.C. Fields, whom I have admired since the day he advanced upon Baby LeRoy with an ice pick, is this: any man who hates dogs and babies can't be all bad.''[227]

Rosten's observation was the hit of the evening:

> The appearance of Mae West in a G-string would not have produced a more explosive cachinnation. The laughter was so uproarious, the ovation so deafening, the table-slapping shoulder-punching were so vigorous, that I [Rosten] cleverly collapsed onto my chair.[228]

Rosten's apt description of Fields became news throughout the United States and parts of Great Britain. Not surprisingly, Rosten thought that he was on the verge of something big, but such was not the case. Very soon the line was being attributed to the comedian, and since that time ''hardly a week passes in which I [Rosten] do not run across some reference to 'Fields's immortal crack.' ''[229]

You Can't Cheat an Honest Man was Fields's first Universal film, and it reunited him with former radio partners Bergen and McCarthy. Fields plays aforementioned circus owner Larson E. Whipsnade, who again has both a loyal daughter and a financially troubled company. Bergen and McCarthy are one of the acts in the show, while Whipsnade's daughter (Constance Moore) is Bergen's love interest. Moore, however, nearly marries rich kid Roger Bel-Goodie (James Bush) in order to help her forever monetarily harrassed con-man father. Appropriately, the high point of the film is the Bel-Goodie party, where Whipsnade—by merely being his unorthodox self (including participating in a wild ping-pong match)—destroys any chance of a wedding. His daughter arrives late, but just in time to defend her father. While deflation of the upper class frequently occurs in Fields's work, the Bel-Goodie comeuppance is most reminiscent of the party scene in *Her Majesty Love,* where the unorthodox actions of another Fields father shock the rich potential in-laws of his daughter, who also defends her father.

Since Bergen and McCarthy's ''Chase & Sanborn Hour'' was still leading in the radio ratings,[230] it is not surprising that *Variety* suggested they, instead of Fields, would be the key to the film's box office. Yet the original story is by Fields (alias Charles Bogle), and he receives both top billing and a more than fair share of the laughter. For today's viewer, *Newsweek*'s closing commentary is more fitting: ''In giving one of the funniest performances of his career, Fields allows plenty of footage to Edgar Bergen, who handles the romantic assignment as well as Charlie McCarthy and Mortimer Snerd [a country hick, Bergen's newest dummy]—Charlie's rival for Bergen's knee.''[231]

Bergen and McCarthy share fewer scenes with Fields than the success of their radio rivalry would have suggested, though there is no let-up in murderous intent. In fact, Fields throws McCarthy to the circus alligators after the little guy filches the gate receipts. (The viewer sees only the recovery, not the actual act itself, which would have made even Fields seem too dastardly.) Still, it is undoubtedly this type of situation that provoked *New York Times* critic Frank S. Nugent into labeling Whipsnade a "completely unsympathetic" character.[232] Part of this is due to the successful continued illusion of McCarthy's reality (much easier to do on radio). For example, "Bergen seldom tees up McCarthy on his knee—dummy is generally beside him on suitable . . . prop to create illusion that 'Charlie' is a personality rather than a ventriloquial stooge."[233]

Biographer R.L. Taylor states the film's title was Fields's favorite slogan, though "a rough synthesis of his friends' opinions" on this suggests the comedian really believed the opposite because these same friends felt he "considered himself almost the model of the honest man and that as such he had been cheated with regularity throughout his life."[234] Thus one might call his periodic huckster characterization poetic justice for a personal life too often antiheroic in nature.

The following year more Fields vernacular made its way into a film title—he costarred with Mae West in *My Little Chickadee*. With Fields playing Cuthbert J. Twillie (a con-artist hair oil salesman) and West as Flower Belle Lee (a displaced saloon girl), Universal would have its biggest-grossing Fields film (earning more than *You Can't Cheat an Honest Man* and the later *Bank Dick* and *Never Give a Sucker an Even Break*).

My Little Chickadee is a broad satire of the western genre, the *Blazing Saddles* (1974) of its time. In fact, an original Fields story, "Honky-Tonk or Husband in Name Only" (an early Fields version of what would become, after much input from others, *My Little Chickadee*), contains a comedy scene premise which Mel Brooks uses in *Blazing Saddles:* Jewish Indians in full "Indian make-up with headger [sic] of feathers tailing down the back . . . [who] all talk Jewish."[235]

There was nothing new about satirizing westerns. For example, Mack Sennett and Hal Roach had done comedy send-ups of such early classics of the genre as 1923's *The Covered Wagon* (parodies: *The Uncovered Wagon,* 1923; and *Two Wagons, Both Covered,* 1924) and 1924's *The Iron Horse* (*The Iron Nag,* 1925).[236] *My Little Chickadee* was refreshing, however, for three specific reasons. First, it was timely. Though countless "B" westerns had been made in the 1930s, the "A" western was just begining a return to prominence at the decade's close.

Second, as William Everson has suggested, the film's early scenes closely resemble the outset of John Ford's 1939 western classic *Stagecoach,* which opened shortly before the Fields-West film began shooting.[237] Both movies start with prostitute figures (Claire Trevor and Mae West respectively) being driven from town by blue-nosed women's groups. In each case her journey brings her in romantic contact with another outcast of society (John Wayne and Fields). Both films also feature actor Donald Meek as a character mistaken for a minister. (In fact, he performs the fake marriage of Fields and West in *My Little Chickadee*.) And each movie includes an epic running battle (from a stagecoach and a train respectively) with a seemingly endless supply of Indians. Thus *My Little Chickadee* actually parodies several key scenes from what is now often considered the archetypal western.

Third, the teaming of West and Fields in a western satire drew upon several natural strengths. Both performers had comedy personae (and costumes) strongly linked with the late nineteenth century—well within the time frame of the genre. And their screen characters were equally tied to satire, especially of the hypocritical small-town women's club variety, an unofficial ruling clique often associated with the western. Moreover, because the western is considered one of only two native American genres (the other being the gangster film), it has become almost an unwritten law (which peaked during the genre's height of popularity in the 1950s) that major American comedians satirize the genre at some time in their careers. Silent film star Buster Keaton lampooned westerns in *The Frozen North* (1922, which parodied film cowboy William S. Hart) and *Go West* (1925); Bob Hope had a string of takeoffs: *The Paleface* (1948), *Fancy Pants* (1950), *Son of Paleface* (1952), and *Alias Jessie James* (1959).

My Little Chickadee was made possible in part by Universal's attempt to utilize former major stars to upgrade their current productions. In the previous year, for example, Universal had successfully relaunched Marlene Dietrich's career with *Destry Rides Again* (1939), another tongue-in-cheek western. *My Little Chickadee* attempted the same thing with West, who had not made a film since *Every Day's a Holiday* (1937). But while *Chickadee* was popular, the prevailing censorship code forever stalled a West comeback.

Fields and West shared the original screenplay credit on *My Little Chickadee,* and the film often fluctuates between their separate scenes with an even more pronounced division than the Fields versus Bergen-McCarthy scenes in *You Can't Cheat an Honest Man.* But the film is still an effective showcase for two performers whose frequently cynical humor reflected the tenor of depression America. Moreover, when they played scenes together, the viewer was not unfulfilled, from their opening-reel abbreviated "courtship" to a finale which has them exchanging trademark lines—Fields invites West to "come up and see me sometime" while she coos "my little chickadee."

Chickadee was a critical and commercial success, though critics then and now often expressed disappointment about what might have been. For example, "the war of temperaments failed to come off, and if *My Little*

Chickadee isn't the comedy riot it promised to be, it is hilarious enough."[238] Purists for both comedians have also argued that the teaming compromises the possibilities of their favorite, a position film comedy historian Donald W. McCaffrey takes (favoring Fields) in *The Golden Age of Sound Comedy: Comic Films and Comedians of the Thirties* (1973).[239]

The consensus today, however, is that Fields fared best in *My Little Chickadee,* a view shared by George Eells and Stanley Musgrove, authors of the excellent 1982 study *Mae West: A Biography.*[240] The Eells-Musgrove book also provides an interesting overview of the behind-the-screen maneuvering on the script, which included writing by both Fields and West (who charmed him into being a surprising ally for her script), as well as uncredited material by screenwriter Grover Jones and *Chickadee* producer Lester Cowan. In fact, Cowan (who also produced *You Can't Cheat an Honest Man*) observed that while West claimed "she sold the original story [for *Chickadee*] to Universal . . . you'll notice no one is credited with the original story. And for good reason. I'll now confess for the first time that I took the plot from Ferenc Molnar's *The Guardsman.*"[241] (In her autobiography, *Goodness Had Nothing to Do with It,* West had claimed *Chickadee* "was produced from my original script entitled, *The Lady and the Bandit* or *My Secret Lover.*"[242]

The year 1940 also saw the publication of the comedian's own book, *Fields for President.* This was a presidential election year, and while there is no record of Franklin D. Roosevelt becoming unduly nervous about Fields's candidacy, the comedian certainly offered the public some provocative thinking. For example, "I shall, my fellow citizens, offer no such empty panaceas as a New Deal, or an Old Deal, or even a Re-Deal. No, my friends, the reliable old False Shuffle was good enough for my father and it's good enough for me."[243]

Ironically, despite this opening combination of politician and con man (possibly a redundancy of terms), the book is more a comic celebration of the nonpolitical antihero. After a beginning "Let's Look at the Record," six of the seven remaining chapters address domestic frustration: "My Views on Marriage," "How to Beat the Federal Income Tax—and What to See and Do at Alcatraz," "Fields, a Man of Firm Resolve," "My Rules of Etiquette," "How I Have Built Myself into a Physical Marvel," and "The Care of Babies."

In the chapter "Man of Firm Resolve," which Fields also labels "Inquiry into Self-Imposed Tortures," he states:

> Ninety-three per cent of the New Year's resolutions fail because they are based on frustration. Tell a person he must no longer eat pomegranates, and he'll be a nervous wreck until he does eat them. . . . [But] under the Fields Plan, you can swear off, swear on—or just swear.[244]

As might seem fitting for the theme of antiheroic frustration, the book was only a modest success, with *Newsweek* probably summing up the situation best: "The whole thing would come off better delivered in person, or on the screen. One can imagine how this would sound coming from under the old Fieldsian topper."[245] Moreover, as Fields himself once observed, "pity the poor book and magazine writers, for it's much easier to get a laugh from physical [screen] action than from the printed word."[246]

The book has since been reissued (1971), however, and is now appreciated as both an important and a unique (his only published book) collection of his comedy writing. Moreover, the work's focus is consistent with the frequently antiheroic nature of his earlier stage and screen work. It underlined the ongoing thirties increase in importance of the comic antihero, a figure of frustration with which an ever increasing number of people could identify. For example, when Irving Thalberg resurrected the film career of the Marx Brothers in the second half of the 1930s, it was largely through the on-screen antiheroic posturing of Groucho. Thus while the mustached one had been president of both a college (*Horse Feathers*, 1932) and a country (*Duck Soup*, 1933) in the team's earlier Paramount years, at MGM he is reduced to being a lowly agent (*A Night at the Opera*, 1935) and a second-class horse doctor (*A Day at the Races*, 1937).

The comic antihero is also an easier figure by which to lure sympathetic *readers,* as opposed to stories featuring the black-comedy inclinations of a Fieldsian con man such as Larson E. Whipsnade, who tosses Charlie McCarthy to the alligators. Again one might use Groucho Marx as further evidence. Another master of the cinematic wisecrack, Marx generally assumed an antiheroic stance in the comedy books he wrote. In the case of one, *Many Happy Returns: An Unofficial Guide to Your Income-Tax Problems* (1942), he was possibly influenced if not inspired by the income tax-Alcatraz chapter in Fields's book. Interestingly, the delightful comedy caricatures which complement both works were drawn by the same artist, Otto Soglow.

Late in 1940 Universal released Fields's last antiheroic cinema classic, *The Bank Dick*. Fields, as Egbert Sousé (as already noted, a name whose mis-pronouncing by characters within the film again accents his underdog status), is an unhappy family man in small-town America. The name chosen for the town, Lompoc, reveals much about Fields. First, it sounds funny, which reflects his fascination for comic-sounding words. Second, funny or not, there actually is a Lompoc (in California), which mirrors Fields's attempt to keep one foot in reality. And finally, the fact that Lompoc sounds like a comic disease (a cross between lumbago and chicken pox?) articulates perfectly his ongoing message about small-town America.

Luckily for Sousé, this Lompoc has some redeeming characteristics: it is home for the Black Pussy Cat Café (where Fields frequently drinks his meals), and Tel-Avis Picture Productions is on location doing a film. Add to this two bank robberies and a spectacular car chase, and even an antihero will not get bored.

The original story and screenplay were by Mahatma Kane Jeeves (Fields). An examination of the latter provides a unique commentary on basic comedy types long prevalent with Fields. For example, Egbert is described as "a scholar, gentleman, and judge of good grape." Mrs. Brunch, his mother-in-law, "is an old nag and a scold."[247]

Moreover, since a number of scenes did not survive the final cut, *The Bank Dick* script also allows one a fuller look at the original comedy possibilites of the film. For instance, the script detached itself from reality a bit more than the final film: Egbert has conversations with Nicodemus, a talking raven, and it is revealed that a fly named Tom once forged the governor's signature to get Egbert pardoned.[248]

While a more realistic world prevailed in the film, as was in keeping with Fields's thoughts on comedy theory, it makes more understandable those periodic bits of absurdity which do occasionally surface in his films. For example, in *The Bank Dick,* Sousé loses bank examiner J. Pinkerton Snoopington (Franklin Pangborn) out of an upper-story hotel window, only simply to retrieve him like some cartoon character.

The deleted scenes with the fantasy overtones also reveal, just as Fields's recycled routines do, that his work was always rather an ongoing potpourri of past and present. That is, Tom the fly was in the same spirit as Willie the ant in *The Comic Supplement* (1925); the talking raven is reminiscent of the bird puppet that was to have set and talked on Fields's shoulder in Grover Jones's version of *My Little Chickadee.*[249]

The film was roundly applauded. *Time* called *The Bank Dick* "the long-awaited reward for followers of [the] cob-nosed comedian"; *Variety* characterized it as "a decided showcase for his individualistic talents in both pantomime and buffonery [*sic*]."[250] But his greatest praise came from his most poetic of champions, *New Republic* film critic Otis Ferguson. His lengthy review ended with a description of a dream he had long had that Fields would one day do a film worthy of his comedy genius. Ferguson then added:

> The end [of the dream] would be that he [Fields] made a picture called *Bank Dick* in which he was a good part of his old and indomitable self, and which he was fully himself in writing, [self] directing, acting and atmosphering in the face of almost everything that ever happened in the movies. He was W.C. Fields in it, the trouper of all troupers once again.[251]

In the autumn of 1941, nearly a year after the release of *The Bank Dick,* Fields's last starring feature was released. Entitled *Never Give a Sucker an Even Break*, it was not so much a film as a celebration of Fields the living legend. In fact, the *New York Times* confessed, "We are not yet quite sure that this . . . is even a movie—no such harum-scarum collection of song, slapstick and thumbnail sketches has defied dramatic law in recent history."[252]

Like the giant caricatures of Fields in the opening credits, he towers over the vaguest of plots in this film about filmmaking. Appropriately, he plays himself and first appears under a billboard advertisement for *The Bank Dick*. And whereas the latter film's story included a B-movie crew on location in Lompoc, *Sucker* is set at the fictitious studio of Esoteric Pictures, Inc., where Fields is trying to sell a script to the always flighty Franklin Pangborn, who plays a producer.

By periodically visualizing Fields's in-story script, triggered by its being read aloud, a film within a film is created. This makes possible two key phenomena. First, it gives a qualified legitimacy to any flights of fantasy Fields wants to include in the interior film because it is merely the visualization of a *real* plot element—a script for sale. Thus when Fields's bottle of alcohol falls from an in-flight airplane, he is able to dive out after it without a parachute and suffer no ill effects.

Second, despite the defensibility of including the fantastic, it still encourages Fields to be viewed as something bigger than life—a comic muse, with the nonbreakable physical characteristics of a cartoon character. Also, the *mere-movies-are-too-small-to-contain-W.C. Fields* atmosphere of *Never Give a Sucker an Even Break* is reinforced by the comedian's direct address to the camera, especially when he attacks part of the then-motion picture establishment, the censorship office. That is, shortly after Fields enters an ice cream parlor and orders a soda (from which he will blow the creamy top, as if it were foam off a beer), he turns to the camera and reveals, "This scene was supposed to be in a saloon, but the censor cut it out. It'll play just as well."

Direct address gives the comedy performer added impact; he now exists on two levels, as both actor *and* audience member, independent of the film. Instead of being frozen in time and place, he is able to step outside the film and enter the forever *now* each time the movie is shown. Moreover, because of the added intimacy made possible by direct address, there is a shared-joke comradery between viewer and performer, a comradery that intensifies the comedy spirit. (The typical Fieldsian mumbled aside—there for only the viewer to hear—creates much the same bond as that of direct address.)

Sucker also intensifies the Fields *bigger-than-life* phenomenon because he has the nerve to attack the hand that feeds him—the movies. While Hollywood satires were hardly new even when Chaplin did *Behind the Screen* (1916), a comic attack by Fields had a special sweet revenge because critics had long thought Hollywood had been misusing him.[253] And his professional differences with the Hollywood powers that be were hardly unknown, especially when there was a comic twist, such as his disagreement with MGM as to whether Dickens's Micawber should juggle in the film adaptation of *David Copperfield.* And even *Sucker* had such an example. Fields's choice for a title had been *The Great Man,* but Universal preferred the more Fieldsian label. The comedian, consistent with his frequently antiheroic private life, observed, "What does it matter? They can't get that on a marquee. It will probably boil down to 'Fields-Sucker.'"[254]

Contemporary critics praised the man but damned his film's lack of structure, though a modern statement like "the film's form is its very formlessness" seems more fitting.[255] That is, the most predictable thing about a Hollywood film is its plot, and the most effective element of Fields's movie satire is its attack on all that is anticipatable. Consequently, while it is still possible for the post-1941 critic to assume an anti-intellectual position on *Sucker* (as Everson does with his attack on the "high-browed"),[256] to deny the inherent Hollywood satire of a film which even lables the studio in its story "Esoteric" seems rather naive. Moreover, the close of Fields's original story outline for *Never Give a Sucker an Even Break* should forever end the argument—Hollywood producer Pangborn is painted as a fool's fool when he sees Fields's purposely bizarre in-film script as potential Oscar material.[257]

While all Fields films find room for recycled material from earlier in his career, *Sucker* sometimes has an eerie, almost *Fields's-greatest-hits* quality, since it was his last starring feature. Though the use of golf and pool material is minimal (he plays golf momentarily in Pangborn's office and then begins to read a scripted pool scene aloud to the producer), there are reappearances of a wealth of other Fields comedy. For example, the film's biggest laugh is drawn from *Sally of the Sawdust.* Fields has just advised his in-film niece, Gloria Jean (also playing herself), against throwing a brick at the troublesome Butch and Buddy (boy comedians Billy Lenhart and Kenneth Brown). Fields seemingly admonishes Gloria Jean: "Hold your temper. Count ten!" Gloria obeys and the poised brick starts to come down. But then Fields, who has just appeared the model of parental wisdom, advises, "Now let 'er go. You got a good aim!"

Other repeats include both an airplane variation of his copyrighted sketch "The Pullman Sleeper," which was previously best showcased in *The Old-Fashioned Way,* and an abbreviated shaving scene reminiscent of the bathroom sketch in *It's a Gift.* And besides a required "drat!", "my little chickadee," and "Godfrey Daniel!", Fields verbalizes again his cure for insomnia: "Get plenty of sleep"; his thoughts on a blonde who drove him to drink: "the one thing I'm indebted to her for"; and his pep talk to a person bitten in the leg by a daschund: "rather fortunate that it wasn't a Newfoundland dog that bit you."

Fields had planned to have trapeze artist Madame Gorgeous (Anne Nagel), who plays Gloria Jean's mother, die in the film within a film and pass on the girl's guardianship to Fields. Though this is cut from the movie,

Fields still assumes the parental role in both the film within the film and *Sucker*'s regular narrative. (Gorgeous just inexplicably drops out of the film.) The plot device of Fields undertaking the responsibility for a young orphaned girl goes back to the relationship between Poppy and Professor Eustace McGargle in the play *Poppy*. Besides Fields's two film versions of *Poppy,* there had been frequent cinema teamings of the comedian with young heroines in real or quasi father-daughter relationships. but in the case of *Sucker*, the death of trapeze artist Madame Gorgeous is drawn directly from a Fields story outline for *You Can't Cheat an Honest Man.*[258]

Unfortunately, Fields's desire for this scene and its pathos possibilities, as the comedian assumes sole parental responsibility, did not happen in *You Can't Cheat,* either. In early 1939 Fields had even complained to Universal (by letter) on this very subject: "This is a transition from low comedy to pathos."[259] Later in the year Fields also included the scene in "Honky-Tonk or Husband in Name Only," an early story version of the comedian's ideas on teaming with Mae West.[260] But of course, it did not end up in *My Little Chickadee.*

Fields's compulsion about this scene is noted for two reasons. First, it contradicts the popular notion that anything even close to sentimentality in a Fields picture is the product of an oppressive studio. Studios had the right to be dictatorial with him, but by frequently axing instead of adding moments of pathos, sentimentality was lessened. And second, it again demonstrates the lengths to which his stubbornness would take him— writing the same scene into story outlines for three successive films.

After *Never Give a Sucker an Even Break,* Fields's poor health and the resulting riskiness of building a feature around him limited his film activity to guest appearances in four films: *Tales of Manhattan* (1942), *Follow the Boys* (1944), *Song of the Open Road* (1944), and *Sensations of 1945* (1944). Sadly, Fields's sequence from *Tales of Manhattan* was eliminated, in order to reduce running time, before the film went into release. *Follow the Boys* has him doing a variation of his pool routine one more time for the cameras. *Song of the Open Road* features a return bout of a sketch with Edgar Bergen and Charlie McCarthy, including a surprise appearance of one Charlie McCarthy, Jr. Fields's train routine in *Sensations of 1945* starts out promisingly, as he rehashes a number of trademark lines, but it quickly fails as he is reduced to a second banana when a comedy team is added to the scene. Ironically, an earlier but more Fields-focused version of the routine had been scratched, with the comedian being uncharacteristically congenial: "I don't want him [Producer and Director Andrew L. Stone] paying me twenty-five grand and not getting his money's worth. I'll go back and do anything else that Andy wants me to do."[261]

In his last years Fields had the continued companionship and care of Carlotta Monti and longtime secretary Magda Michael and the ongoing friendship of such people as author Gene Fowler, painter John Decker, director Gregory LaCava, and restaurateur David Chasen. (Close friend John Barrymore died in 1942). However, as drama critic Ashton Stevens once said of Barrymore, "Nobody can run downhill as fast as a thoroughbred"—something close friend Fowler saw as equally true of the self-destructive Fields.[262]

The comedian had been able to stay on the wagon only a short time in the late 1930s before succumbing again to his need for alcohol, particularly his favorite intimate, the martini. Furthermore, Fields was, if anything, even less fond of doctors than he had been earlier in his life. Fowler even overheard Fields advising a mutual friend, whose doctor was asking him to abstain from alcohol: "Pay no attention to those dastardly fee-splitters. When doctors and undertakers meet they always wink at each other."[263] And this was at a time when the comedian himself was "doggedly resisting the [alcoholic] inroads on his liver and kidneys."[264]

The physical deterioration of Fields is already apparent in *The Bank Dick* and *Never Give a Sucker an Even Break,* and unretouched studio publicity stills from the period are even more shocking. As Fowler's apt yet strikingly macabre pronouncement states, Fields and certain of his friends "were their own executioners."[265] Yet "they blamed no one but themselves for the outcome of their follies; self-pity was a stranger to them. They paid all penalties without welshing and lived their last hours without cringing."[266]

The Man in the Bright Nightgown, Fields's epithet for death, came for him on Christmas Day in 1946. He who once defined recovery as being discovered "blowing the foam from his medicine"[267] had dodged the big sleep for the last time. But in his short span he had grown from a child with merely a name reminiscent of royalty (Dukenfield) to an adult whose pseudonym would forever symbolize true royalty in God's greatest gift—laughter. The Man in the Bright Nightgown had been fooled after all.

NOTES

1. "Rogue's Progress," *Newsweek,* January 6, 1947, p. 19.

2. Robert Lewis Taylor, *W.C. Fields: His Follies and Fortunes* (Garden City, N.Y.: Doubleday, 1949), p. 337.

3. Carlotta Monti (with Cy Rice), *W.C. Fields & Me* (1971; rpt. New York: Warner Books, 1973), p. 227.

4. Fields's alleged dislike for Christmas is cited in any number of sources, but the most pointedly specific is Will Fowler's "Why W.C. Fields Hated Christmas," *Show Business Illustrated,* January 2, 1962, pp. 115-116. This later appeared, with slight variations, as "A Holiday Visit with W.C. Fields," *Life,* December 15, 1972, p. 42.

5. Alva Johnston, "Profiles: Legitimate Nonchalance—I," *New Yorker,* February 2, 1935, p. 26.

6. Taylor, *W.C. Fields: His Follies and Fortunes,* p. 10.

7. Ronald J. Fields, ed., *W.C. Fields by Himself: His Intended Autobiography* (Englewood Cliffs, N.J.: Prentice-Hall, 1973), pp. 3-4.

8. Corey Ford, "The One and Only," *Harper's*, October 1967, p. 65.

9. Johnston, "Profiles: I," p.23.

10. Mary B. Mullett, "Bill Fields Disliked His Label, So He Laughed It Off," *American Magazine*, January 1926, p. 19. Largely an interview with Fields.

11. R.J. Fields, *W.C. Fields by Himself*, p. 450.

12. Johnston, "Profiles: I," p. 24.

13. Monti, *W.C. Fields & Me*, p. 229.

14. R.J. Fields, *W.C. Fields by Himself*, pp. 6, 23.

15. Ibid. p. 8.

16. Johnston, "Profiles: I," p. 23. The Fields profiles appeared in the February 2, 9, and 16, 1937, issues of the *New Yorker*.

17. Ibid., p. 23.

18. R.J. Fields, *W.C. Fields by Himself*, pp. 4-5, 8-9.

19. Jim Tully, "The Clown Who Juggled Apples," *Photoplay*, January 1934, p. 60.

20. Ibid.

21. Alva Johnston, "Profiles: Legitimate Nonchalance—II," *New Yorker*, February 9, 1935, p. 25.

22. Ibid., p. 24.

23. Helen Hanemann, "He Hated Alarm-Clocks," *Motion Picture*, August 1926, pp. 39+.

24. Mullett, "Bill Fields Disliked His Label," p. 144.

25. Ibid., p. 145.

26. Ibid.

27. Taylor, *W.C. Fields: His Follies and Fortunes*, p. 40.

28. Ibid., p. 37.

29. Mullett, "Bill Fields Disliked His Label," p. 145.

30. Maude Cheatham, "Juggler of Laughs," *Silver Screen*, April 1935, p. 30.

31. Selbit (pseud. for Percy Thomas Tibbles), *The Magician's Handbook: A Complete Encyclopedia of the Magic Art for Professional and Amateur Entertainers* (London: Dawbarn and Ward, 1901), title page.

32. Taylor, *W.C. Fields: His Follies and Fortunes*, p. 86.

33. Ibid., p. 142.

34. R.J. Fields, *W.C. Fields by Himself*, p. 40.

35. Ibid., p. 24.

36. Ibid., p. 48.

37. Ibid., p. 21.

38. Ibid., pp. 62, 65, 445, 446, 490.

39. "W.C. Fields Files" (source unnoted), Billy Rose Theatre Collection, New York Public Library at Lincoln Center.

40. Ibid.

41. Taylor, *W.C. Fields: His Follies and Fortunes*, p. 30.

42. R.J. Fields, *W.C. Fields by Himself*, pp. 16-17.

43. William K. Everson, *The Art of W.C. Fields* (New York: Bonanza Books, 1967), p. 22. See also *Moving Picture World*, September 25, 1915, p. 2162.

44. "W.C. Fields Files" (source incomplete), Billy Rose Theatre Collection.

45. Nicholas Yanni, *W.C. Fields* (New York: Pyramid Publications, 1974), p. 23.

46. Taylor, *W.C. Fields: His Follies and Fortunes,* p. 172.

47. "'Follies of 1921' Best of Them All," June 22, 1921, in *New York Times Theatre Reviews, 1920-1926,* vol. 1 (New York: New York Times and Arno Press, 1971), n.p.; Taylor, *W.C. Fields: His Follies and Fortunes,* p. 173.

48. Frank "Kin" Hubbard, *Abe Martin: Hoss Sense and Nonsense* (Indianapolis: Bobbs-Merrill, 1926), p. 56.

49. W.C. Fields, "The Family Ford" ("W.C. Fields Papers," Library of Congress, copyrighted October 16, 1919—first of three versions), p. 6.

50. W.C. Fields, "Off to the Country" ("W.C. Fields Papers," Library of Congress, copyrighted May 25, 1921—first of three versions), p. 1.

51. Ibid., p. 6.

52. W.C. Fields, "10,000 People Killed" ("W.C. Fields Papers," Library of Congress, copyrighted May 29, 1922—first of two versions), p. 4.

53. Ibid., p. 5.

54. Ibid., p. 1.

55. W.C. Fields, "The Mountain Sweep Stakes" ("W.C. Fields Papers," Library of Congress, copyrighted March 21, 1919), p. 1.

56. Ibid., pp. 2, 10.

57. Lita Grey Chaplin with Morton Cooper, *My Life with Chaplin* (New York: Bernard Geis Associates, 1966), p. 143.

58. Monti, *W.C. Fields & Me,* p. 74.

59. Ibid., p. 69.

60. W.C. Fields, "Mountain Sweep Stakes," p. 8.

61. Sara Redway, "W.C. FIELDS Pleads for Rough HUMOR" *Motion Picture Classic,* September 1925, p. 33.

62. Walter Blair, *Native American Humor* (1937; rpt. San Francisco: Chandler Publishing Company, 1960), p. 168. See also Wes Gehring, *Leo McCarey and the Comic Anti-Hero in American Film* (New York: Arno Press, 1980); Wes Gehring, "The Comic Anti-Hero in American Fiction," *Thalia: Studies in Literary Humor,* Winter 1979-1980, pp. 11-14.

63. Heywood Broun, "The New Play," *New York World Telegraph,* September 4, 1923, p. 9.

64. Everson, *Art of W.C. Fields,* p. 27.

65. See Taylor, *W.C. Fields: His Follies and Fortunes,* p. 182; Everson, *Art of W.C. Fields,* p. 27; Yanni, *W.C. Fields,* p. 25.

66. Seemingly every review of *Poppy* mentioned patented Fields carryover materials. See especially *Poppy* review, *Variety,* September 6, 1923, p. 17.

67. Floyd Clymer, *Those Wonderful Old Automobiles* (New York: Bonanza Books, 1953), p. 151.

68. W.C. Fields, *W.C. Fields in The Bank Dick* (New York: Simon and Schuster, Classic Film Scripts Series, 1973, though basis for 1940 film), p. 15.

69. All references to *Poppy* programs are drawn from copies in the "W.C. Fields Files," Billy Rose Theatre Collection. A star billing date of June 2, 1924, is noted in R.J. Fields, *W.C. Fields by Himself,* p. 74.

70. "'Poppy' is Charming," September 4, 1923, in *New York Times Theatre Reviews, 1920-1926,* n.p.

71. Harold Cary, "The Loneliest Man in the Movies," *Colliers,* November 28, 1925, p. 26. The article appeared in a slightly abbreviated form as "How the Films Fought Shy of 'Bill' Fields," *Literary Digest,* February 20, 1926, pp. 52, 54.

72. Cary, "Loneliest Man in the Movies," p. 26.

73. Ibid.

74. "New Spring Follies Is Rich in Humor" (March 11, 1925) and "Ziegfeld Follies Bloom for Summer," July 7, 1925, in *New York Times Theatre Reviews, 1920-1926.*

75. Donald Deschner, *The Films of W.C. Fields* (1966; rpt. Secaucus, N.J.: Citadel Press, 1974); pp. 44, 103; Yanni, *W.C. Fields,* pp. 147, 150. The original screen credit is democratically ambiguous: "From the J.P. McEvoy *Comic Supplement,* based on the Charles Bogle [Fields synonym] story."

76. Everson, *Art of W.C. Fields,* p. 42; Yanni, *W.C. Fields,* p. 30.

77. J.P. McEvoy, *Slams of Life: With Malice for All, and Charity toward None* (Chicago: P.F. Volland, 1919).

78. Ibid., pp. 37, 38, 39, 44-45, 72, 100-101.

79. J.P. McEvoy, *Denny and the Dumb Cluck* (New York: Simon and Schuster, 1930), p. 143.

80. J.P. McEvoy, *The Comic Supplement* (1924), Library of Congress Copyright Department (Madison Building).

81. J.P. McEvoy, *The Comic Supplement* (dress rehearsal copy, 1925), Billy Rose Theatre Collection.

82. "J.P. McEvoy File" (source unnoted), Billy Rose Theatre Collection.

83. J.P. McEvoy, "W.C. Fields' Best Friend," *New York Herald Tribune, This Week* magazine section, July 26, 1942, pp. 15-16.

84. McEvoy, *Comic Supplement* (1924), p. 2.

85. Ibid., p. 3.

86. Ibid.

87. McEvoy, *Comic Supplement* (1925), unnumbered page preceding p. 1.

88. Ibid., p. 17.

89. Ibid., p. 17.

90. Ibid., p. 8.

91. Ruth Waterbury, "The Old Army Game," *Photoplay,* October 1925, p. 102.

92. James Thurber, "The Night the Bed Fell" and "The Day the Dam Broke," in *My Life and Hard Times* (1933; rpt. New York: Bantam Books, 1947), pp. 19-31, 49-65; James Thurber, "A Box to Hide In," in *The Middle-Aged Man on the Flying Trapeze* (1935; rpt. New York: Harper & Row, 1976), pp. 224-227; Robert Benchley, "Exercise for Those at Sea" and "Penguin Psychology," in *The Treasurer's Report: And Other Aspects of Community Singing* (New York: Grosset & Dunlap, 1930), pp. 140-148, 220-231.

93. Everson, *Art of W.C. Fields,* p. 28.

94. W.C. Fields, "Come, Come, My Little Chickadee," CBS Biography Service, p. 3.

95. This was no doubt encouraged by the general and continuing unavailability of the play itself. *Poppy* was never published for commercial sales. The Union

Catalog of major United States library holdings does not list it. And the Library of Congress has lost its copyright edition of *Poppy.* In order to note key differences between the original play and Griffith's adaptation, the plot analyses of numerous play reviews of *Poppy* were compared with the film.

96. *Sally of the Sawdust* review, *Variety,* August 5, 1925, p. 30. Also in this issue (p. 28) is a short but interesting article on the stage prologue for the film.

97. Ibid., p. 30.

98. Walter Kerr, "The Demiclowns," in *The Silent Clowns* (New York: Alfred A. Knopf, 1975), pp. 295-296.

99. McEvoy, *Comic Supplement* (1925), p. 100.

100. Robert Coleman, "'God Loves Us' Opens," *New Daily Mirror,* October 20, 1926, p. 26.

101. Sinclair Lewis, *Babbitt* (1922; rpt. New York: Signet Classic, 1980), pp. 6-7.

102. Ibid., p. 6.

103. W.C. Fields, "An Episode on the Links" ("W.C. Fields Papers," Library of Congress, copyrighted August 30, 1918), p. 5. The copyrighted routine had a wayward hunter shoot and drop a turkey on Fields. But the original sketch continued beyond this point. For example, when Fields finally manages to get up he looks into the sky and says, "I wish those aviators would fasten themselves in more securely."

104. Julia Ralph's nose-in-the-air portrayal of Mrs. Murchison in *So's Your Old Man* anticipates the Marx Brothers's celebrated use of Margaret Dumont by several years. Dumont will later team with Fields in *Never Give a Sucker an Even Break* and an unreleased segment of *Tales of Manhattan,* 1942.

105. Heywood Broun, Preface to *The Potters: An American Comedy,* by J.P. McEvoy (Chicago: Reilly & Lee Co., 1924), p. ix.

106. McEvoy, *Potters,* p. 24.

107. Ibid., p. 112.

108. Ibid., p. 106.

109. Ibid., p. 211-212.

110. James Agee, "Comedy's Greatest Era" (from *Life.* September 3, 1949), in *Agee on Film,* vol. 1 (New York: Grosset and Dunlap, 1969), p. 14.

111. For a further examination of this comparison see Wes Gehring, "Inspector Clouseau: In the Tradition of Harry Langdon," *Ball State University Forum,* Autumn 1979, pp. 57-60.

112. For a detailed examination of the antiheroic nature of Laurel & Hardy see Gehring, *Leo McCarey and the Comic Anti-Hero in American Film.*

113. Wes Gehring, *Charlie Chaplin: A Bio-Bibliography* (Westport, Conn.: Greenwood Press, 1983).

114. Jack Spears, *Hollywood: The Golden Era* (New York: Castle Books, 1971), p. 143.

115. Wes Gehring, "Berman on Hollywood during the 1930s: An Interview," forthcoming from *Paper Cinema.*

116. R.J. Fields, *W.C. Fields by Himself,* p. 446.

117. Mordaunt Hall, *Two Flaming Youths* review, January 2, 1938, in *New York Times Film Reviews, 1913-1931,* vol. 1, project manager Abraham Abramson (New York: New York Times and Arno Press, 1970), p. 413.

118. Review, of Earl Carroll's *Vanities,* August 7, 1928, in *New York Times Theatre Reviews, 1927-1929,* vol. 2, (New York: New York Times and Arno Press, 1971), n.p.

119. Francis R. Bellamy, "The Theatre," *The Outlook,* August 22, 1928, p. 670.

120. R.J. Fields, *W.C. Fields by Himself,* p. 76.

121. Everson, *Art of W.C. Fields,* p. 48.

122. Taylor, *W.C. Fields: His Follies and Fortunes,* p. 154.

123. *Vanities* program, August 27, 1928, in the "W.C. Fields Files," Billy Rose Theatre Collection.

124. "W.C. Fields Files" (source incomplete), Billy Rose Theatre Collections. All descriptions of Bessie Poole's death are from here.)

125. Taylor, *W.C. Fields: His Follies and Fortunes,* p. 174.

126. *W.C.Fields Speaks* (Los Angeles: Price/Stern/Sloan Publishers, 1981), p.22.

127. R.J. Fields, *W.C. Fields by Himself,* p. 138.

128. J. Brooks Atkinson, *Ballyhoo* review, *New York Times,* December 23, 1930, p. 24.

129. See *Ballyhoo* out-of-town review, December 14, 1930, in *New York Times Theatre Reviews, 1930-1934,* vol. 3, New York: New York Times and Arno Press, 1971, n.p.; Atkinson, *Ballyhoo* review, ibid., p. 24; *Ballyhoo* review, *Variety,* December 24, 1930, p. 54.

130. Heywood Broun, "W.C. Fields and the Cosmos," *Nation,* January 7, 1931, p. 25.

131. See "First $8,000 to 'Ballyhoo' Labor, 'Smiles' Bows Out This Saturday," *Variety,* January 7, 1931, p. 64; "'Ballyhoo' Cast Gets 84% of Regular Pay," *Variety*, January 14, 1931, p. 52; "Bank Foreclosing on Hammerstein Theatre Building" and "Five Shows Going Out," *Variety,* February 25, 1931, pp. 55, 58.

132. "'Ballyhoo' Cast Gets 84% of Regular Pay."

133. R.J. Fields, *W.C. Fields by Himself,* p. 138.

134. Ibid., p. 137.

135. "Guest Names Keep 'Ballyhoo,'" *Variety,* January 21, 1931, p. 21.

136. Yanni, *W.C. Fields,* p. 42.

137. *Million Dollar Legs* review, *Time* magazine, July 18, 1932, p. 19.

138. Andrew Bergman, Chapter 3, "Some Nihilist Laff Riots," in his book *We're in the Money: Depression America and Its Films* (1971; rpt. New York: New York University Press, 1972), p. 35.

139. Monti, *W.C. Fields & Me,* p. 16.

140. Sara Hamilton, "A Red-Nosed Romeo," *Photoplay,* December 1934, pp. 32+.

141. Everson, *Art of W.C. Fields,* p. 85.

142. *It's a Gift* review, *Variety,* January 8, 1935, p. 18.

143. Palace review, March 24, 1930, in *New York Times Theatre Reviews, 1930-1934,* vol. 3, n.p.

144. Review of Earl Carrol's *Vanities,* August 7, 1928, in *New York Times Theatre Reviews, 1927-1929,* vol. 2, n.p.; *Vanities* review, *Variety,* August 8, 1928, p. 48; Bellamy, "The Theatre," p. 670; Palace review, March 24, 1930.

145. See Cheatham, "Juggler of Laughs." Also see Chapter 4 herein, the "Fields on Fields" shorter works section.

146. Sara Redway, "W.C. FIELDS Pleads for Rough HUMOR," *Motion Picture Classic*, September 1925, p. 33.

147. Robert Redding, *Starring Robert Benchley: Those Magnificent Movie Shorts* (Albuquerque: University of New Mexico Press, 1973), p. 187. *The Sex Life of the Polyp* utilized three Benchley comedy essays: "The Social Life of the Newt" (from *Of All Things,* 1921), "Do Insects Think?" and "Polyp with a Past" (both from *Love Conquers All,* 1922).

148. See *The Dentist* review, *Variety,* January 3, 1933, p. 19; *The Fatal Glass of Beer* review, *Variety,* July 11, 1933, p. 15; also Deschner, *Films of W.C. Fields,* pp. 76, 77, 79.

149. Frank "Kin" Hubbard, *Abe Martin's Town Pump* (Indianapolis: Bobbs-Merrill Co., 1929), p. 183; See also Wes Gehring, "Kin Hubbard's Abe Martin: A Figure of Transition in American Humor," *Indiana Magazine of History,* March 1982, pp. 26-37.

150. See also "W.C. Fields Files" (the Andrew C. McKay additions), Billy Rose Theatre Collection; Everson, *Art of W.C. Fields,* p. 97.

151. "No Outstanders; Dressler 1st," *Variety,* January 3, 1933, p. 1.

152. *International House* review, *Time,* June 5, 1933, p. 20.

153. Marie Dressler was the number-one box-office draw in movies during 1932 and 1933, while Wallace Beery ranked seventh and fifth those years. Corrett Steinberg, *Reel Facts: The Movie Book of Records* (New York: Vintage Books, 1978), pp. 403-404.

154. W.C. Fields, "10,000 People Killed" ("W.C. Fields Papers," Library of Congress, copyrighted October 10, 1922—second of two versions), p. 3.

155. Mordaunt Hall, *Tillie and Gus* review, November 13, 1933, in *New York Times Film Reviews, 1932-1938,* vol. 2, project manager Abraham Abramson (New York: New York Times and Arno Press, 1970), p. 999.

156. Mordaunt Hall, *Alice in Wonderland* review, December 22, 1933, in *New York Times Film Reviews, 1932-1938,* vol. 2, p. 1012.

157. ARGUS, *Six of a Kind* review, *The Literary Digest,* March 24, 1934, p. 45.

158. Gerald Mast, *Film/Cinema/Movie: A Theory of Experience* (New York: Harper & Row, 1977), p. 226.

159. Lewis Carroll, *Through the Looking-Glass,* in *Alice's Adventures in Wonderland & Through the Looking Glass* (originally published separately, 1865 and 1871; rpt. New York: Bantam Books, 1981), p. 169.

160. "W.C. Fields Files" (unidentified article), Billy Rose Theatre Collection.

161. *Alice in Wonderland* review (cover article), *Time,* December 25, 1933, pp. 22-23.

162. Grace Kingsley, "Hobnobbing in Hollywood," *Los Angeles Times,* December 8, 1933, sect. 1, p. 7.

163. Ibid.

164. Ibid.

165. *The Old-Fashioned Way* review, *Time,* July 23, 1934, p. 24.

166. Otis Ferguson, *The Old-Fashioned Way* review, *New Republic,* August 1, 1934, p. 320.

167. Everson, *Art of W.C. Fields,* p. 122.

168. ARGUS, *You're Telling Me* review, *Literary Digest,* April 21, 1934, p. 40;

Andre Sennwald, *It's a Gift* review, January 5, 1935, in *New York Times Film Reviews, 1932-1938,* vol. 2, p. 1132.

169. Otis Ferguson, "The Great McGonigle" (*The Man on the Flying Trapeze* review), *New Republic,* August 21, 1935, p. 48.

170. See especially ARGUS, *It's a Gift* review, *Literary Digest,* January 19, 1935, p. 30.

171. See also Pauline Kael, *Going Steady* (Boston: Little, Brown, 1968), p. 94.

172. W.C. Fields, "Anything For a Laugh," *American Magazine,* September 1934, p. 73.

173. Blair, *Native American Humor,* pp. 102-124.

174. Artemus Ward (Charles Farrar Browne), "Interview with President Lincoln," in Blair, *Native American Humor,* p. 403.

175. Jack Grant, "THAT NOSE of W.C. Fields," *Movie Classic,* February 1935, p. 60.

176. Ibid.

177. Ibid.

178. Monti, *W.C. Fields & Me,* p. 48.

179. Ibid., p. 51.

180. Charles Dickens, *David Copperfield* (1848-1849; rpt. New York: Penguin Books, 1981), p. 143.

181. Ibid., p. 192.

182. Monti, *W.C. Fields & Me,* p. 48.

183. Dickens, *David Copperfield,* p. 211.

184. Monti, *W.C. Fields & Me,* p. 50. See also Dickens, *David Copperfield,* p. 213.

185. Dickens, *David Copperfield,* p. 227.

186. Ibid., p. 98.

187. Taylor, *W.C. Fields: His Follies and Fortunes,* p. 95.

188. Ibid.

189. Ibid., p. 278.

190. Ibid.

191. Andre Sennwald, *David Copperfield* review, January 19, 1935, in *New York Times Film Reviews, 1932-1938,* vol. 2, p. 1137; *David Copperfield* review, *Newsweek,* January 26, 1935, p. 27.

192. *David Copperfield* review, *Time,* January 28, 1935, p. 32; Sennwald, *David Copperfield* review, p. 1137.

193. Taylor, *W.C. Fields: His Follies and Fortunes,* p. 237.

194. *Mississippi* review, *Variety,* April 4, 1935, p. 12; Andre Sennwald, *Mississippi* review, April 18, 1935, in *New York Times Film Reviews, 1932-1938,* vol. 2, p. 1167.

195. *Mississippi* review, *Variety,* p. 12.

196. *The Man on the Flying Trapeze* review, *Variety,* August 7, 1935, p. 21.

197. "W.C. Fields Files" (unidentified October 25, 1935, article), Billy Rose Theatre Collection.

198. Everson, *Art of W.C. Fields,* p. 149.

199. Ibid., p. 150; Yanni, *W.C. Fields,* p. 86.

200. "W.C. Fields Files" (*New York Sun,* June 13, 1936—both article and citation incomplete), Billy Rose Theatre Collection.

201. Monti, *W.C. Fields & Me,* p. 160.

202. Sara Hamilton, "Dangerous Days For Bill Fields," *Photoplay,* July 1936, p. 30.

203. Sara Hamilton, "That Man's Here Again," *Photoplay,* August 1937, pp. 103-104.

204. Charles Darnton, "Mr. Fields Wins by a NOSE!" *Screen Book Magazine,* November 1937, p. 34.

205. Ibid., p. 35.

206. Hamilton, "That Man's Here Again," pp. 16 + .

207. Ibid., p. 104.

208. Darnton, "Mr. Fields Wins by a NOSE!" p. 34.

209. "W.C. Fields Files" (*Los Angeles Times,* June 26, 1933 article—citation incomplete), Billy Rose Theatre Collection.

210. Taylor, *W.C. Fields: His Follies and Fortunes,* p. 253.

211. *Poppy* review, *Variety,* June 24, 1936, p. 29.

212. Frank S. Nugent, *Poppy* review, June 18, 1936, in *New York Times Film Reviews, 1932-1938,* vol. 2, p. 1294.

213. John Dunning, *Tune In Yesterday: The Ultimate Encyclopedia of Old-Time Radio, 1925-1976* (Englewood Cliffs, N.J.: Prentice-Hall, 1976), p. 125. See also "Charlie McCarthy Is the Most Objectionable Young Man in America," *Life,* July 26, 1937, p. 57.

214. Annabelle Gillespie-Hayek, "Oh What a Dummy! The Torment of Bill Fields and Don Ameche," *Silver Screen,* December 1937, p. 18.

215. Dunning, *Tune In Yesterday,* p. 126.

216. Martin J. Porter, "Gay Old Rascal Makes Good," *New York Evening Journal-Saturday Home Magazine,* June 5, 1937, p. 17.

217. Yanni, *W.C. Fields,* p. 94.

218. "Saucy Charlie," editorial, *New York Times,* July 10, 1937, p. 14. See also "Charlie McCarthy Is the Most Objectionable Young Man in America."

219. See note 218.

220. "Charlie McCarthy Is the Most Objectionable Young Man in America," pp. 57-58.

221. James Reid, "Nobody's Dummy," *Motion Picture,* October 1937, pp. 37 + .

222. In order of appearance: "The Skunk Trap," from the record album *The Best of W.C. Fields* (Columbia CG 34144); "Children" and "Feathered Friends," both from the record album *W.C. Fields on Radio: With Edgar Bergen & Charlie McCarthy* (Columbia CS 9890).

223. Dunning, *Tune In Yesterday,* p. 220.

224. "W.C. Fields Files" (CBS Biographical Service, September 30, 1938, p. 1), Billy Rose Theatre Collection.

225. *The Big Broadcast of 1938* review, *Variety,* February 9, 1938, p. 14; *The Big Broadcast of 1938* review, *Time,* February 28, 1938, p. 64.

226. Leo Rosten, "My Most Embarrassing Moment," *Saturday Review,* June 12, 1976, p. 12.

227. Ibid.

228. Ibid.

229. Ibid.

230. Dunning, *Tune In Yesterday,* p. 126; *You Can't Cheat an Honest Man* review, *Variety,* February 22, 1939, p. 12.

231. *You Can't Cheat an Honest Man* review, *Newsweek,* February 27, 1939, p. 25.

232. Frank S. Nugent, *You Can't Cheat an Honest Man* review, February 20, 1939, in *New York Times Film Reviews, 1939-1948* (vol. 3), project manager Abraham Abramson (New York: New York Times and Arno Press, 1970), p. 1580.

233. *You Can't Cheat an Honest Man* review, *Variety,* February 22, 1939, p. 12.

234. Taylor, *W.C. Fields: His Follies and Fortunes,* p. 320.

235. R.J. Fields, *W.C. Fields by Himself,* p. 334.

236. Gerald Mast, *A Short History of the Movies,* 3d. ed. (1971; rpt. Indianapolis: Bobbs-Merrill Educational Publishing, 1981), p. 80; Kalton C. Lahue, *World of Laughter: The Motion Picture Comedy Short, 1910-1930* (1966; rpt. Norman: University of Oklahoma Press, 1972), p. 135.

237. Everson, *Art of W.C. Fields,* p. 177.

238. "Mae and Bill Out West," *Newsweek,* February 26, 1940, p. 30.

239. Donald W. McCaffrey, Chapter 9, "The Latter-Day Falstaff," in his *The Golden Age of Sound Comedy: Comic Films and Comedians of the Thirties* (New York: A.S. Barnes and Company, 1973), p. 171.

240. George Eells and Stanley Musgrove, Chapter 13, in *Mae West: A Biography* (New York: William Morrow and Company, 1982), p. 198.

241. Ibid., p. 195.

242. Mae West, Chapter 24, "Still the Queen of Sex," in *Goodness Had Nothing to Do with It* (1959; rpt. New York: A MacFadden-Bartell Book, 1970), p. 287.

243. W.C. Fields, *Fields For President* (1940; rpt. New York: Dodd, Mead and Company, 1971), pp. 11-12.

244. Ibid., pp. 76 + .

245. *Fields For President* book review, *Newsweek,* April 22, 1940, p. 41.

246. Monti, *W.C. Fields & Me,* p. 72.

247. W.C. Fields, *The Bank Dick* (New York: Simon and Schuster, 1973), pp. 7, 10.

248. Ibid., pp. 7 + , 15-16.

249. McEvoy, *Comic Supplement* (1925), p. 109; Eells and Musgrove, p. 195.

250. *The Bank Dick* review, *Time,* December 4, 1940, p. 35; *The Bank Dick* review, *Variety,* December 4, 1940, p. 12.

251. Otis Ferguson, "The Old-Fashioned Way," *New Republic,* December 30, 1940, p. 900.

252. *Never Give a Sucker an Even Break* review, October 27, 1941, *New York Times Film Reviews, 1939-1948,* vol. 3, p. 1818.

253. See especially Otis Ferguson, "The Great McGonigle," *New Republic,* August 21, 1935, p. 48.

254. Yanni, *W.C. Fields,* p. 113.

255. Ibid.

256. Everson, *Art of W.C. Fields,* p. 210.

257. R.J. Fields, *W.C. Fields by Himself,* p. 409.

258. Ibid., p. 307.

259. Ibid., p. 322.

260. Ibid., pp. 329-330.

261. Monti, *W.C. Fields & Me,* p. 224.

262. Gene Fowler, *Minutes of the Last Meeting* (New York: Viking Press, 1954), p. 172.

263. Ibid., p. 173.

264. Ibid.

265. Ibid., p. 170.

266. Ibid., p. 31.

267. Yanni, *W.C. Fields,* p. 120.

2.

THE GREAT MAN

When once asked if he had ever had DT's, Fields replied: "I don't know. It's hard to tell where Hollywood ends and the DT's begin."[1]

Shortly after Fields's death some of his friends ran the following full-page ad in the *Hollywood Reporter:*

> The most prejudiced and honest and beloved figure of our so-called "colony" went away on a day he pretended to abhor— "Christmas."
> We loved him, and—peculiarly enough—he loved us.
> To the most authentic humorist since Mark Twain, to the greatest heart that has beaten since the Middle Ages—W.C. Fields, our friend.
>
>
> Dave Chasen
> Billy Grady
> Eddie Sutherland
> Ben Hecht
> Grantland Rice
> Greg LaCava
> Gene Fowler
>
>
> Requiescat in Pace[2]

Though this tribute displayed some of the exaggerations known to any circle of friends who has lost a fellow reveler—it is so hard to compare heartbeats

5. An original group caricature of W.C. Fields in three pivotal roles: as con-man McGargle of *Poppy* (center), flanked by *Bank Dick* antihero Sousé (left) and *It's a Gift* antihero Bissonette (right). (Drawn by Paul Montgomery for this volume in 1983.)

between the Middle Ages and 1946—the general thrust of the salute seems to have become more apt with the passing years. Fields was "authentic" because while the man could fluctuate between prejudice and honesty, just as his personae could fluctuate between con man and antihero, the message remained the same: laughter can make survivors of everyone.

Fields has had a major, continuing impact upon American comedy and upon American popular culture in general. But before examining the more philosophical ramifications of the comedian and his work, it is important to discuss his significance as a cultural icon. After Chaplin's Tramp figure (Charlie), a caricature of Fields in the con-man attire of Professor Eustace McGargle or the Great McGonigle is probably the most universally recognized of American film icons.

Variations on the Professor, in top hat and long coat, have been celebrated in diverse ways: as a national advertising campaign for a potato chip manufacturer (Fields became W.C. Frito) and in an appearance on a United States postage stamp. (Fields supporters were disappointed that the government would not approve martini-flavored backing on the stamps.)

Appropriately for a comedian who was both adept at cartooning and upon whom cartooning had had a major impact (see Chapter 1 comments on J.P. McEvoy's *The Comic Supplement*), the figure of Fields is no stranger to newspaper comic strips. During the comedian's lifetime he was the inspiration for the Great Gusto, a prominent character in the strip "Big Chief Wahoo" (1936).[3] Wahoo played the stooge to Gusto, who had a medicine show—the classic con-man setting for Fields since his success as a medicine show huckster in the Broadway production of *Poppy* (1923). In fact, Fields starred in the second film adaptation of *Poppy* in the same year "Big Chief Wahoo" first appeared—1936.

Fields was a fan of the strip, and its creators Allen Saunders and Elmer Waggon eventually visited Hollywood to receive praise from the comedian.[4] "Big Chief Wahoo" quite possibly influenced Fields's later film *My Little Chickadee* (1940), in which Cuthbert J. Twillie (Fields) also has an Indian sidekick who functions as a stooge, Clarence (George Moran). Twillie is first seen in *Chickadee* as he naps in comfort on a litter behind Clarence's horse. And one of *Chickadee*'s most comic exchanges is between Twillie and Clarence:

> My brave—go upstairs and pary your stoical presence outside the teepee of Mrs. Twillie. Number eight [the hotel room of Mae West]. I'll proceed to the local gin mill and absorb a beaker of firewater.
> Big Chief gottum new squaw?
> New is right. She hasn't been unwrapped yet.

More recently, Fields was the genius for the character of crooked lawyer Larsen E. Pettifogger in Johnny Hart and Brant Parker's newspaper strip,

6. W. C. Fields is honored with a U.S. postage stamp appearance in 1980 to commemorate the one hundredth anniversary of his birth.

"The Wizard of Id" (1964). The Fields caricature is that of his con man and further borrows from the comedian by recycling part of his character's name from the "Your Hit Parade" radio show—Larsen E. Whipsnead (Fields played Larson E. Whipsnade in *You Can't Cheat an Honest Man,* 1939).

A Fieldsian Pettifogger actually represents the most obvious metaphor for the frequently black-humor style of the strip. Id is a kingdom run by a midget monarch solely interested in exploiting his subjects. The subjects, however, like a Fields family, have few redeeming qualities. Thus it is a comic tradeoff, with the reader never letting sympathy get in the way of the "me first" humor, a cynical philosophy which might just as appropriately have labeled the strip "Never Give a Sucker an Even Break."

A pint-sized king is also consistent with Fields's cartoonlike "fancy for people out of the common run physically."[5] For example, the skinny-as-a-rail American Gothic-type Bill Wolf seemingly was given a number of cameo parts in Fields films just because of his physique; on more than one occasion an unusually small person was cast so that the comedian could utilize the line, "Is he standing in a hole?" And as is so often true of Fields, his cinema inclinations were true in real life, also. During his California years he had once hired a stooge with an extremely small head, telling friends, "With that head, he'll own Hollywood."[6] While working for Ziegfeld he had even employed a dwarf known as "Shorty" to be his valet and general man Friday.[7] Originally hired to spook a superstitious Ziegfeld, Shorty eventually crossed the line of reality versus illusion when Fields also included him in his golf routine.

The comedian's ultimate newspaper cartoon recognition occurred in October 1982, when the *Los Angeles Times* Syndicate started the "W.C. Fields" strip.[8] It was done by artist Frank Smith and writer Jim Smart, but after June 27, 1983, it was produced by artist Fred Fredericks and writer Ron Field. As with the "Wizard of Id," the new strip focused on Fields as con man, complete with late nineteenth-century attire, à la *Poppy.* The image was so strong that while the figure of Fields was done in period costume, the strip itself was contemporary in setting.

Why does Fields as icon, particularly con-man icon, continue to have such a strong impact on America, from commercials to comics to the sale of countless products on which his likeness is reproduced? There are two key reasons.

First, his is a genuinely funny image, as demonstrated by its propensity to turn up in newspaper comic strips. The rounded body, the flamboyant costume, the tomato nose produce an immediate comic environment. Moreover, the exaggeration which makes the Fields icon amusing also reinforces the frequently tall-tale nature of his comedy. In addition, it is very difficult to view an image of Fields without hearing his nasal drawl, probably the most imitated vocalism in America. Consequently, while a

7. The panels of this W.C. Fields newspaper cartoon strip portray three comic standbys of his repertoire: the battle of the sexes, the juggling of the language, and the imbibing of alcohol. (© W.C. Fields Productions. Reprinted with permission, Los Angeles Times Syndicate.)

commercial is more effective if it can get the viewer to finish a product jingle, the Fields icon can go beyond this by producing an auditory response from a purely visual stimulus. (It can be especially challenging to reevaluate Fields's silent films without mentally adding his voice.)

The second reason Fields as icon has an ongoing comic love affair with the American public is the well-defined nature of his personae and the uniformly high quality of his surviving works. Despite a gift for ad-libbing, he finely honed a number of now-celebrated routines over a fifty-plus-year career. His work was further polished by adapting the same or similar situations for a number of different media: stage, screen, radio, and print. And in the late 1930s he even talked of "a career in television."[9] (His 1933 film *International House* had, of course, an early television device at the center of its wacky plot.)

His most complete gift to the world of entertainment was his sound motion pictures, with film being the medium which best combined his unique visual and auditory gifts in the most sustained presentation of his routines. While he did not control his film productions in the unquestioned total auteur manner of a Chaplin, he was, like the Marx Brothers, largely undirectable. As a result, there have been minimal references to his directors in this text, because their primary act of creativity was to maintain some containment of Fields. The comedian's view of the position's overrated nature would seem to be articulated beautifully in *Never Give a Sucker an Even Break* (1941): Fields's character takes over the film within a film from the constantly inebriated director, *A. Pismo Clam* (Jack Norton), and is pompously carried aloft on a ceremonial litter by four strongmen.

Unlike the Marx Brothers, Fields was much more responsible for authorship of his personae and general comedy surroundings. While there is no denying the genius of the Marx Brothers, particularly that of Groucho, their best films were shaped by some of the age's most gifted comedy minds, such as George S. Kaufman, S.J. Perelman, and Morrie Ryskind. But without the right material, even the Marx Brothers could be unfunny, as was frequently the case in their RKO picture *Room Service* (1938) and the MGM films which followed.

Fields owed an unquestionable debt to writers Dorothy Donnelly and J.P. McEvoy. But Donnelly's *Poppy* opened comic con-man possibilities more than it provided the comedy itself. Fields seems to have done much of the fleshing out over the years as he performed comic variations on the huckster. And even the *New York Times* review of the original Broadway production of *Poppy* stated the Dorothy Donnelly book was not intrinsically funny.[10] The play's own debt to the world of Dickens no doubt encouraged Fields to utilize better his own great appreciation of the novelist.

McEvoy's antiheroic *The Comic Supplement* (1924) was, on the other hand, funny to begin with, and the revised *Supplement* of 1925 would seem to display a strong Fields influence. Moreover, as Fields's copyrighted comedy material (generally of an antiheroic vein) demonstrates, the McEvoy-Fields union was much more a meeting of common minds than merely a contact of author and gifted performer. Fields's copyrighted sketches, in fact, are the ultimate evidence which separated him from most 1930s comedians of personality. The Marx Brothers, for example, seem to have left no copyrighted comedy floor plans of their own, though Groucho eventually authored several loosely autobiographical humor books.

Because Fields seldom ventured far from his own material or liberally peppered anything new with patented, established bits of his own, his films maintain—at least when he is on screen—a consistently high level of comedy. This is something censorship, after 1934, kept even from the highly original Mae West, often her own chief author.

All in all, the success of Fields as icon points toward three primary influences on American film and popular culture. The first is that he has become a universal symbol as important in today's mass communication age as the celebrated literary characters of the past. The other two key influences are that he was a pioneer in both the development of the American antihero and in "the revolt from the village."[11]

The most famous analogous argument is probably film theorist André Bazin's interrelating of Chaplin's Charlie with epic characters of literature: "For hundreds of millions of people on this planet he [Charlie] is a hero like Ulysses or Roland in other civilizations."[12] A character of this type transcends any one story or collection of stories, whether they are printed or cinematic. Such a character has withstood the test of time, and the works in which he is showcased are "read" and "reread" through the years. All of this applies to the art of W.C. Fields.

Fields has been equated with many important literary characters. But as if to justify the appropriateness of singling out Fields as equally unique, it should be noted that he has most frequently been compared with Charles Dickens's Micawber and Shakespeare's Falstaff, the two most significant literary comedians in the English language. And without trying to be sacrilegious in the halls of literature, Fields is now unquestionably more universally applicable by the general public, and he has been for some time.

Fields and the world of Dickens's Micawber have already been compared closely as an outgrowth of the examination of the 1935 film adaptation of *David Copperfield* in which Fields plays the character of Micawber. Fields's personae (and the comedian himself) also encompass key comedy characteristics of Falstaff and the comic peculiarities of players who are satellites of Falstaff.

This comparison does not imply that the character of Falstaff directly affected Fields, as seems to have been the case with Micawber. Instead, it puts into perspective the significance of Fields as a modern-day Falstaff, for when critics linked the film comedian with the Shakespearean character, they were using a literary comedian ranked above even Micawber. In fact, according to honored literary critic and historian J.B. Priestley, "With the exception of Hamlet, no character in literature has been more discussed than this Falstaff, who is, like Hamlet, a genius, fastening immediately upon the reader's imagination, living richly in his memory."[13]

Unfortunately, a detailed comparison of Falstaff amd Fields (personae and individual) never seems to have been done. Therefore, they will be examined according to the following criteria: (1) celebration of alcohol, (2) bragging and telling of tall tales, (3) quickness of wit and gift for language, (4) physical incongruity of their being men of action, (5) performance of the cowardly act, and (6) characteristics and general ties between Falstaff's circle of supporting players and Fields's.

Falstaff's and Fields's personae frequently are tall tale-telling revelers who like nothing better than the comradery of male drinking companions, just as Gene Fowler chronicled the real Fields inner circle in *Minutes of the Last Meeting*.[14] Fascination with drink would seem the best starting point for comparison. After all, a beer was even named for Falstaff. And not surprisingly, in the fourth act of Shakespeare's *Henry the IV, Part II,* Falstaff expands at length on the merits of alcohol:

> A good sherris sack [wine] hath a twofold operation in it. It ascends me into the brain; dries me there all the foolish and dull and crudy vapors which environ it; makes it . . . delectable shapes, which, delivered o'er to the voice, the tongue, which is the birth, becomes excellent wit. The second property of your excellent sherris is the warming of the blood.[15]

Fields's films represent a nonstop celebration of drinking, but he best articulates the importance of imbibing (in preference to man's best friend, the dog) in the essay "Alcohol & Me," which is examined at length in Chapter 4 herein. Probably his most comic exultation of alcohol, however, is "The Temperance Lecture," the title notwithstanding. Easily the most anthologized of all his radio recordings, it provides a Fieldsian version of the past which makes him a much closer historical neighbor to Falstaff:

> Throughout the Middle Ages the use of liquor was universal. Drunkenness was so common it was unnoticed. They called it the middle ages because no one was able to walk home unless they were between two other fellows. I was the middle guy.[16]

Alcohol was just as important in Fields's private life as in his professional one, though he always claimed his red nose was a product of numerous childhood beatings, because his runaway freedom was a source of envy to some boys. Serious drinking came later as a way of coping with the stress of nearly nonstop juggling practice and performing. And while there were few drinks he had not tried, eventually the martini became his staple. His martini intake was massive; during the California years most sources suggest nearly two quarts daily.[17]

Fields claimed martinis were best for him because "they work fast, and the sensations are lasting. They prick my mind like the cut of a razor blade. I work better with them inside me."[18] And they seemed to have this positive effect, for he drank continuously, even during film productions, and did not become drunk. (In fact, he strongly disliked drunks.) During film production Fields's only cover-up for his martini cocktail shaker was to claim that it was full of pineapple juice—a hoax generously accepted by all, though pranksters once filled it with real pineapple juice, causing him to boom, "Somebody's been putting pineapple juice in my pineapple juice."[19]

And while Falstaff takes a symbol of the tavern onto the battlefield in Act V of *Henry the IV, Part I* (Prince Hal discovered Falstaff is carrying a bottle of wine in his pistol case),[20] Fields's excursions on the estate or in his Cadillac were complete with a portable bar. (His in-house stock could have doubled for a commercial outlet store.)

In the second comparison, both Falstaff and Fields are also excellent at bragging and telling tall tales. Possibly the most comic example involving Falstaff occurs in the second act of *Henry the IV, Part I,* just after Prince Hal and Poins have robbed Falstaff and several companions—only moments after the latter gang has done some robbing of its own. Falstaff's initial response is to claim the gang was beset by a hundred robbers, though the prankster Prince keeps Falstaff on a braggart's defensive: "if I fought not with fifty of them, I am a bunch of radish! If there were not two or three and fifty upon poor old Jack, then am I no two-legged creature."[21]

Fields, of course, is never far from the tall tale. The antiheroic Ambrose Wolfinger of *The Man on the Flying Trapeze* (1935) claims to have a wrestling hold so unique "there isn't a man or boy born in the United States or Canada that could get out of . . . [it]"; the con-man Commodore of *Mississippi* (1935), relating his Indian-fighting career, is forever describing how he "cut a path through this wall of human flesh."

In real life Fields was also forever spinning tales, which, as he admitted in a 1934 article, were starting to catch up with him.[22] That is, he had been creative with so many facts that when friends and associates requested rehashes of specific stories, he was frequently at a loss. However, there is no denying the ties between Fields's public and private yarns. For example, Carlotta Monti observed:

> At dinners Woody [Fields] sometimes grew verbose knowing he had a captive audience, and would grossly exaggerate happenings that supposedly occurred to him in far-off and generally unheard-of spots in the world. The "Rattlesnake" story [about

the close friendship of a particular man and his snake] from *You Can't Cheat an Honest Man* [the mere word "snake" always made the film's stuffy Mrs. Bel-Goodie wail and faint] is a good example.[23]

Third, while the tales of Falstaff and Fields sometimes got both in trouble, their quick wit and continued gift for language often came to the rescue. For instance, Prince Hal eventually calls out Falstaff's yarn about bravely fighting a veritable army of robbers on the highway—an army only of the disguised Prince and Poins—by stating, in part, "Falstaff, you carried your guts away as nimbly, with as quick dexterity, and roared for mercy, and still run and roared, as ever I heard bullcalf. . . . What trick . . . canst thou now find out to hide thee from this open and apparent shame?"[24] Falstaff smoothly replies, "By the Lord, I knew ye as well as he that made ye. . . . Was it for me to kill the heir apparent? . . . Why, thou knowest I am as valiant as Hercules, but . . . I was now a coward on instinct."[25]

In a similar manner, the bravery of Fields's former Indian-fighting Commodore is called into question on the point of his character having pulled out a revolver during a battle royal years before. Revolvers had not been invented at that time, interjected some skeptic, to which Fields's Commodore coolly replied, "I know that but the Indians didn't know it." (Regarding the verbal magic of Fields's personae, one should not, of course, fail to mention his ability to sell someone a talking dog in *Poppy,* 1936.)

The private Fields was, if anything, even more determined not to lose a point of debate on any issues. A typical example can be drawn from the comedian's earlier tendency during touring years to open banking accounts all over the world as a safety-valve reflection of both his poor beginnings and the hazards of being stranded on the road. Thus during a World War II gathering of friends, Fields revealed he had approximately ten thousand dollars in a Berlin bank. David Chasen thought he must be kidding, while Gene Fowler volunteered, "Or else you're nuts. With the war on, and the inflation in Germany, how do you expect to get your dough from Hitler?"[26] Fields, never one to underestimate a villain, "put on a superior expression, and the toothpick [in his mouth] stopped moving."[27] (A motionless toothpick meant he was disgruntled. Fowler compared it to a "readied stinger.") The comedian then replied, "Suppose the little bastard wins?"[28]

It should also be noted that the real world frequently echoed (and continues to echo) the words of this performer—words which frequently also represented clever bypasses of difficult situations, such as Fields's use of "Godfrey Daniel" as a substitute for "god damn" in the censorship era, or his often blanket endorsement of both the pretty and the not so pretty with terms of endearment such as "my little chickadee," "my glowworm," and "my dove." Of course, many of Fields's nationally acclaimed statements or catchwords merely turn a traditional observation on its ear, such as his widely quoted *Bank Dick* (1940) comment on bathing. Fields, as Egbert Sousé, is having a scotch and water at a bar. He downs the alcohol, dips his fingers in the small water chaser, and methodically wipes them off on a napkin. Sousé then requests of the bartender, "Make it another one, and another chaser. I don't like to bathe in the same water twice."[29]

Fourth, while Falstaff and Fields look and feel most natural in taverns and other locations of leisurely debauchery, they often are called upon to be men of action—obviously a visual source of much of their humor. To see the big-bellied, uncourageous Falstaff on a battlefield—despite his position as a soldier—is the most delightful of comic incongruities, probably best captured by Orson Welles (in the title role) in his own outstanding film production *Falstaff* (1967, sometimes titled *Chimes at Midnight*).

Comedian Fields is not unknown to military settings. In *Janice Meredith* (1924) he plays a drunken British sergeant during the American Revolution; in the 1928 remake of *Tillie's Punctured Romance* Fields's circus assists the World War I Allied cause by a slapstick involvement with the German Army. One might say the comedian even improves upon Falstaff's military incongruity, because in both noted cases Fields's greatest involvement is with the losing side. (Fields also cowrote and copyrighted, with coauthor Mortimer M. Newfield, a three-act army farce set on an American base at the time of United States entry into World War I. The farce was entitled "Just Before the Dawn."

Despite these comedic army involvements of Fields, he is much better known for his civilian skirmishes, all showcasing admirably the comic incongruity of Fields in battle. In *The Man on the Flying Trapeze* (1935), the gun-toting, pajama-clad Ambrose Wolfinger falls down the cellar steps (in the best tradition of the antihero) as he hunts for burglars. Professor McGargle takes it on the lam in *Poppy* when a posse materializes. In *My Little Chickadee,* Cuthbert J. Twillie attempts to fight Indians with a slingshot. And in *The Bank Dick,* Egbert Sousé is at his uniformed-guard best when he attempts to strangle a cowboy-clad child toting a toy pistol.

The real Fields maintained his own private war with the world, a war that sounds as if he were direct from the antihero pages of James Thurber. For instance, like Thurber's eccentric collection of relatives in "The Night the Bed Fell," Fields had his own established routine when he was especially aroused by fears of burglars.[30] He would prowl the grounds of his estate, gun in hand, frequently adding a monologue suggesting someone was with him—no doubt intended to further intimidate any crooks in the area, yet also lessening the chances of a direct confrontation.[31] During another period his fears of being kidnapped caused him to multiply his fictitious companion to several equally fictitious bodyguards. And in the middle of the night he would give his crew, who answered to names like "Joe, Bull, and Muggsy," directions such as: "I know you boys are former prize fighters and gunmen but I'd rather you didn't shoot to kill. Try to get them in the spinal cord or the pelvis. Ha ha ha ha ha. . . ."[32]

There was also a comic military air in the daylight manner in which Fields frequently surveyed his estate from the house with a large pair of binoculars. Gene Fowler even went so far as to liken Fields to "an admiral on the bridge of a flagship."[33] In addition, the comedian had a loudspeaker over the main door, and thanks to his binoculars, he was more than prepared for unwanted visitors. For Fields, just about the whole world was the enemy. Thus, he once scared away two nuns collecting for a charity by impersonating

> the violent quarrel of lovers—snarled in his own voice, then answered in falsetto. There were threats by the male voice, piteous entreaties by the artificial voice, such as, "I'll murder you with this baseball bat, you double-crossing tart!" "Don't! Please don't beat me again, Murgatroyd! Think of poor little Chauncey, our idiot child!"[34]

(Fields also played spy, having all his rooms wired so that he could monitor any potentially dangerous conversations from his servants, who were people he rarely trusted.)

Real war did, however, touch Fields's private life. During World War II (at sixty-plus years of age), he and several drinking companions, all of whom were suffering from various physical ailments, appeared at an army center prepared to register for home defense. While they were given forms to fill in (Fields is said to have requested a commando assignment), the woman on duty caught the comic absurdity of the event quite nicely when she inquired: "Gentlemen, who sent you? The enemy?"[35]

Fifth, not only are Falstaff's and Fields's personae comically incongruous to "battle," they are very capable of performing the cowardly deed, if it serves their purposes. Thus, in Act IV of *Henry the IV, Part I,* Falstaff first plays dead during battle and later stabs an already-deceased Hotspur, claiming credit for his death.[36] Fields's entertainment alter egos are just as apt to do such deeds, from booting Baby LeRoy in *The Old-Fashioned Way* (1934) to pushing his rival (Leon Errol) for Margaret Dumont off a mountain in *Never Give a Sucker an Even Break* (1941). But probably the best example of this, and certainly the one in which the on-screen Fields projects the most pride, occurs in *My Little Chickadee* (1940).

Twillie, tending bar, tells a customer how he knocked down Chicago Molly. But when someone else claims credit, Fields replies yes—but he was the one who started kicking her. Then he tops the black-comedy effect of this proud admission by going into depth on the kicking experience: "So I starts to kick her in the midriff. Did you ever kick a woman in the midriff that had a pair of corsets on?" The customer replies, "No. I just can't recall any such incident right now." Twillie continues, "Why I almost broke my great toe. I never had such a painful experience." (Later, however, it is revealed that Twillie and another man were eventually beaten up by the victim and an elderly gray-haired woman with her.)

One would not say the real Fields performed cowardly acts, but his methods could be dangerously eccentric. Probably the most famous case in point is the night he was doing his pool routine in the Ziegfeld Follies and found the laughs were not coming at the right times. Eventually he discovered a mugging Ed Wynn under the table. Fields was not amused, and he promised fatal consequences if it happened again.

It happened again. This time Fields brained Wynn with his pool stick during the routine, knocking him unconscious. The audience thought it was a set piece and loved it. Fields continued his popular pool routine, which still received additional laughs when Wynn uttered unconscious moans. Fields later offered to incorporate the whole thing into his act, but Wynn declined.[37]

In later Hollywood years, Fields had a musclebound butler who worked out on still rings in the garage. The comedian was intimidated by him and eventually sensed disrespect. Thus Fields acted . . . maybe. That is, the next time this live-in Charles Atlas took a swing on his rings, they gave way at the most inopportune of times. "As he lost consciousness, he said later, he heard a kind of hoarse, maniacal laughter from a darkened corner of the building."[38] The two parted company.

These, then, have been the obvious parallels between Falstaff and Fields. But the comparison does not stop there. Several of Falstaff's supporting players also seem to have similarities or ties with Fields. Most obvious is the case of Bardolph, attendant to Falstaff and possessor of an impressive red nose which invites witty comment. For example, when Bardolph suggests Falstaff is too heavy, the latter directs an attack against the attendant's nose: "Do thou amend thy face, and I'll amend my life. Thou art our admiral [flagship], thou bearest the lantern in the poop—but 'tis in the nose of thee: thou art the Knight of the Burning Lamp."[39]

Fields, of course, owned quite a "Burning Lamp" too, and references to it are frequent in his comedy, from the radio rivalry with Charlie McCarthy to numerous films. Except for Jimmy "Schnozzola" Durante, no major comedian probably ever better utilized his proboscis (the term Fields preferred over nose). Strangely enough, however, he was unusually sensitive about his nose in private life and could become easily offended, even when the cracks were from close friends. One such offending comment was actually reminiscent of Falstaff's aforementioned jab at Bardolph's nose. After John Barrymore's death, his friends had difficulty convincing Fields to serve as a pallbearer, because he felt the time to help pals was when they were alive. But when Fields continued with his "why me" manner, painter-friend John Decker replied, "Well, in case it gets dark, your nose would make an excellent tail light."[40]

Prince Hal's companion Poins, who devises the comic robbing of the robbers (Falstaff and company), suggests Fields's con-man persona. Pistol, the tavern warrior whose overblown speeches cover a coward, can be like a boastful Fields. Silence, the truly "silent" partner-stooge to country justice Shallow, is like any number of stooges Fields had on stage and in films, as well as in real life. And Dame Quickly, hostess of Boar's-Head Tavern and lender of money to Falstaff, rather anticipates those gullible women whom a conning Fields could manipulate.

This extended comparison to Falstaff hopefully has dramatized the most significant legacy of Fields today—a universal symbol in American film and popular culture—on an equal footing with the greatest figures of literature.

Fields's second-greatest influence also has literary ties—his nearly groundfloor participation in the popularization of the comic antihero in American humor. Fields's natural writing inclinations were toward the antihero character, as best demonstrated in his copyrighted sketches. The antihero's attempt to find sanity where only insanity reigns nicely describes most domestic situations in which the antihero Fields persona found himself.

The mid-1920s founding of the *New Yorker* made possible a pivotal blossoming of the antihero during the decade, as would the films of Leo McCarey's Laurel & Hardy. But Fields's earlier sketches, like the newspaper cartoon strips mentioned in Chapter 1 and like other comedy pioneers of modern frustration, laid the groundwork for the antihero. Recognition of Fields as an antihero pioneer could be said to have been acknowledged, though not by name, in Albert F. McLean, Jr.'s *American Vaudeville as Ritual,* which notes that early twentieth-century critics frequently implied a "new humor" (often centered in urban frustration) had developed. While McLean refers to other media, he gives the greatest credit to vaudeville, because it "was both the major market and the leading innovator in this revolution in popular taste."[41] Unfortunately, vaudeville, unlike film or literature (where the event is preserved for the ages), has left very little documentation. That is why the discovery of Fields's copyrighted sketches represents such a gift to antiheroic scholarship, as well as a more complete understanding of the pre-*New Yorker* germination period of the movement.

It should also be noted that Fields, though a world-famous comic juggler since the turn of the century, had been showcasing his antiheroic talents annually, since 1915, in all-important New York City—the eventual center for the ultimate literary articulation of the movement. Moreover, Fields was doing this in probably the city's most visible entertainment marketplace, the Ziegfeld Follies.

The antihero is nonpolitical, urban, childlike, leisure-oriented, and frustrated—often at the hands of a domineering wife and machines in general. This is practically a blueprint for Fields's copyrighted sketches, which generally embrace all these characteristics. For example, "Off to the Country" (1921, detailed earlier) is a frustrating attempt to leave the city by subway for a rural holiday, with man/child Fields saddled with a henpecking wife, a troublesome family, and an irritating tickettaker.

Leisure activity, which America was discovering in a big way during the 1920s, has a key two-pronged placement in Fields's sketches. First, there are leisure athletics—his comic frustrations playing golf and tennis, as in the 1918 copyrighted routines "An Episode on the Links" and "An Episode of Lawn Tennis." (People also had more time to follow major sporting events; thus golfer Bobby Jones and tennis player Bill Tilden were major athletic stars of the decade.) Second, leisure travel, especially by car, was growing in frequency during the twenties, and Fields was there with "The Sport Model" (1922) and three versions of "The Family Ford" (1919-1920). Still another, "The Midget Car," was copyrighted in 1930. Routines like these also provided an important source of comic aggrevation based on mechanical breakdowns.

If travel was not by car in the 1920s, chances were good that people went by rail. Fields examines comic frustration here with "The Pullman Sleeper" (1921, which he later adapted to plane travel), as well as the comic difficulty of even getting on a train in "Off to the Country." (The very antiheroic Laurel & Hardy would later develop their own Pullman sleeper routine in the film *Berth Marks,* 1929.)

The defeat of leisure at home occurs in "The Sleeping Porch" (1925), where the central character is just trying to get some rest, and "10,000 People Killed" (1922), a saga of the family disruptions caused by the mass communication marvel of the 1920s—the radio. (The latter also adds more humor from mechanical frustrations.)

These and other copyrighted sketches by Fields also had a generous sprinkling of irritating females and children and a comic frustration with more of an undercurrent of anger than is present in his sound films of the 1930s. The stage routines have been initially focused upon here, despite the equally antiheroic (and more famous) nature of many of his later films (frequently drawn from the same routines), because of their timeliness—the beginning of the national transition to a comic antihero. However, such later classic Fields renderings of the antiheroic as *It's a Gift* (1934) and *The Bank Dick* deserve equal billing with the most acclaimed literary works of such pivotal antiheroic authors as Clarence Day, Robert Benchley, James Thurber, and S.J. Perelman.

Fields's interest in the antihero obviously spilled into the comedy world of his con men, who, though generally having more in common with the nineteenth century's capable comedy figures of American humor (particularly of the old southwest), still frequently exhibited antiheroic characteristics, such as even the Great McGonigle's inability to get away from Cleopatra Pepperday's unending warbling of a sea shell song in *The*

Old-Fashioned Way. (The time setting for most of Fields's con-man roles was also the nineteenth century.)

Fields's third-greatest influence was his unrecognized involvement in what literature terms "the revolt from the village," a movement of the late 1910s and the 1920s that focused on small-town hypocrisy and emptiness but "was in actuality an over-all attack on middle-class American civilization."[42] The new wave was precipitated by Edgar Lee Master's *Spoon River Anthology* (1915), "though it required five years for the influence of that book to pass thoroughly over from poetry to prose."[43]

There were earlier precedents in American literature, such as Mark Twain's complex, biting short story "The Man That Corrupted Hadleyburg" (apparently Twain was Fields's favorite author after Dickens).[44] Masters's haunting collection of free-verse poems—each one spoken from the grave by a different individual whose life had often been wasted—found the early twentieth century a much more receptive environment. And while the contents of *Spoon River Anthology* might not sound like vintage Fields, the general metaphor of Master's examination of wasted—that is, buried—lives is a cornerstone of any artist's work which (like Fields's) attacks hypocrisy and its frequent companion, smugness. There are, however, black-comedy moments in Masters's work which sound quite Fieldsian. One such is prohibitionist Deacon Taylor admitting his death was not watermelon related (as reported) but rather cirrhosis of the liver—the result of a thirty-year passion for a drug store bottle labeled "'spiritus frumenti.'"[45]

Carl Van Doren's watershed article "The Revolt from the Village" begins with a brief overview on how "For nearly half a century [prior to 1915] native literature has been faithful to the cult of the village, celebrating its delicate merits with sentimental affections."[46] And Anthony Channell Hilfer's overview of the movement, *The Revolt from the Village: 1915-1930,* examines even more deeply the roots of America's affection for the village.[47] Understandably, this reinterpretation of a basic American institution created a storm of controversy. But while other important works followed *Spoon River Anthology* (especially Sherwood Anderson's *Winesburg, Ohio,* 1919), it took Sinclair Lewis's *Main Street* (1920) "to bring to hundreds of thousands the protest against the village which these [earlier revolt] books brought to thousands."[48] And Lewis would soon follow *Main Street* with his equally significant *Babbitt* (1922).

Lewis is of central importance to both the movement and a better understanding of Fields's ties with it. As noted in Chapter 1, there are a number of parallels between Fields's antiheroic persona and Lewis's Babbitt, with even the possibility that the novelist influenced Fields's "Sleeping Porch" routine. Moreover, one could posit that the comic antihero movement has direct ties with "the revolt from the village," because the *New Yorker* (so important in the birth of the antihero) was founded with a pledge that stated, in part: "The New Yorker will be the magazine which is not edited for the old lady in [small-town] Dubuque. It . . . is a magazine avowedly published for a metropolitan audience."[49]

Regardless of just how closely related these two movements are, Lewis's entry into the revolt group is dependent upon his use of a more direct and broad comic attack, precisely the style Fields brought to the movement during the same time period (1920s), as well as later. Both Fields and Lewis are caricaturists who produce cartoonlike portraits of a frequently proud shallow-mindedness which anticipates by years painter Grant Wood's real portraits of the same subject (see especially Wood's *American Gothic*, 1930, and *Daughters of Revolution,* 1932).

Lewis's *Main Street* characters are also said to be "indistinguishable because, though some are kinder or better-natured, they all think in the same clichés . . . the group mind thinks in stock formulas and . . . group conventions."[50] Yet through this Lewis underlines a key thrust of this and other 1920s revolt texts—the inherent dullness of these tunnel-minded burgs. This is certainly true of the characters who inhabit Fields's sketches and films of the decade, from the comedian's own Fliverton tribe to the Jones family of *The Comic Supplement* (1924 and 1925).

It has been observed also that "the dominant metaphor of the book [*Main Street*] is the machine. The villagers sit 'in rocking chairs . . . listening to mechanical music, saying mechanical things about the excellence of Ford Automobiles.'"[51] Again, this is true of other revolt texts (Lewis's 1929 *Dodsworth* will actually have a car magnate for its central hero). And as already noted, Fields territory is just as taken with the mechanical, from flivvers and radios to martini shakers which can be attached to pogo sticks. Fields (both the man and his antihero persona) are just as enamored of the family motor outing as Will Kennicott (*Main Street*) and George F. Babbitt. In fact, the Fields-influenced *Comic Supplement* of 1925 beautifully combines a motor picnic with the fundamental materialism also inherent in the stereotypical village America from which these artists were revolting. That is, after the Jones family finishes their trespassing picnic on the lawn of a sumptuous estate, Pa (Fields) puts one of the children in the house for some basics in stealing: "she might just as well start learning how to get along in the world. Nothing like training children right when they're young."[52]

Fields's *So's Your Old Man* (1926, loosely adapted from Julian Street's award-winning, Sinclair Lewis-like short story "Mr. Bisbee's Princess") nicely combines many of these issues when it presents Fields as the inventor of unbreakable automobile glass, living in the most class-conscious of small American towns. And just as Fields would remake *So's Your Old Man* in the 1930s, the comedian would continue his "revolt from the village" theme throughout the decade. His ongoing attack was somewhat unique, because the Great Depression had diffused many of the revolt issues, and the pendulum actually swung back (at times) to the celebration of small-town values, as in Thornton Wilder's *Our Town* (1938) and the cinema of Frank Capra. Thus, as stated in the poem which opens this book:

> While Capra celebrated small-town
> America Fields was busy deflating
> Big wheels on Main Street,
> Making W.C. a red-nosed hero
> To all blue-nose victims.

Carlotta Monti has observed that in private life Fields enjoyed "thrusting at the mores and hypocrisy of society with a sharp-edged tongue which never cut two ways."[53] Consequently, just as the antiheroic frequently surfaced in the world of his con men, Fields also addressed small-town hypocrisy in period costume. And while his "revolt from the village" connections have been placed behind his significance as a universal American figure and a comic antihero pioneer status, for many these rebel ties would still come to mind first, especially for people who discovered him in the 1960s.

The antiestablishment sixties were a time, of course, when the equally antiestablishment Fields was rediscovered in a big way. Monti also offers commentary on the even bigger dissident the comedian was in real life, where "single-handedly he wanted to fight the entire social system."[54] For instance, the performer who comically railed against income tax in *Fields for President* (1940) was obsessed with beating the tax system in real life.

Fields's two comedy personae could even be said to have offered models for 1960s dissidents. After all, student radical leader Abbie Hoffman's *Steal This Book* (a compendium of ways to rip off the establishment) is really nothing more than a "how-to" book for the con man of the former Now Generation. And while Fields's antihero could never be as direct about his opposition, he, too, represented a nonconforming spirit, from muttering asides to making illegal alcohol. Both Fields personae have "fifth-columnist" tendencies,[55] but it is more apparent in the antihero.

These, then, have been the key thrusts of Fields's influence on American humor and popular culture. Yet this is only a survey chapter on the impact of a man probably best described as America's greatest native-born comedian. More needs to be written on a number of subjects, for example, his apparent influence on such important but diverse figures in American comedy as film writer-director Preston Sturges and actor Walter Matthau.

For this author, Sturges's greatest film is the screwball classic *The Lady Eve* (1941), which showcases a truly delightful Fieldsian trickster named "Colonel" Harrington (Charles Coburn), who refers to his daughter (Barbara Stanwyck) as "my little minx."[56] The "Colonel" travels the world fleecing suckers in cards, and to the card question "Is this a game of chance?'' one always expects him to drawl Fields's priceless reply "Not the way I play it, no." In true Fields fashion, the "Colonel" is accompanied by his beautiful and loving daughter, who manages to fall in love with the story's wealthy young man (Henry Fonda).

Fonda is the son of Mr. Pike (Eugene Pallette), an antiheroic (though wealthy) father in the tradition of Fields's antiheroic and neglectful fathers of the 1920s. Appropriately Fieldsian also is the fact that the Pike fortune is the fruition of a brewery—"Pike's Pale, the Ale That Won for Yale." Word games, like the Pike advertising jingle or the given name of Fonda's bodyguard—Ambrose Murgatroyd (William Demarest, who is equally anti-heroic and prefers the nickname "Muggsy")—also put the viewer into a Fieldsian environment.

At the time of *The Lady Eve,* Fields was no longer at Paramount, the parent company for Sturges, but both individuals had been employed for most of the decade by that studio. And both had had close ties with producer William LeBaron (in charge of Paramount productions under Y. Frank Freeman at the time of *The Lady Eve).* LeBaron was responsible for giving both men much of their creative freedom in a period when studio supervision was generally much tighter. But regardless of just how it happened, *The Lady Eve* is very much a Fields-like creation. And the Sturges film world in general reflects much that is Fieldsian, particularly the frequency with which the director satirizes small-town America (see especially *Hail the Conquering Hero,* 1944). Moreover, as comedy historian Raymond Durgnat has suggested, "It's no accident that before Sturges, he [Fields] used Franklin Pangborn and other preferred denizens of the Sturges world."[57]

Such behind-the-scene ties between Fields and Walter Matthau are not as readily apparent, but on screen Matthau frequently seems to borrow. This is most apparent in Matthau's greatest role, his Academy Award-winning performance as the con-man lawyer in *The Fortune Cookie* (1965) who exaggerates client Jack Lemmon's injuries for insurance purposes.[58] Other Matthau roles which are reminiscent of Fields are the oddball aristocrat of *A New Leaf* (1971, in which Matthau "frequently delivers his lines like W.C. Fields")[59] the crotchety ex-vaudevillian of *The Sunshine Boys* (1975, an adaptation of a Neil Simon play), the nonstop-drinking Little League coach of *The Bad News Bears* (1976, unorthodoxically leading a team of comically foul-mouthed, problem kids), the initially very reluctant father figure of *Little Miss Marker* (1980, a remake of the Damon Runyon story with Matthau as the bookie), and the comically contrary antihero of *Survivors* (1983).

The general spirit of Fields's outrageousness, such as his bass fiddle having a litter of illegitimate little bass fiddles in *The Barber Shop* (1933) or really putting the toe to Baby LeRoy in *The Old-Fashioned Way,* best lives on today, however, in the films of Mel Brooks. In fact, Fields's belief that comedy needs a certain degree of vulgarity[60] works equally well as a philosophy for Brooks's world.

The Brooks film which best carries on this mood besides *Blazing Saddles* (1974) is his greatest work to date—*The Producers* (1968, an Oscar winner for best original screenplay). Zero Mostel plays a down-and-out theater con man who goes for one big score by selling more than one hundred percent of a play he is sure will fail—*Springtime for Hitler*. It is, of course, a hit, and the antiheroic Mostel is "held over" in prison. In addition to this stock Fields situation, Mostel must con an innocent but simple-minded young man (Gene Wilder) into being his partner (shades of Fields conning Grady Sutton into a get-rich scheme in *The Bank Dick*), while Mostel wines and dines little-old-lady investors—a frequent Fields ploy for raising capital.

Fields is honored, not despite his vulgarity, but by virtue of it. His unorthodox, at times even irresponsible, comedy manner has been well earned in both a real life and a screen life that have been frequently antiheroic. And unlike the usually so-similar Falstaff, who was eventually banished by a king, Fields films inevitably close with him in the kingly position—before a public bowing with laughter. Fields has left a unique comedy heritage for an ever-expanding following. It seems a miracle that so much laughter could be born of so much pain, particularly (like Chaplin) from his early years. But that is often the tradition, the bittersweet beauty, the preciousness, of comedy.

NOTES

1. "Rogue's Progress," *Newsweek,* January 6, 1947, p. 19.

2. Robert Lewis Taylor, *W.C. Fields: His Follies and Fortunes* (Garden City, N.Y.: Doubleday & Company, 1949), p. 341.

3. Maurice Horn, ed., *The World Encyclopedia of Comics* (1976; rpt. New York: Avon Books, 1977), pp. 636-637.

4. Ibid., p. 637.

5. Taylor, *W.C. Fields: His Follies and Fortunes,* p. 255.

6. Ibid.

7. Ibid., p. 174.

8. Correspondence between the *Los Angeles Times* Syndicate and the author.

9. James Reid, "Nobody's Dummy," *Motion Picture,* October 1937, p. 85.

10. "'Poppy' Is Charming" (September 4, 1923), in *New York Times Theatre Reviews, 1920-1926,* vol. 1, (New York: New York Times and Arno Press, 1971), n.p.

11. Carl Van Doren, "The Revolt from the Village," *Nation,* October 12, 1921, p. 407.

12. André Bazin, "Charlie Chaplin," in *What Is Cinema?*, vol. 1, selected and trans. by Hugh Gray (1958; rpt. Los Angeles: University of California Press, 1967), p. 144.

13. J. B. Priestley, *The English Comic Characters* (New York: Dodd, Mead, 1931), p. 69.

14. Gene Fowler, *Minutes of the Last Meeting* (New York: Viking Press, 1954).

15. *Henry the IV, Part II,* act 4, sc. 3, lines 97-105.

16. *The Best of W.C. Fields,* previously released recordings (Columbia, BL 34145), 1976.

17. Carlotta Monti (with Cy Rice), *W.C. Fields & Me* (1971; rpt. New York: Warner Books, 1973), p. 205.

18. Ibid., p. 206.

19. Taylor, *W.C. Fields: His Follies and Fortunes,* p. 242.

20. *Henry the IV, Part I,* act 5, sc. 4, lines 52-55.

21. *Henry the IV, Part I,* act 2, sc. 4, lines 185-188.

22. Sara Hamilton, "A Red-Nosed Romeo," *Photoplay,* December 1934, p. 33.

23. Monti, *W.C. Fields & Me,* p. 78.

24. *Henry the IV, Part I,* act 2, sc. 4, lines 258-261, 263-265.

25. Ibid., lines 268-274.

26. Fowler, *Minutes of the Last Meeting,* p. 101.

27. Ibid.

28. Ibid.

29. Monti, *W.C. Fields & Me,* p. 184.

30. James Thurber, "The Night the Bed Fell," in *My Life and Hard Times* (1933; rpt. New York: Bantam Books, 1947), pp. 19-31.

31. The domestic private battles of Fields often figure in the biographical literature on the comedian. See Taylor, *W.C. Fields: His Follies and Fortunes,* p. 313.

32. Fowler, *Minutes of the Last Meeting,* p. 257.

33. Ibid., p. 152.

34. Ibid.

35. This story also appears frequently in Fields material. See Taylor, *W.C. Fields: His Follies and Fortunes,* pp. 264-265; Fowler, *Minutes of the Last Meeting,* pp. 204-205.

36. *Henry the IV, Part I,* act 4, sc. 4, lines 75, 119, 127-128.

37. This is another oft-reported incident. See Alva Johnston, "Profiles: Legitimate Nonchalance—II," *New Yorker,* February 9, 1935, p. 26; Taylor, *W.C. Fields: His Follies and Fortunes,* pp. 150-151.

38. Taylor, *W.C. Fields: His Follies and Fortunes,* p. 259.

39. *Henry the IV, Part I,* act 3, sc. 3, lines 25-28.

40. Fowler, *Minutes of the Last Meeting,* p. 222.

41. Albert F. McLean, Jr., *American Vaudeville as Ritual* (Lexington: University of Kentucky Press, 1965), p. 106.

42. Anthony Channell Hilfer, *The Revolt from the Village: 1915-1930* (Chapel Hill: University of North Carolina Press, 1969), p. 5.

43. Van Doren, "Revolt from the Village," p. 407.

44. Monti, *W.C. Fields & Me,* p. 48.

45. Edgar Lee Masters, "Deacon Taylor," in *Spoon River Anthology* (1915; rpt. New York: Collier Books, 1962), p. 80.

46. Van Doren, "Revolt from the Village," p. 407.

47. Hilfer, *Revolt from the Village,* pp. 3-136.

48. Van Doren, "Revolt from the Village," p. 410.

49. Walter Blair, *Native American Humor* (1937; rpt. San Francisco: Chandler Publishing Company, 1960), p. 168.

50. Hilfer, *Revolt from the Village,* pp. 162-163.

51. Ibid., p. 163.

52. J.P. McEvoy, *The Comic Supplement* (1925), Billy Rose Theatre Collection, New York Public Library at Lincoln Center, p. 112.

53. Monti, *W.C. Fields & Me,* p. 90.

54. Ibid., p. 53.

55. Penelope Gilliatt, *Unholy Fools: Wits, Comics, Disturbers of the Peace: Film & Theater* (New York: Viking Press, 1973), pp. 262-263.

56. Douglas McVay, "Elysian Fields," *Film,* Winter 1967, p. 23.

57. Raymond Durgnat, "Suckers and Soaks," in *The Crazy Mirror: Hollywood Comedy and the American Image* (1969; rpt. New York: Dell Publishing Co., 1972), p. 145.

58. McVay, "Elysian Fields," p. 23.

59. Pauline Kael, review of *A New Leaf* in *Deeper Into the Movies* (Boston: Little, Brown and Company, 1973), p. 269.

60. Sara Redway, "W.C. FIELDS Pleads for Rough HUMOR," *Motion Picture Classic,* September 1925, pp. 32, 33, 73.

3.

FIELDS ON FIELDS: AN INTERVIEW/ARTICLE COLLAGE

Since no in-depth examination of an artist would be complete without including some of his own observations, this chapter includes the reprinting of extensive excerpts (the Cheatham piece is complete) from six interview/articles with Fields over the course of twelve years.

The interview/articles are Sara Redway's "W.C. FIELDS Pleads For Rough HUMOR" (*Motion Picture Classic,* September 1925), Ruth Waterbury's "The Old Army Game" (*Photoplay*, October 1925), Helen Hanemann's "He Hated Alarm-Clocks" (*Motion Picture,* August 1926), Jack Grant's 'THAT NOSE of W.C. Fields" (*Movie Classic*, February 1935), Maude Cheatham's "Juggler of Laughs" (*Silver Screen,* April 1935), and James Reid's "Nobody's Dummy" (*Motion Picture,* October 1937). The pieces are arranged in chronological order, starting with pivotal 1925—the real beginning of Fields's film career—and closing with 1937, the year of his amazing health/career comeback after a near fatal illness. A collage approach utilizing these articles was chosen because of the richness with which this framework can showcase key characteristics of both Fields and his comedy personae during a period in which the vast majority of his films were made.

The real meat of these articles is when Fields reflects on the nature of comedy, which, in turn, is analyzed in the shorter works section (under "Fields on Fields") of Chapter 4. But the interview/articles also unleash the Fieldsian spirit on a menagerie of other subjects, ranging from the Follies to a delightful tongue-in-cheek discussion of Fields's "proboscis" (that is, his nose). All in all, the informal Fields is often the most insightful.

W.C. FIELDS Pleads for Rough HUMOR

SARA REDWAY

Summer after summer, a tired, hot and impatient audience has sat in the New Amsterdam Theater in New York watching Mr. Ziegfeld glorify the American girl. They watched girls slink down staircases pretending to be "Love Thruout the Ages," or sometimes they were "Sirens of History," or sometimes they sank so far as to be named "Miss Deauville" or "Miss Palm Beach." Still, the audience sat thru it all, looked at them and waited.

They waited for a man with very light hair, a vague face and a small unconquered black mustache. His name is W.C. Fields. To me he is the funniest man in the world, and he is no mean juggler.

FIELD'S FOOTLIGHT COMEDY

I like him because the minute he steps on the stage, things go from bad to worse with him. If he plays pool, the cues bend and the balls fly back and hit him; if he plays golf, the clubs turn to rubber and the balls to putty; when he does his act with the flivver, the tires fall off and the top collapses on him. He is wonderful.

8. A caricature of W.C. Fields while being interviewed. (Done by Charles Bruno for the original Charles Darnton article "Mr. Fields Wins by a NOSE!" *Screen Book* magazine, November 1937.)

Reprinted from *Motion Picture Classic*, September 1925, pp. 32, 33, 73.

Now he is in a picture. It is D.W. Griffith's "Sally of the Sawdust." When you see it, you will wonder why you ever laughed before. Both Mr. Griffith and Mr. Fields should be crowned with laurel wreaths. More than that, they should be knocked cock-eyed by them, for Mr. Fields has dared to be vulgar and Mr. Griffith has dared to let him, and he has added a few kicks of his own.

Whether all the beautiful rough stuff will be allowed in the picture or not, I do not know. It will more likely be taken out. The master minds who stand for Elinor Glyn and blush at a broken suspender button, are capable of almost anything.

A COMEDY BUM TO THE END

I told Mr. Fields that I had liked him in the picture because he was such an old bum from start to finish.

"That is the way I should be," he said, "But I dont [sic] think audiences like it. Just the way a girl will marry a bad egg because he is a bad egg, and then want to reform him, audiences will like some no-account character, but they want him to turn out all right in the end.

"I was offered a part in a play a while ago. The man in it was an old souse, but in the last act, he reformed and dedicated his life to fighting the bootleggers."

"Are you thinking of taking the part?" I asked.

"No, I couldn't. There may be old souses who reform, that's neither here nor there, but the old souses who reform and jump on the other side of the fence cant [sic] expect to endear themselves to anyone."

DOESN'T LIKE NICE HUMOR

"I don't like to have to be too nice. I'm not. No one is, or if they are no one likes them. Things should be a little rough on the stage or in pictures just to be consistent.

"Every day I go down and stand and watch the crowds on Broadway about half past two in the afternoon. If I dressed on the stage the way some of the people I see are dressed, I'd be accused of exaggerating. People are funnier than their caricatures.

"I have talked to several successful moving picture comedians about this same niceness that is in such great demand. I have suggested things to them that they might use, and they have told me that their audiences would not stand for anything vulgar. Yet Chaplin, the greatest of all comedians, is vulgar.

"I think the funniest scene I almost ever saw was in one of Chaplin's old pictures. He is eating some ice-cream and it falls down his trousers. You remember the one. . . ."

With all his stage experience, Mr. Fields never played a real speaking part [his stage routines were largely pantomime, but some contained dialogue] until two years ago [Poppy]. . . .

MAKING AUDIENCES LAUGH

"What do they like the most?" I asked.

"The rough stuff," said Mr. Fields. "I hope I never get too nice for them."

Mr. Fields in "Sally of the Sawdust" is vaguely reminiscent of the happy days when two-reel comedies were really funny, when hilarity had not turned to amusement.

Dont [sic] expect, after all I have said, to find a funny man with a pair of comedy trousers, steamboat shoes, and a hat that doesn't fit. Mr. Fields only wears a mustache to deceive, and he is as funny as a bad fall. He is as funny as a kick in the pants.

THE OLD ARMY GAME
RUTH WATERBURY

W.C. Fields, the
overnight comedy sensation
of "Sally of the Sawdust"
knows his stuff

"My ambition is to bring back slapstick two dollared up."

Mr. W.C. Fields speaking, Mr. Fields, the newest comedian of the silver screen, a gentleman long of the Follies and the overnight movie sensation in "Sally of the Sawdust," which Griffith made.

A unique character this, very simple, very direct, very charming. Most unexpected back stage at the Follies. Since "Sally of the Sawdust" was released the Eastern studios have been calling him the coming comedian of filmdom. He has been offered his own production unit with three major companies. On the speaking stage, two managers are claiming contracts for his services and four others are trying to outbid one another for his signature.

All of which pleases Mr. Fields but causes him no need to change his hatter.

It has taken him more than ten years to break into the movies. "That is because I am a pantomimist," he says with a smile.

"Movie directors, as a whole, think of comedy in terms of stage comedy with the words left out," explains. "Griffith doesn't. Chaplin doesn't. I'm convinced the others do. They recognize comedy through their ears, not through their eyes.

"I've been here in the Follies since 1914 and constantly during that time I have been trying for a movie chance. I never got a look-in until 'Janice Meredith.' The bit I did in that was very small in the actual filming and much smaller in release. But it gave me my opportunity."

No heartbroken clown hiding his sorrow behind a mask of laughter. Not on your life. Fields would call that the old hoke, the old army game. He has spent so many years in the land of hokum he is not even to be kidded into taking himself with undue seriousness. He is very interested in his own career, but it is the same sort of balanced interest a bank president has in the bonding department. . . .

"I prefer pantomime [over dialogue]," Fields insists. "It's the better medium, much funnier than speech can ever be. The laughs can come quicker. In spoken comedy, you must wait for the laugh. Follow one line

Reprinted from *Photoplay*, October 1925, pp. 68+

too quickly with another and you kill both laughs, the one that should have come and the one you're working toward. In pantomime, the laughs can come as fast as an audience can shake them out of their throats.

"That's why I believe so firmly in the great future for the movies. There are no racial, language, time or distance barriers for them. That's why I'm so excited about having landed in them at last—that and the fact they'll let me travel again.

"The character I want to portray is the American husband, the boy of the newspaper cartoons. He's so comic he's pathetic and pathos is the true base of all laughter.

"At least," Mr. Fields smiles again, "that's what I think. But take all this with sufficient salt. After all in this movie game I'm only a neophyte."

Imagine a man eleven years in the Follies and six months in the studios calling himself a name like that!

Real intelligence? Well, rather.

HE HATED ALARM-CLOCKS

HELEN HANEMANN

And Proves That Old Saying about the Early Worm
Is Not to Be Taken Too Seriously

Behind the counter of a country store, a soda jerker jerked at his saccharine calling. Necessary, but hardly inspiring, the perpetual blending of chocolate, strawberry and vanilla, of more chocolate, strawberry and vanilla, of finally still more, long after the proper count had been lost. To be sure, the monotony was varied once; the soda clerk tried to mix a glassless soda, but that would scarcely pad a letter home. Strong the personality that could have stood out in this medley of syrup bottles, and used, still fuzzy glasses. Yet this man succeeded. He belonged definitely to that small class of persons conspicuous anywhere, even behind a soda counter. Here stood still another possessor of Elinor Glyn's famous "it."

Perhaps this vague quality arose from the tremendous solemnity with which he quizzically effected his task; possibly the secret lay in the kindliness with which he nodded in the direction of an occasional passer-by, a kindly nod which had seen and experienced much sadness, even aged a little, but was not discouraged. More likely it was a mixture of both mellowed with a singular wealth of charm.

The country store was set in a tiny portion of the lot enclosed by Famous Players for its Long Island Studios, and the picture, "The Old Army Game," first starring vehicle of William C. Fields. Strangely, prophetically enough, Bill Fields, comedy juggler, named this present triumph in previous engagements with the "Follies." "The old army game" was a favorite byword of his. The story of his world pilgrimages, of his ten years at the "Follies," doing a juggling act against the grim fear of an old age when he would again wander from town to town, from continent to continent with returns which diminished steadily, has become almost as well known as that of his sudden ascent to stardom. Two pictures, "Sally of the Sawdust," and "That Royle Girl" [though '20s critics felt Fields was wasted in the latter film—a weak Griffith melodrama], started producers outbidding each other for what they realized would prove the gilded services of W.C. Fields. Anyone, well, almost anyone, they argued from the depths of their wealth of hard-boiled experience, can be a pretty girl, but a man like Fields is a comedian. There is further testimony of these hard-boiled gentlemen's

---

Reprinted from *Motion Picture*, August 1926, pp. 39, 98.

appreciation in the fact that Julian Street's short story, "Mr. Bisbee's Princess," winner last year of the O. Henry memorial prize, is being made into a picture for Mr. Fields. It will appear under a title suggested by the current favorite maxim of a wise-cracking stage: "So's Your Old Man."

"I've tried for years to break into pictures," said Bill Fields, as they stopped shooting for a moment, "but no one would give me a chance. . . ."

Here Bill parked his cigar stub, and returned to his ministrations at the soda fountain, or as one might better say in speaking of him, to his soda juggling. And here I got an insight into one of the unusual features of Fields' work: it is practically undirected. There was an occasional suggestion of "Bill . . ." from Kleig bronzed young Edward Sutherland, who spoke from the eminence of a stool beside the soda counter and from the deep absorption of folded arms and bent brow. Not that one is casting any slurs on a director who has the good judgment to leave swell enough alone. And so much, incidentally, for the screen critics who say that the art of acting is in pictures supplanted by a simian following of mechanical directions.

When Fields had once more returned, as in the bleachers, some astute admirer asked how it felt to become a star, and at that, overnight. W.C. Fields, then, was to epitomize his triumph with a few well-chosen words, cue if ever for an avalanche of ego. I liked the man, and I shivered. It wasn't pleasant to foresee the swift shattering of a favorite ideal. With a trace of that smile which is going so large just now among the fans, Bill briefly replied: "It doesn't feel any different. Acting is acting the world over. It doesn't suddenly change just because you happen to have a better part."

"But dont [sic] you miss all the hands you used to get at the theater?" It was my turn to scintillate.

"Not a bit," was the swift reply. "That's all there was to it, the applause; seeing if I could make each audience laugh harder than the one that went before and then the next one louder than that. I always go to see my pictures two or three times, and if people laugh, I am perfectly satisfied. In fact, I love this work. There's always something different here. I used to get sick of doing the same thing night after night, year after year. I dont [sic] want to go back to the stage—not for a long time, anyway. There're so many things I'd like to try out in pictures first. I want," continued the seasoned showman with surprising naïveté, "to do some slapstick comedies, and also some work of a more subtle character."

"Mr. Fields," interposed one of the studio staff who had been listening, "knows all there is to be known about gags. No matter which one they think of using, he can tell you just where and when and by whom it was originated. He can even list the number of times it's been used since."

"Oh, I only know what I've seen around at shows in my spare time," Fields deprecated. "The gags I really meant were a lot of little incidents I've watched on the street, things totally unimportant, but full of humor and human-interest. I've always had the best luck with gags I've actually seen take place."

"I know one good gag of yours, that never took place on the stage or street," said I, looking at it admiringly.

"Oh, my mustache!" and to the accompaniment of a chuckle, Mr. Fields exhibited his first sign of pride. "That is my own idea. Want to see how it works?" He unclamped a bit of mustache to which had been attached a substantial hook-eye. "I got tired of taking the glue off my face, and I think this is just as good, even a littler funnier."

Once we had agreed on that, Bill fell into a confidential mood:

"Say, do you know what's responsible for any success I've had?"

"Great industry and talent, combined with an undying desire to get ahead?" I nodded a sagacious head.

"Not a bit of it. It's been a case of pure laziness. I went on the stage as a kid of eleven—I'd run away from home, you see, and I never went back—so that I could sleep late in the mornings. Now I'm in the movies partly because I've changed and hate going to bed late. There's little doubt that if I'd persisted long enough I could have got someone to give me a chance in pictures before this, but I didn't, again because of inherent laziness—my great failing, or merit, or whatever you want to call it. And a good thing the delay was, too. I'm that much surer of myself, and just that much better qualified for my new work. Of course, I did very little talking on the stage, and the training that I got in pantomime is invaluable to me now."

THAT NOSE of W.C. Fields

JACK GRANT

"Some folks are born with big noses. Others acquire them. Mine was cultivated. And with loving care. I feel I should have another treatment now. Will you join me? Shall we make a loving cup of the one I see Tammany bringing?" [While Fields would utilize his nose for comedy in public, he was very sensitive of what was said privately—among friends— about his "proboscis." Moreover, as noted earlier, he really attributed his impressive nose to boyhood beatings rather than a lifetime of drinking.]

"Tammany" was Tammany Young, once one of the world's most famous gate-crashers, now Bill Fields' constant companion and Man Friday and Saturday, Sunday and the rest of the week. It is Tammany who is always on hand with a highball when Bill's nose needs a "treatment."

The quaffing habits of Bill Fields are without parallel in the movie colony. His dressing-room at the studio is as well stocked as any first-class bar. He has had a trailer built for his car on location trips. It carries a hundred pounds of ice and is equipped with a portable cellarette. Also, a folding bed, in case Bill prefers to recline while enjoying the scenery. He is an avid Nature-lover, living at Toluca Lake for no other reason than the beautiful vista it affords.

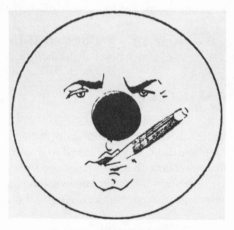

9. Another version of the distinctive nose. (Done by Charles Bruno for the original Charles Darnton article "Mr. Fields Wins by a NOSE!" *Screen Book* magazine, November 1937.)

Reprinted from *Movie Classic*, February 1935, pp. 56, 60.

"I have been with him on his last four pictures," a fellow-worker told me, "including 'Mrs. Wiggs of the Cabbage Patch,' and I have yet to see him affected in the slightest by what he drinks. He never blows up on a line of dialogue, most of which he writes for himself, nor does his tongue become thick. He keeps on drinking and he keeps on being funny, so whose business is it except his own?"

It was during the making of "Mrs. Wiggs" that I witnessed a very funny sample of Bill's off-stage humor. Norman Taurog was directing one of those scenes that seem destined for trouble from the first take. One thing after another went wrong, although no one was at fault. Finally, proceedings were stopped by the necessity of camera reloading.

Fields walked off the set and had a drink. Two takes later, things stopped again while "sound" reloaded. Bill went away to have another drink.

"Company on stage," called Taurog. "Where's Bill?"

"Fields reloading," answered Bill from his dressing room.

"I'm an advocate of moderation," Bill later told me. "For example, I never drink before breakfast."

"During the morning, I have fifteen or twenty highballs. Then comes lunch. But I don't eat lunch. Bad for the waistline. I drink it instead—oh say, a gallon of cocktails.

"In the afternoon, which is longer than the morning, I have possibly thirty or forty highballs. With dinner I have ten or twelve bottles of wine or something to drink. In the evening, I like a case of sherry or maybe fifty to sixty highballs.

"Beside my bed there is always a keg of beer. If I awaken during the night, I have a quart or two. But I never drink before breakfast!"

THEY CAN'T BELIEVE IT'S REAL

Coming back to his nose, as who can help doing when writing of Bill Fields, there are several stories he cherishes concerning it.

Once, when on shipboard, he was persuaded to do his juggling act as the feature of the impromptu show that ship passengers always stage the night before landing. After the show was over, one gushing lady came to him to say, "Oh, Mr. Fields, I just loved your act. And that putty nose you wore was a perfect scream. . . ."

"My pride, my joy," Bill mourns. "Some people do not like it."

"I think it's swell," I said.

"Thank you, my friend, thank you. Let's have another."

We were having it when Jack Coogan, father of Jackie Coogan, arrived to visit his old friend, Fields.

"What's the matter with your nose?" was Bill's greeting.

"I was kicked by a horse last week," Coogan replied. "The swelling has gone down considerably. At first, it was nearly as big as yours."

"Good thing it didn't happen to me," Fields observed, "or folks would have said, 'Who is that two-headed boy?'"

The longer you know Bill Fields, the more you are amazed by the conflict of his interests. About his love of beauty and of Nature, I have previously remarked. But did you know that this prince of jesters, this man whose education ended before he had graduated from grammar school, is one of the best-read men in Hollywood to-day?

WHERE HE GETS THOSE NAMES

I asked him where he had got the insane names of the characters he plays on the screen. . . . [Fields credits Dickens as being the father of the phenomenon, noting:]

"In 'David Copperfield,' there are Mr. and Mrs. Micawber"—Bill, by the way, is now playing *Micawber* in the picture version—"Tommy Traddles, Mrs. Gummidge, Charley Pyegrave, Mr. Peggotty and Miss Mowcher, to recall just a few. In "Oliver Twist," the parade of grand surnames includes Bumble, Crackit, Grimwig, Sowerberry and Bedwin. 'Pickwick Papers' has Augustus Snodgrass, Esquire, Sergeant Buzfuz, Mr. Skimpin, Mr. Phunky, and Alfred Jingle. And for 'Bleak House,' Dickens invented Volumnia Dedlock, Mr. Guppy, Mr. Tulkinghorn and Harold Skimpole." Bill Fields enjoyed the mouthing of every syllable of these names as only he can mouth them. . . . [From this Fields was inspired to collect names, which he drew from real life.]

"As a boy in Philadelphia, I had neighbors named Fushwantz and Muckle. So I have used them in the movies. I remember Fushwantz owned a goat that he would never let me ride.

"Posthlewhistle I got from a town in England where half the population is named Posthlewhistle. Sneed Smunn is a lawyer, but I don't remember where I met him. Chester Snaveley is an undertaker in Washington. And, believe it or not, there are many families called Turnipseed in the South."

JUGGLER OF LAUGHS
MAUDE CHEATHAM

W.C. Fields Can Balance a Plug
Hat On A Cane Or An Audience
On a Gale of Laughter.

Twenty million film fans can't be wrong and they've acclaimed W.C. Fields funny, *very* funny!

He's convulsed them with his hilarious characterizations in "You're Telling Me," "The Old-Fashioned Way," "It's a Gift," and others, and he'll do it again soon in "Mississippi," while his *Micawber,* in "David Copperfield," stands out as the gem of comedy portraiture that crowns him King of Laughter.

Hearing it from his own lips, however, the road that led to his capturing of this laugh-kingdom wasn't so funny.

Sprawling across the big blue davenport in his dressing-room at the Paramount studio, he startled me by saying in his quiet way, *"A comedian is best when he's hungry!"*

"Paradoxically," he continued, "to understand humor, to know what laughs are made of, one must suffer. Every laugh is built on heartaches, sometimes tears. Funny, isn't it? But it is true.

"I don't know whether I'd start out again to be a comedian or not. As it was I more or less drifted into it. I happened to have a yen for jokes and, also, I was always juggling tin cans, marbles or pebbles, and the neighborhood gang laughed at everything I did or said. The truth is, I was probably the unfunniest kid anywhere around but, naturally, their appreciation of my antics tickled me, and, when at nine, I ran away from home to build my own life, I quickly found that if I could make people laugh I could get more out of them.

"Lord, those were hard years. I slept in parks and was always hungry. When I could stand it no longer I'd swipe fruit or vegetables from the street stands. So, you see, I never over-ate, never had a chance at sweets or rich foods. I was fifteen when I had my first real meal; steak and fried potatoes. And I still get a thrill out of steak and fried potatoes!

"The first thing I remember figuring out for myself was that I wanted to be a definite personality. I had heard a man say he liked a certain fellow because he always was the same dirty damn so and so. You know, like *Larsen* in Jack London's 'Sea Wolf.' He was detestable, yet you admired him because he remained true to type.

Reprinted from *Silver Screen*, April 1935, pp. 30, 31, 62.

"Well, I thought that a swell idea so I developed a philosophy of my own, *be your type*! I determined that whatever I was, I'd *be* that, I wouldn't teeter on the fence."

Bill must have been a funny little figure, a bit pathetic, too, only nine, and starting out to win his fortune selling newspapers on the street corners and forever juggling anything he could lay his hands on. Just because his humor bubbled despite the hardships, he always added an amusing flip of the hand, a grotesque swing of the body that sent the crowds hovering around him, shrieking with glee.

So, his career started. With this gift of comedy he couldn't stay down and the first thing he knew he had a job in a beer garden at five dollars a month, with orders to keep the gang laughing.

Now, Billy says juggling is a terrific job. You work twelve to fourteen hours a day, with muscles and nerves taut. You perfect your trick. You try it out again just for luck and it eludes you. It may be hours or even days before you capture it again. It is this mental hazard that tortures a juggler, for, no matter how well he knows the trick, there is always a time when it fails him.

He was hungry so much of the time, and if he wanted to eat he had to keep the crowd laughing, so he began studying comedy, made it his tool and gradually developed comic pantomime to add to the juggling acts.

Turning his blue eyes upon me, he said, "I never go out for a gag. I base my comedy on humanness, so I just watch people. We're all very funny only we don't know it. No one is original, and we all do about the same things, so I take the simplest, every day incidents, exaggerate them and turn them into an act and, people seeing themselves, laugh.

"You go into a grocery and buy some eggs. Coming out of the shop you drop them. Now, if that actually happened to you it wouldn't be funny, but when it happens to someone else, it visualizes the very fear you have so often had and it becomes highly amusing.

"While hanging around pool halls as a kid, I noticed that every player went through the same gyrations. He elaborately chalks his cue, he sights the ball, he wiggles around and sights it again, and he always preens and struts when he makes a shot. So, I enlarged upon this routine and it became one of my bright spots of pantomime, for everyone who ever played pool recognizes himself and laughs heartily.

"The same with my golf act. Every move I make, every hazard I encounter is only too familiar to all golfers, and this incites merriment.

"People laugh at another's embarrassment, at frustrated plans, at timidity, at the underdog. Why? Blest if I know. But they do.

"There is plenty of comic material around. I can sit in my parked car on the street, or here in my dressing room, and watch people going by and see dozens of amusing situations. But it takes hard work to build them into a comedy act. It keeps me thinking all the time and I spend most of the night hours thrashing out new angles for familiar situations. It is work, not luck

10. W.C. Fields performing his celebrated cigar box juggling routine in *Sally of the Sawdust*, 1925. (Courtesy of Museum of Modern Art/Film Stills Archive.)

that brings any success. Of course, when Opportunity knocks at your door you must be ready, the music going, and your make-up on so that you can grab your place in the spotlight.''

Well, Fields grabbed off a good many triumphs during his colorful career. Billed as the *Tramp Juggler*, he performed in thirty foreign countries where he discovered comedy to be a universal language. As he pantomimed and never talked, he was welcome in every land.

He was on the same bill in South Africa that introduced Will Rogers as a lariat wizard; was top attraction at the *Folies Bergere,* in Paris, when a slim young dancer, Maurice Chevalier, began his career. In Copenhagen, a little tow-headed boy hung around the stage door to beg for his picture, now—Carl Brisson (who was that boy) and Fields have adjoining dressing rooms at the same picture studio in Hollywood!

"It was in Copenhagen that I had one of my funniest experiences," chuckled Bill. "I had a pet juggling act in which I balanced a cane on my chin, put a top hat on my foot, then kicked the hat and caught it on the tip of my cane. Well sir, one night when the theatre was packed, I missed that trick seven times. I always had a running comedy gag to use in such cases trying to cajole the audience into believing these delays were intentional. But when I missed the trick the eighth time I gave up and, tossing the hat into the air, I smacked it viciously with the cane. It soared high above the stage, twirled dozens of times, hit the back curtain and bounced right onto a peg in the hat rack placed beside me.

"It was the most spectacular thing I ever saw. The audience went wild. Many knew it was a fluke but some credulous souls were thrilled at my skill. In any case it was an exciting trick and they applauded several minutes.

"Laughs and applause are all a comedian can hope for, that spells his triumph, so I decided to use this stunt. I had a back curtain made of net and when I'd hit the hat into the air it would do a series of somersaults and drop into the net, then a replica of the first hat would be thrown onto the hat rack. It proved a sensation and the act over which I had worked and sweated blood for three years to perfect was supplanted by this simple contrivance."

Of course, it was inevitable that Fields and his unique talents would come to the screen but he didn't answer the call until he had won honors for nine seasons as top liner in the Ziegfeld Follies and other stage successes.

"When I first came to Hollywood," drawled Bill, "I thought I had landed in Heaven. They told me my days of worry and toil were over, that specialists would write my stories and dialogue and for me to run along now and play golf and when the party was ready they'd call me in to make a few faces before the camera and recite the lines they had written.

"I tried it and in six months was out of a job. After making a few two-reelers came 'International House,' and the studio suddenly decided I might do after all. But I'd learned my lesson. I wouldn't sign a contract until I was allowed to help with my own stories and dialogue as I had always done on the stage. Whatever my comedy is it is my own and, evidently, it can't be sifted through the medium of another one's thought.''

So don't be fooled when you see that a certain Charles Whoosis is given screen credit for the story and dialogue of the Fields pictures, for Whoosis is none other than the actor himself. He's a story teller, not a wise-cracking comedian and he still employs much pantomime, knowing that actions are often more illuminating than a raft of words. But Bill doesn't hoard his merriment for his pictures, he scatters it freely and is one of the most popular and loved men around the studio.

"I like the screen, especially," he added, with a grin, "when I have a *Micawber* role to do. Funny, but all my life 'David Copperfield' has been a favorite book and I've laughed my fool head off over Micawber many times, never dreaming I'd ever bring him to life. It is such coincidences that make acting a thrilling game.

"Yes, I like making pictures and it is no more heartbreaking than any other phase of this profession. Too, it gives me a chance to settle down. I'm tired of traveling around. I'm crazy about the sunshine. I like to play golf the year around and I enjoy beautiful scenery. Here's the secret. I moved to a ranch in Encino, in the foothills back of Hollywood, just so I could see the sun set over the ocean and watch the cloud effects and rolling valleys on every side. God, it's a sweeping canvas of breath-taking beauty!

"A Finnish couple takes care of my house. Thomas is my chauffeur, and I'm one of those detestable back-seat drivers but I never, never kick about his wife's cooking. So, life is pretty sweet for me and I'm very contented."

During our long chat there were just two subjects he wouldn't discuss; his age and his marriage.

Well, birthdays will never dim the Fields' humor, he can go on indefinitely cheering up the world's tempo. About his marriage, all I know is that it happened a long time ago and was but a brief interlude.

Perhaps that's the tear on which he has built his laugh-kingdom!

NOBODY'S DUMMY

JAMES REID

Bill Fields—little chickadees—is no
termite's flophouse, sitting on a
ventriloquist's knee. He's a born comic
who stands on his own hind legs,
passing wisecracks and quick on the pickup

His last picture was *Poppy*, made fourteen months ago. During its filming, he had a bout with something that he thought was rheumatism or "petrified jitters." It was painful, trying to move normally—but the show had to go on. He finished the picture. Then he went down to Saboba Hot Springs, in the sun-drenched hills back of San Diego, "to steam the poison out."

He had been there only a few days, when he came down with pneumonia. Double pneumonia. Nobody thought he was in any condition to win the battle. He was unconscious when he was rushed to the nearest town with a hospital. The newspapers had obituaries all prepared. . . .

The inactivity of those months, he says today, nearly killed him.

For Christmas [1936], someone [mistress Carlotta Monti] gave him a combination radio, phonograph and recording device. "That saved my life," he says.

He lay there, thinking of gags, telling them to the recording machine, then finding out how they sounded when they came back at him, trying to improve on them. And he discovered radio. He had never paid much attention to it before. Now, he had it on most of his waking hours. He made an amazing (to him) discovery: there was some pretty good talent on the air. But he still didn't have any ideas about a radio career for W.C. Fields.

"I had had radio offers for years," he says, "and turned 'em all down. I didn't think radio was a regular business—not for show folks. It was the same when movies came along. I didn't think they were a regular business, either. Now, "—he grins that satanic-cherubic grin of his, with his cigarette holder pointed skyward—"now I'm looking forward to television."

The sanitarium had therapeutic machines operated by electricity. When they went on, they shot Bill's radio full of static. Invariably, during one of his favorite programs. He lived for the day when he could get outdoors, out to his car, in which he had a radio installed. . . .

Before his enforced acquaintance with hospital beds, he had never taken a rest in his life. "I got to liking it so much after a while, I got so contented, that I said to myself, 'Here, here! This will never do! I've got to go out and

Reprinted from *Motion Picture,* October 1937, pp. 37, 84-86.

do some work! I'm getting rusty'. . . . I took the [Chase & Sanborn radio hour] offer.

"Sure I like it [radio]—even if it is the toughest work I've ever had," he says, crushing out one cigarette and immediately lighting another, an old habit of his. "The shorter the time you have to get laughs the more difficult it is to get them. On the stage, if you flop in the first part of a show, you may make it up in the last part. But on radio, when you have just ten minutes, you have to make every minute count, squeeze down every gag to its minimum wordage, and, on top of that, be nonchalant. As if you're adlibbing."

Which, part of the time, Bill is. It's another old habit of his, which has made him the ad-libber par excellence of our times. But it's highly disconcerting to his radio cohorts—Don Ameche, Dorothy Lamour, and Edgar Bergen, not to mention Charlie McCarthy. When Bill ad-libs, they all lose track of their lines and their scripts. So far, they've always been able to find them again. But what if, sometimes, they couldn't? What then?

They're trying to reform him, trying to get him to ad-lib before the broadcast, not during it.

"It doesn't matter where I am—I can usually run off the mouth," he says, in apology.

Nobody's dummy himself, he finds Edgar Bergen's dummy, Charlie McCarthy, a new reason for living. Even if he does call him "a termite's flop house." (That's just one of the lines Bill has got away with on the radio.)

"Funny thing," he says. "Everybody thought ventriloquism was all washed up years ago. And along comes Bergen with that kid and cleans up."

Accuse Bill of talking as if Charlie is alive, and he says, "Everybody believes he's alive. Dorothy kisses him goodnight after every broadcast. Bergen pretends that Charlie is just a dummy, but he doesn't believe any such nonsense. He has another dummy, exactly like Charlie, in case somebody should steal Charlie—but he can't use him. He isn't alive, like Charlie."

Bill is thoroughly sold on radio, even if it *is* the hardest work he has ever had. But it hasn't made him less sold on the movies. He still thinks comedy that can be seen, as well as heard, is funnier than comedy that can only be heard.

As soon as he has recovered a few more of his vanished pounds, and looks like his former movie self again, he will do a skit for Paramount's *Big Broadcast of 1938*, then start *Things Began to Happen*.

But he shakes his head, in mild amazement, that after forty-two years in show business, he has a new career. He thought he had done everything there was to be done, in the show line. He had been in medicine shows, circuses, county-fair acts, burlesque, vaudeville, musical comedy, movies. But now, he's in radio. Now, nothing can surprise him. Not even a career in television.

4.

A FIELDS
BIBLIOGRAPHICAL ESSAY

Fields once observed: "I do believe it was Carry Nation
or Mrs. Carry Catt who said 'Take a little wine for thy stomach's
sake, but don't get blotto.'"[1]

This bibliographical essay furnishes, in a logical manner, those key
reference materials which are most helpful in studying W.C. Fields's life
and career. All works are divided first by length and then by subject.

Section one is devoted to book-length sources written about or by the
comedian. The materials are then subdivided into four categories: Fields
viewed by insiders, Fields on Fields, Fields critical biographies, and Fields
references.

The second section considers shorter works and includes articles,
interviews, book chapters, and monographs. It is subdivided into three
parts: Fields critical film analysis, Fields on Fields, and Fields's world view.

BOOKS

Fields Viewed by Insiders

Robert Lewis Taylor's *W.C. Fields: His Follies and Fortunes* (1949) is the
oldest and undoubtedly the most influential book on the comedian,
regardless of category. Few Fields references since then have neglected to
note the biography. Taylor was assisted greatly by several close friends of
Fields, including author Gene Fowler (who shared his notes on the
comedian with Taylor and to whom the book is dedicated) and film director
Gregory LaCava (who made two films with Fields). Fowler's involvement is

especially significant since he would later do a unique group biography of Fields's inner circle, *Minutes of the Last Meeting* (1954).

In writing about a master comedian, Taylor has created a *comic* masterpiece of a biography. However, the reader must occasionally digest the book with more than a grain of salt, because it is often biography by anecdote. In all fairness Taylor, whose skill as a writer would eventually be rewarded with a Pulitzer Prize for *The Travels of Jamie McPheeters* (1957), was writing about a man who had few equals in yarn spinning. Moreover, considering both the time (1949) and type of biography (from an insider's perspective), one hardly expects footnotes and a bibliography. *Time* magazine's review of the book probably summed it up best when it stated Taylor was "content to be entertaining about one of America's greatest entertainers."[2]

Film historian William K. Everson's pioneer critical work on the comedian, *The Art of W.C. Fields* (1967), notes several of the key mistakes in Taylor's work—mistakes generally focusing on the production of specific films.[3] And while Everson's points are well taken (and though he first pays tribute to Taylor's "affectionate" portrait),[4] the overall suggestion is a negation of *W.C. Fields: His Follies and Fortunes.* Such a position is unfortunate for two reasons.

First, with the more recent publication of such works as *W.C. Fields & Me* (by Fields's mistress Carlotta Monti with Cy Rice, 1971) and *W.C. Fields by Himself: His Intended Autobiography* (a collection of Fields's writings—from correspondence to script ideas—edited by his grandson Ronald J. Fields, 1973), all those seemingly exaggerated Fields anecdotes are beginning to sound not so exaggerated. For example, biographer Taylor makes an insightful but comically off-hand observation on Fields's tendency to assume "persecution complexes."[5] Yet after one has read the more recent volumes, a phrase like "persecution complexes" can no longer quietly slide by in an aside.

The second reason a blanket negation of Taylor's biography would be a mistake deals with the spirit of his work. True, there are historical inaccuracies in the text, especially pertaining to specific films. But the book never was meant to be a guide to Fields's films, and proportionately the author spends little time on them. Taylor was stalking much bigger game—a case study of America's greatest native-born comedian. And the biographer's gift is the ease with which he throws off those penetrating asides—so much in the tradition of his subject—and his ability to draw the most perceptive parallels. For example, Taylor compares young Fields's difficulty in returning to an overly civilized home life after an extended period of total freedom to that of Huckleberry Finn's sojourn at Widow Douglas's.[6] The comparison is insightful, elevating Fields to a level of literary importance that only now is achieving recognition. Thus if Taylor's work is not without the broad strokes of exaggeration, it is best to remember that the truest picture is often the caricature.

Chronologically, Gene Fowler's *Minutes of the Last Meeting* (1954) is the next insider's biography of Fields to appear. As previously stated, the book chronicles not just Fields but also four additional kindred spirits with whom he kept company in his last years: actor John Barrymore, painter John Decker, vagabond poet Sadakichi Hartmann, and Fowler himself.

Originally the biography was to be only of Hartmann, a project suggested half in jest to Fowler by Barrymore and Decker. Hartmann, a "self-proclaimed genius" and a controversial "jack-of-all-arts," might best be described as "a bamboo bridge connecting the artistic and the literary scene of the 1880s with that of our own time [1940s]."[7] The only vote against this most eccentric of biography subjects was cast by Fields, who frequently damned Hartmann as "a no-good bum."[98]

Fields's pique at the introduction of this literary oddity into the equally odd circle of Fowler's friends possibly was more self-serving than even Fowler realized. That is, Hartmann seems the very personification of Fields's personae—independent to the extreme of contrariness, archetypally cynical, and utilizing the most comically biting of asides. For example, Hartmann coined such observations as "Other people talk about dying. I'm doing it," and "If you think vaudeville is dead, look at modern art."[9] Hence, it is more than just a little possible that Fields feared a rival. Of course, any such anxieties he might have had were unnecessary (as were most of his fears); time has shown that while Hartmann was a self-proclaimed genius, Fields was a real one.

While Hartmann was more mascot than equal partner in the group's escapades, he was never the "court jester" to the band that *Time* magazine described him as in its review of Fowler's book.[10] No doubt a mock-worshipful tone existed at times toward the eccentric poet, but in the final analysis he was too much the ultimate iconoclast for the group not to appreciate him. After all, there was no philosophy more celebrated by Hartmann's Hollywood patrons.

This common iconoclasm, with occasional doses of misanthropy, proved the real catalyst for a group portrait. Fowler captures this spirit wonderfully when he calls Decker's Bundy Drive studio (where the group normally met) an "artists' Alamo."[11] But besides opening a window to their last stand, Fowler also movingly records a case study of artists who "lived too much in conflict with . . . [their] talents," artists who were "their own executioners."[12]

As with Robert Lewis Taylor's biography of Fields, the best thing about Fowler's book is his ability to seize the spirit of his characters. And though again we are dealing with anecdotes, we have moved one generation closer to the source, because our teller was also part of the group.

Unlike Taylor, Fowler does not attempt to touch upon Fields's film career. Instead, he focuses entirely on his own experiences with the private man. While one always hopes for as much insight into Fields's film work as possible, Fowler's avoidance of the subject eliminated what had been a key source of error in the Taylor book. Because of this, and because the book does not attempt to be a full-blown Fields biography, one is even more inclined to trust Fowler's always metaphorically insightful stories.

This work certainly does not deserve comparison with Fowler's book on Mack Sennett, *Father Goose* (1934), probably his most "creative" biography of an entertainer. Anyone who has read Sennett's own *King of Comedy* (with Cameron Shipp, 1954) knows the film comedy pioneer was not unfamiliar with the tall tale. Quite possibly, Fowler was acknowledging the imaginative nature of Sennett by selecting an in-joke title so close to childhood's greatest collection of fantasy tales. (It should also be noted that Taylor's biography of Fields most frequently erred when it came in contact with Sennett.)

The third and most recent insider's biography of the comedian, *W.C. Fields & Me* (1971) by his mistress Carlotta Monti (with Cy Rice), is the most revealing. Monti, who spent fourteen years with Fields (a period that encompasses most of his career in sound films) and doubled as his nurse and an occasional supporting player in his films, draws upon both notes and sound recordings she made during their relationship. Adding more anecdotes, she creates a true *insider's* biography.

As with the Taylor and Fowler volumes, the thrust of Monti's book is that the cinematic Fields "was just playing himself."[13] Like Lita Grey Chaplin's *My Life with Chaplin: An Intimate Memoir* (1966), Monti's book also seems to offer unique new insight on an already long-established personality. Unlike Chaplin's second wife, however, she had no scores to even. Monti's recounting of Fields's views on favorite author Charles Dickens, for example, offers fresh observations on a subject forever linked with Fields (especially after his portrayal of Micawber in *David Copperfield,* 1935) but never before recorded at such length.[14] And while Fields's pontifications on Dickens sometimes flirted with hyperbole (such as his suggestion that Ebenezer Scrooge replace Washington and Lincoln as schoolbook model heroes),[15] the general tenor of his remarks seems quite heartfelt.

Monti, whom *Newsweek*'s review of the book would label "His Last Chickadee," also includes an excellent section dealing with Fields on comedy.[16] And though some of his comedy theories had surfaced years before in a handful of 1920s and early thirties journal articles, there was little readily available information on the subject until the appearance of Monti's book.[17]

The memoir also provides a more well-rounded study of Fields in the 1930s and 1940s, especially in terms of the comedian's dark side—an area not addressed in Taylor's biography and only touched upon by Fowler. For example, Monti's picture of the comedian's death, when he curses everyone and everything but her, describes a much more embittered man than the one normally showcased as W.C. Fields.[18]

These, then, have been the insider's books on Fields, each successive one providing a closer look at the man behind the screen. Because there is much less written about Fields than, for instance, Chaplin, especially in terms of critical biographies, insider's references have played a greater than normal part in the construction of his image. In fact, added to the monumental impact of the Taylor biography over the years, Monti's book resulted in the 1976 movie of the same name, *W.C. Fields & Me,* with Rod Steiger and Valerie Perrine playing the title roles. While too frequently fictionalizing reality, it was a sometimes engaging film because of Steiger.

Fields on Fields

The most important written work by the comedian are the copyrighted sketches that constitute the "W.C. Fields Papers" in the Manuscript Division of the Library of Congress. There are twenty-three separate documents on sixteen subjects (some sketches were copyrighted more than once when changes were made). Generally written for the stage, several of the sketches, or variations of them, later turned up in the comedian's films.

The "W.C. Fields Papers" provide a unique opportunity to examine the comedy evolution of a great comedian, especially variations on a single theme. An example would be his classic sketch "An Episode at the Dentist's," which was copyrighted three times (1919 and twice in 1928) and later preserved on film in still another variation as *The Dentist* (1932). Much of Fields's most celebrated material had been on the drawing board since the 1910s, enabling him to tune finely his almost clinical dissection of the comic antihero, the frustrated modern man. (A number of the sketches are examined in detail in Chapter 1. And the conclusion of Chapter 5 lists every one in chronological order, with both the copyright date and the Library of Congress document number.)

W.C. Fields by Himself: His Intended Autobiography (1973), an anthologylike collection of Fields's writings edited by his grandson, Ronald J. Fields, happily does include variations on some of these sketches, the first time any of them had been published. (However, the multiple copyrighting of a single yet changing property is neither included nor alluded to, and specific dates are generally absent.) It is one of the most important *published* works on or by the comedian, but its vaudeville scripts section cannot be substituted for the Library of Congress's "W.C. Fields Papers."

Only one book was published by the comedian during his lifetime: *Fields for President* (1940). But with rediscovery of the man in the 1960s, Fields fascination zoomed. Besides the appearance of the epic 510-page *W.C.*

Fields by Himself, numerous short joke books of Fields aphorisms have appeared, such as *W.C. Fields Speaks* (1981).

Fields for President, originally serialized in the *New York Herald Tribune* Sunday magazine supplement *This Week,*[19] is an invaluable source for two specific reasons. First, coming late in his career, the book is a compendium of Fields material gathered over a lifetime—a comedic well from which he would do some extra drawing in his final features.

Second, *Fields for President* represents an excellent guide to the essentially comic antihero nature of his work. Like contemporary humorists Robert Benchley and James Thurber, Fields's art is drawn from the little, yet irremediable, frustrations of life—so nicely exemplified by Chapter 3, "How to Beat the Federal Income Tax—and What to See and Do at Alcatraz."[20]

While politics normally is not associated with comic antiheroes (being more the domain of crackerbarrel humorists like Fields's longtime friend Will Rogers), Fields merely uses the premise of a political platform as a showcase for a comic attack on the frustrations of a lifetime. And politics per se receives very little direct attention, though an occasional absurdist detour through politics is also true of other comic antihero writers. Benchley, for example, writes a fanciful account of interviewing Mussolini, discovering they both went to Syracuse High.[21]

There are many targets in *Fields for President,* including such classic Fields nemeses as doctors and lawyers. But like all good antiheroes, he has a special fear of the female: ". . . over 80% of reckless resolutions made by American husbands occur at a moment when the wife is standing over the bed with a putter in her hand, giving advice and making certain demands."[22]

If there is a hero to the story other than Fields himself, it would be that greatest of medicinal fluids—liquor. Thus Fields suggests that when applying for a job, "Remember to have no liquor bottles visible on your person; but if you *should* forget, at least have the decency to offer your prospective employer a pull."[23]

Fields's book was only a modest success when it first appeared. Michael M. Taylor's introduction in the 1971 reissuing of the volume explains: "The problem was that it was received as an ordinary book written by a novelist, which it definitely is not."[24] While marketing might have been part of the book's problem, a more logical explanation is that Fields simply had become more of a popular culture cult figure by the 1970s. Regardless of explanations, however, Taylor seems to have addressed the sales question by interspersing throughout the book dozens of Fields stills, generally from the comedian's films, as well as selecting captions from the Fields text for each photograph. As for many personality comedians whose mere appearance solicits laughter, Taylor's mixing of Fields's verbal comments with his visage adds to the book's comedic success. Not surprisingly, the 1971 version was successful enough to be reissued again the following year, this time in paperback.

Paralleling and no doubt contributing to this renewal of interest in Fields were both Carlotta Monti's *W.C. Fields & Me* (1971) and the compilation by his grandson Ronald J. Fields, *W.C. Fields by Himself: His Intended Autobiography* (1973).

The latter volume attempts, more than anything else, to be a revisionist biography of Fields, contending that "in this book we can let W.C. speak and clear up the incessant fictions surrounding his life."[25]

Ironically, while the book is most insightful, it seems to endorse rather than contradict the "incessant fictions surrounding" the comedian. For example, his grandson suggests Fields was not the misogynist he was always labeled, but rather was a closet family man.[26] Yet there is little love lost in the elder Fields's numerous letters to his estranged wife Hattie, whose constant requests for money certainly must have helped spawn his misogynist nature: "You have been a lazy, ignorant, bad-tempered, arguing troubling [sic] making female all your life."[27] This is just one of several contradictions between family claims and W.C. Fields's written word. His grandson finally seems to concede this in a 1973 article on the book: "I've learned there was not a great difference between what he was on the screen and what he really was."[28] In all fairness to a revisionist stance, however, the comedian does show some initial interest in his son, W.C. Fields, Jr. Yet he allowed his work to keep them forever apart, even in summers when most vaudeville performers took an extended holiday. Moreover, once Fields felt that his wife had poisoned the boy against him, he made even less of an attempt to play the role of father.[29] (This is reflected in all his quasi film sons, who were invariably hopeless disciples of their mothers.) Thus not only do Fields's words seem refreshingly uncensored by the family, they often seem to have been unexamined.

This tendency of the family to interpret the comedian's writing in a manner at odds with the conclusions of a general reader echoes the frequency with which biographies of the comedian cast aspersions upon Field's wife and their son. For example, while the bulk of the comedian's large estate was to have gone for an orphanage, his wife and son successfully fought the will, becoming its chief beneficiaries.[30] Fields's will, in addition, specified both that his body be immediately cremated and that there be no type of funeral. Again, wife and son overruled his wishes (though Carlotta Monti also had a funeral for Fields).

Regardless, however, of the grandson's understandable though failed attempt at a revisionist stance, the volume represents a wealth of information. The text is divided into six parts: "Part One: Life and Letters, 1880-1929"; "Part Two: Vaudeville Scripts, 1920s and '30s"; "Part Three:

Notes, Articles, and Public Issues, 1930s and '40s''; "Part Four: Radio Scripts and Scenarios, 1930s and '40s''; "Part Five: The Movies, 1932-1943,'' and "Part Six: Life and Letters II, 1933-1946.''

From this Fields compendium several things can be surmised. First, he had much more to do with those cinematic moments of pathos in his film scripts than had been assumed earlier. Second, his voluminous letter writing, a habit acquired during his early touring days, often served as a testing ground for new comedy material. Third, he tended to rework old routines even more than his cinematic repetitions would suggest. And fourth, despite the efforts of family to the contrary, no volume makes a more convincing argument that Fields's screen personae closely paralleled the real man.

A final unexpected bonus of *W.C. Fields by Himself* is the inclusion of numerous drawings by the comedian, frequently self-caricatures. These were often used as ad copy during his career in vaudeville and the Ziegfeld Follies. And there are also a number of apparently never-before-seen photographs of Fields—photographs generally taken away from the footlights. Hence, despite the aforementioned reservations on family commentary, this is an indispensable Fields reference.

A minor though always enjoyable aspect of any Fields on Fields category must be directed at the short joke books of Fields aphorisms (or ones attributed to him). There have been several of these collections: *Drat! Being the Encapsulated View of Life by W.C. Fields in His Own Words* (edited by Richard J. Anobile, 1968), *I Never Met a Kid I Liked* (edited by Paul Mason, 1970), *Never Trust a Man Who Doesn't Drink* (also edited by Paul Mason, 1971), *Fields' Day: The Best of W.C. Fields* (Hallmark, 1972), *The Quotations of W.C. Fields* (edited by Martin Lewis, 1976), and *W.C. Fields Speaks* (Price/Stern/Sloan Publishers, Inc., 1981).

To paraphrase Fields's favorite author, Charles Dickens, *Drat!* is both the best and the worst of these books. It is superior because it is the most ambitious of the collections. Excerpts are presented from Fields's article "Alcohol and Me" (from the October 13, 1942, issue of *PIC* magazine), the complete version of the comedian's essay "From Boy Juggler to Star Comedian" (October 1928 issue of *Theatre* magazine), an abridged (though this is unnoted) Christmas interview with Fields (December 8, 1933, *Los Angeles Times*), a better-than-average introduction by television personality and Fields aficionado Ed McMahon, as essay by *New York Times* reporter Richard F. Shepard, and a preface by editor Richard Anobile.

Drat! also fails, however, because it generally avoids Fields's best-known mainstream aphorisms (the focus of the later collections), substituting excerpts from "Alcohol and Me" in their place. And while the essay is amusing as a whole, there is seldom the page-to-page comic explosion a true aphorism, particularly a Fields aphorism, provides. For example, the celebrated "the best cure for insomnia is to get plenty of sleep"[31] is a no-show in *Drat!* (However, additional captions—aphorisms—for the film stills occasionally correct this deficiency.)

Stills represent a sizable portion of all these joke books, except *Never Trust a Man Who Doesn't Drink,* where caricatures (often based upon famous stills of Fields) serve the same purpose. In fact, one might better christen them joke and picture books.

The most systematic approach to Fields's humor among the six collections is Martin Lewis's *The Quotations of W.C. Fields,* which organizes the barbs into twelve categories: parents and Philadelphia, police and lawyers, money, women/marriage, the presidency of W.C. Fields, advice, dogs, children, odd language, health and death, drinking, and miscellaneous. Each section also has a short introduction sketching Fields's ties with the subject. Consequently, the true Fields connoisseur can move with utmost haste to his favorite bits of iconoclasm.

As is common with most joke books, the Fields volumes not only pad with pictures, they also have rather generous spacing between observations. Thus a page number breakdown would seem to be in order at this point: *Fields's Day* (24 pages), *I Never Met a Kid I Liked* (58 pages), *Never Trust a Man Who Doesn't Drink* (74 pages), *W.C. Fields Speaks* (79 pages), *Drat!* (128 pages), and *The Quotations of W.C. Fields* (160 pages, though *Drat!* actually squeezes more material into fewer pages). All in all, they provide pleasant diversions for both the student of Fields and the fan who is interested in a well-balanced coffee table.

Anobile's two additional Fields books, *A Flask of Fields: Verbal and Visual Gems from the Films of W.C. Fields* (1972) and *Godfrey Daniels: Verbal and Visual Gems from the Short Films of W.C. Fields* (1975), as well as Fields's film scripts published in book form, are dealt with in the reference category herein.

Fields Critical Biographies

Amazing as it may seem, there are at this time only two critical biographies of Fields: William K. Everson's *The Art of W.C. Fields* (1967) and Nicholas Yanni's *W.C. Fields* (1974). While each provides some excellent insights, both also operate under a series of restrictions.

Film historian Everson, who has written extensively on numerous cinema topics from the western to Laurel & Hardy, completed *The Art of W.C. Fields* at a time when most of the comedian's silent films were thought to be lost. Everson was therefore unable to reevaluate them in terms of the comedian's complete career. Moreover, neither of the pivotal studies by Carlotta Monti and editor Ronald J. Fields appeared until after Everson's work.

Quite possibly because of this limitation, Everson opens his text by arguing strongly against autobiographical interpretations of an artist's work.[32] Furthermore, he states that film comedy study can never be consistent if one looks for autobiographical motivations in the work of some (such as Chaplin and Fields) and not others (like Keaton, Langdon, and Laurel & Hardy).[33] However, Everson skates on thin ice when he defends his position by claiming that none of the latter group's films "were in any way autobiographical."[34] (Again, more recent research, especially in the case of Keaton, contradicts this.) While he grants that certain of Fields's personal positions surface in his films, Everson leaves himself very vulnerable when he states, "There seems nothing in Fields' life on which to base this year-in, year-out indictment of The American Family."[35] (To refute the last statement now merely takes an examination of the comedian's barbed letters to wife Hattie in *W.C. Fields by Himself.*)

Though Everson's text-only stance is certainly most legitimate, a potentially richer course would seem to be forever searching out possible autobiographical insight about an artist's work. As Philip Rosen so eloquently stated in his much praised essay "The Chaplin World-View," such examinations not only assist in understanding an artist's work, they also "help illuminate the culture from which the artist has risen and the interaction between art and culture . . . [and perhaps such an] examination will help us understand the psychology of artists in general."[36]

The key thrust of Everson's work is the reminder that "W.C. Fields has suffered from . . . over-simplification of his screen character . . .[he] was a sympathetic underdog on the screen far more than he was a conniving charlatan."[37] In point of fact, Fields's screen personae were more than complex; they fluctuated between two types—the classic Milquetoast husband and the carnival huckster. Nevertheless, Everson's basic reminder on "over-simplification" is well-taken because most of the writing on Fields focuses only on the charlatan. Indeed, this is the key weakness of Nicholas Yanni's *W.C. Fields*—he expounds on the sly but not the shy Fields.

This flaw notwithstanding, Yanni's book is the better critical overview on the comedian. Published in 1974, Yanni was able to draw from the afore-mentioned films and texts not available to Everson. Appearing in the underrated series "Pyramid Illustrated History of the Movies," the volume offers a more pointed and scholarly overview of Fields and includes bibliography, filmography, and index (all conspicuously absent from the Everson text). Yanni also maintains an ongoing critical analysis of Fields's life and times. (Everson, however, provides valuable plot synopses and passing observations on 1930s filmmaking as it related to Fields.)

Each book includes numerous stills of Fields (both in films and at home), as well as frequent examples of his aphorisms—a common characteristic of all material on the comedian. And despite Everson's hesitancy to explore autobiographical interpretations of an artist's work, both authors see little difference between Fields's public and private personae. This is the norm in nearly everything written about the comedian, with the possible exception of the attempted revisionist stance of Fields's grandson and Louise Brooks's "The Other Face of W.C. Fields."[38]

Fields References

There are five key reference texts on Fields: Donald Deschner's *The Films of W.C. Fields* (1966); two film script collections, *W.C. Fields in Never Give a Sucker an Even Break and Tillie and Gus* (1973) and *W.C. Fields in The Bank Dick* (1973); and editor Richard J. Anobile's two picture-book (frame-by-frame) examinations of the comedian's work, *A Flask of Fields* (1972) and *Godfrey Daniels* (1975).

Deschner's work is in the generally excellent "films of" reference series by Citadel Press, following that series' basic organization. Fields's movies are listed in chronological order, with complete cast and credits, plot synopses, excerpts from contemporary reviews, and numerous stills from each production.

The book also contains a short biographical sketch of the comedian; an introduction by celebrated film historian Arthur Knight; two essays by Fields ("Speaking of Benefits," 1923, and "Anything for a Laugh," 1934); Otis Ferguson's comically insightful 1940 review of *The Bank Dick* (which uses the name of another Fields film for its title—*The Old-Fashioned Way*); Heywood Broun's essay of high praise ("W.C. Fields and the Cosmos," 1931), which originally appeared years before the comedian's now most celebrated films; and highlighted commentary on Fields by Andre Sennwald, Alan P. Twyman, and Otis Ferguson. Though supplementary material of this nature is typical of the Citadel series, both the amount and the significance of the support items included here (especially the pieces by Fields himself) are extraordinary.

Deschner's work is the most indispensable of the reference group, with no real flaws, though like most filmography texts there are occasional errors in the synopses. The most notable example is the overview of *Never Give a Sucker an Even Break,* which seems to have been drawn from the original screenplay, not the completed film. For example, the synopsis has Fields meeting his niece (Gloria Jean) at the shooting gallery of the rival (Leon Errol) who eventually will compete with the comedian for the hand of Mrs. Hemogloben (Margaret Dumont). The synopsis also includes the trapeze death of the niece's mother, Madame Gorgeous (Anne Nagel), thus necessitating Fields's responsibility for Gloria (though she is the one who does most of the parenting). While both of these scenes were originally shot, neither made the final print.

Just for the record, *The Films of W.C. Fields* does not include a guest appearance the comedian made in a Warner golfing short subject entitled

Hip Action (1933, the third lesson in the series "How to Break 90"). In Deschner's defense, decidedly few Fields texts note this how-to film, which starred the celebrated golfer Bobby Jones.

The next most important reference works are the screenplays, especially *W.C. Fields in The Bank Dick*. This one-screenplay volume is to be preferred over the aforementioned double collection because it presents Fields's (or should one say Mahatma Kane Jeeves's) original script, with ninety notes on variations that occurred in the final film. Thus the reader is provided with invaluable insights on Fields's initial conception of *The Bank Dick* and its production evolution in which the primary differences between script and film center on fantasy and the forcefulness of Fields.

The script has a number of tall-tale characteristics that do not survive in the film, from Nicodemus (a talking raven that serves as something of a comic Greek chorus) to Fields's story about Old Tom, the fly that forged the governor's signature in order to pardon Egbert Sousé (Fields), who was behind bars for purloining a watch. In terms of forcefulness, Fields's script character is generally more aggressive than the eventual film persona (whether the focus is flirting with pretty girls or showcasing battles royal with the family). Because of this knowledge, the more forceful Fields of the fantasy-oriented *Never Give a Sucker an Even Break* (1941, which followed the release of *The Bank Dick* and was his last starring feature film) does not seem quite the radical departure some would have it be.

While the double-script collection, *W.C. Fields in Never Give a Sucker an Even Break and Tillie and Gus,* merely represents final film dialogue continuities and not original screenplays, the juxtapositioning of the scripts allows the reader to compare the first sound feature film to utilize fully Fields's skills (*Tillie and Gus,* 1933) with the last such production (*Sucker*).

It should be noted that Fields did not receive screenplay credit for either film. However, the original story for *Sucker* is credited to one Otis Criblecobis (Fields), and both movies are generously peppered with patented Fields material, from the observation that he likes children "if they're properly cooked" (*Tillie and Gus*) to his comment to a man bitten in the ankle by a little daschund, "rather fortunate that it wasn't a Newfoundland dog that bit you" (*Never Give a Sucker an Even Break*).[39]

Both this volume and *W.C. Fields in The Bank Dick* were published in Simon and Schuster's generally excellent "Classic Film Scripts Series." *The Bank Dick* text is supplemented by two excerpts from contemporary reviews, while the *Tillie and Gus* double volume includes an insightfully tongue-in-cheek introduction by Andrew Sinclair (which touches briefly on variations from the original script in *Sucker*).

The books edited by Richard J. Anobile—*A Flask of Fields: Verbal and Visual Gems from the Films of W.C. Fields* and *Godfrey Daniels: Verbal and Visual Gems from the Short Films of W.C. Fields*—combine some key elements of the reference sources already examined. Dialogue has been transcribed from the screen and matched to representative film frame enlargements of the scenes under scrutiny.

A Flask of Fields examines verbal and visual scene excerpts from ten films, including the courtroom scene in *Tillie and Gus*; Fields's entry and exit by autogyro (a wonderful sight gag of a vehicle, part plane and part helicopter) in *International House* (1933); buying an ostrich for his wife in *You're Telling Me* (1934); highlights of the "Sleeping Porch" scene in *It's a Gift* (1934); confronting drunken crooks in *The Man on the Flying Trapeze* (1935); doing dinner-table battle with Baby LeRoy in *The Old-Fashioned Way* (1934); the railroad "courtship" of Mae West, Fields as reminiscing bartender, and Fields as master card cutter in *My Little Chickadee* (1940); "making" change and feuding with Charlie McCarthy in *You Can't Cheat an Honest Man* (1939); Fields's run-in with the waitress and the ice cream soda scene in *Never Give a Sucker an Even Break;* and the opening battle with his family, as well as the Mickey Finning of Franklin Pangborn, in *The Bank Dick. A Flask of Fields* also includes a foreword by Anobile and an introduction by film critic Judith Crist.

Anobile's *Godfrey Daniels* follows the same format as *A Flask of Fields,* except the focus is now on short subjects rather than features. More specifically, Anobile limits himself to the comedian's most celebrated shorts—*The Dentist* (1932), *The Fatal Glass of Beer* (1933), *The Pharmacist* (1933), and *The Barber Shop* (1933, all produced by Mack Sennett). In each case, Fields receives the sole screenwriting credit.

Since *Godfrey Daniels* examines fewer as well as shorter films, Anobile's scene selections come closer to being an overview of each short subject instead of the more pronounced "greatest routines" nature of *A Flask of Fields. Godfrey Daniels* also boasts an Anobile preface and an introduction by noted film historian Raymond Rohauer.

As has been the case with the other reference texts described in this section, Anobile's work on Fields compares well with similar studies on other film figures. However, a key reason behind the consistency is that Anobile has become a one-man industry in this type of reference work, having completed nearly a dozen of these volumes, ranging from *A Fine Mess!: Verbal and Visual Gems from the Crazy World of Laurel and Hardy* (1975) to *Woody Allen's Play It Again Sam* (1977).

SHORTER WORKS

Fields Critical Film Analysis

Any number of essay-length critical works on Fields's films might have been chosen for this section; the most important writing is arranged into two categories. First, for the period of Fields's lifetime, the focus is on several film critics, starting with Otis Ferguson and Andre Sennwald, who have had a major effect on shaping the study of Fields through largely mainstream publications. The critics—or if the reviews were unsigned, the magazines—have been examined in order of the significance of their Fields writing.

Second, the more ambitious essays on Fields are examined, chronologically to the present, starting with 1925, the year of Fields's first starring feature film, *Sally of the Sawdust*. These exclude reviews during his lifetime of specific films. This second category, however, does include reviews of some post-1946 (the year of Fields's death) rereleases of his films, because by then few authors could avoid expanding further on their subject.

It is most fitting that a section devoted to shorter pieces on Fields should begin with the writing of Otis Ferguson, author of the most poetically insightful original reviews of the comedian's films. Like James Agee's equally poetic and penetrating observations on Chaplin, Ferguson's *New Republic* musings on Fields occupy a special category among the literature on the comedian.

These reviews were not, however, complete critical hosannas to Fields (unlike Agee's Chaplin work). Ferguson often had problems with individual Fields films. Frequently he turned his reviews into general forums on the greatness of Fields, while admonishing the wastefulness of the film industry, for "Fields is more like a national resource: he should be got into his ace picture before his time is out, because there is a certain savor still lacking in the national salt."[40]

Ferguson's most celebrated Fields essay, "The Old-Fashioned Way" (which focuses on *The Bank Dick* and is anthologized in several works), finds the critic at his lyrical best in describing Fields:

> He is the harried man of family and emperor of the world, his
> address and resource are infinite except when approaching a
> simple flight of steps, he is fastidious to the high point of using
> his chaser for a finger bowl, he is dignity with a red nose.[41]

Ferguson nicely captures the dual nature of Fields's comedy personae—the fluctuation between victim and victimizer. (Most writing on the comedian still focuses on the latter category—Fields as the con man.)

Ferguson is troubled, however, with certain non-Fieldsian aspects of *The Bank Dick*, which the critic notes in his own comic style: "the only pace discernible is in the distance between drinks or the rhythm of the fleeting seconds it takes Fields to size up trouble coming and duck to hell out."[42] Yet more than any of Ferguson's other essays on Fields, "The Old-Fashioned Way" chronicles a critic's delight in a favorite subject achieving even a measure of his potential. And as might be assumed from the piece's title, which puns the name of an earlier Fields film, Ferguson is suggesting that the comedian is at his best when merely allowed adequate time to be W.C. Fields, "the trouper of all troupers once again."[43]

It is not necessary, though, to limit a Ferguson bibliography on Fields to just one essay. Nor would it be complete if one were to add those Fields references in non-Fields essays when Ferguson needed to sketch a quality comedy pantheon. That is, there are numerous Ferguson essays on Fields which consistently showcase the most poetic insights—poetic insights at a time when Fields was not nearly so roundly celebrated. Thus Ferguson observes in his review of *Never Give a Sucker an Even Break*:

> If there was ever a great clown in this time of changeover from the beer and music hall to the universal distribution of radio and films, I would say it was in the person and character and the undying if corny gusto of Bill Fields, who moved mountains until they fell on him, and then brushed himself off and looked around for more.[44]

And as the close of his *Man on the Flying Trapeze* review notes, Fields "is not only a funny man, he is a familiar and endearing figure, to be seen with mirth and remembered with special affection; a minor Jack Falstaff on the sawdust of the twentieth century."[45] Once again, Ferguson is able to juggle Fields's dual comedy nature and be lyrical in the bargain. Moreover, the latter commentary includes a brief but important analogy between Fields and Falstaff, a phenomenon already expanded upon.

Ferguson's nearest rival in the category of Fields's most perceptive contemporary critics was Andre Sennwald of *The New York Times*. Like Ferguson, Sennwald produced a number of insightful reviews of Fields films, but easily his best writing on the comedian occurs in a special character sketch entitled "W.C. Fields, Buffoon":

> Not to be aware of the tragic overtones in the work of this middle-aged, whiskey-nosed, fumbling and wistfully incompetent gentleman is to be ignorant of the same tragic overtones in the comedy of Don Quixote de la Mancha. To be of the belief that Mr. Fields is no more than a funny man is to hold the opinion that *Gulliver's Travels* is a book for children and that the Spanish bullfight is planned as a contest between a man and a beast.[46]

Beyond focusing some much needed attention on the dark side of the Fields personae, the essay also anticipates by years film theorist André Bazin's analogy between a gifted performer of the twentieth century (his example was Charlie Chaplin) and "heroes of old [known] through literary works," the "mythical figure who rises above every adventure in which he becomes involved."[47] It is only after an elevation of this nature that a true appreciation of the unique Fields character is possible. Though there were earlier, more fleeting literary comparisons, Sennwald's position is highlighted because he grants Fields an equality with literary greats rare among contemporary reviewers. (Even Ferguson's later moving tribute from his review of *The Man on the Flying Trapeze* qualifies itself by labeling the comedian a *minor* Falstaff.) Sennwald, moreover, seems to have been more drawn to literary analogies. Thus, just five days after the appearance of "W.C. Fields, Buffoon," he devotes nearly his entire review of *David Copperfield* (1935) to the appropriateness and skill with which Fields plays Dickens's Mr. Micawber—at a time when most other critics spent little time on Fields's participation.[48]

"W.C. Fields, Buffoon" is broken into four segments: Part 1 examines the serious implications of Fields's comedy; Part 2 draws parallels between his real life and his comedy; Part 3 focuses on *It's a Gift* (which Sennwald had reviewed eleven days before on January 2, 1935); Part 4 examines in detail some of the most basic frustrations through which Fields (and by association, the viewer) suffers.

After this pivotal essay, Sennwald's strongest Fields writing is the aforementioned review of *It's a Gift* (also anthologized in Stanley Kauffmann's *American Film Criticism*). The film no doubt triggered "W.C. Fields, Buffoon" since it is probably the comedian's greatest work. Yet Sennwald is to be praised for his foresight in stating: "*It's a Gift* immerses the veery, adenoidal and bulbous-noses [*sic*] star in a variety of situations which he promptly embrolders [*sic*] into priceless and classic comic episodes."[49] It was a time when even the most celebrated of Fields critics (Ferguson) did not recognize the inherent greatness of *It's a Gift*. (Ferguson said the comedian's "presence dignified a magic-lantern show that as it stood could not, without the grace of block booking, have ever made the grade of being double billed into the neighborhood houses of Canarsie.")[50] Although *It's a Gift* had a much better initial response than the Marx Brothers' earlier *Duck Soup* (1933, which almost ended their careers), it took years for the works to be recognized as Fields's and the Marx Brothers' best, or near best, films.

While Ferguson's forte was the broad-stroke overview of Fields's art, Sennwald excelled in penetrating dissections of the film at hand. For example, he nicely demonstrates Fields's ability to draw comedy from the controversial in *It's a Gift*:

> With the one exception of Charlie Chaplin, there is nobody but Mr. Fields who could manage the espisode with the blind and deaf man in the store so as to make it seem genuinely and inescapabling funny instead of just a trifle revolting.[51]

And while many critics found fault with the supporting casts in Fields's films, Sennwald wisely perceived early the significance of the comedian's frequent cinema nemesis Kathleen Howard (who is to Fields what Margaret Dumont is to the Marx Brothers): "As the nagging wife Kathleen Howard is so authentic as to make Mr. Fields's suffering seem cosmic and a little sad despite their basic humor."[52] The observation seems all the richer for a phrasing that brings to mind Heywood Broun's delightful 1931 essay "W.C. Fields and the Cosmos," which was referred to in Chapter 1.[53]

The reason for Sennwald's close attention to the world of Fields probably was best defined in his review of *The Old-Fashioned Way*: Fields "is so much greater than his material that scarcely anything in which he appears can afford to be ignored by students of humor."[54] The statement has become more true with each passing year, if that is possible. And though Sennwald tragically died in the midst of Fields's film career (1936), the living criticism he left behind honors both the comedian and the author.

After Ferguson and Sennwald, one must honor ARGUS of *The Literary Digest*. In Greek mythology, Argus was a giant with a hundred eyes assigned a watchman's job. And because a hundred-eyed watchman is not a bad description of the conscientious film reviewer, *The Literary Digest*, with tongue firmly in cheek, seems to have selected the term as the perfect pseudonym for the author or authors of its cinema column. Since the journal was a digest, it no doubt had a limitless supply of "eyes" at other presses.

Unfortunately, Fields's views on the subject of pseudonymity in critics do not seem to have been recorded. However, for a man who liked nothing better than a good pseudonym, be it Mahatma Kane Jeeves or simply Charles Bogle, a film critic calling himself ARGUS certainly would have garnered some respect from Fields—if Fields could respect anyone in that profession. And if the ARGUS reviews ever used outside "digested" material, Fields—no stranger to "borrowing"—probably would have respected the reviewer(s) even more. Yet in all fairness to *The Literary Digest*, its Fields film reviews seem more a sympathetically thoughtful overview of then-contemporary responses to the comedian rather than an aping of one or two other articles and/or columnists.

When compared to the writing of Otis Ferguson and Andre Sennwald, the *Literary Digest* reviews favor the latter, with detailed looks at each film in question. For example, ARGUS explores the comedian's often neglected ability to play pathos in a review of *Your're Telling Me*: "Probably only Mr. Fields, of all the comedians, including Chaplin, could make that scene of attempted suicide hilarious [he attempts to take iodine with a collapsible spoon], but in some magic way, he does perform the miracle."[55]

Interestingly enough, however, the best Fields review by ARGUS does draw upon the spirit of Ferguson. It uses the subject of *Six of a Kind* as a platform from which to present a brief overview of some elements of the comedian's work.[56] Special attention is paid to the unique Fields voice and to the irony that much of his career was spent as a juggler and pantomimist. Other Fields films mentioned in this review are *Sally of the Sawdust* (1925), *Million Dollar Legs* (1932), and *Alice in Wonderland* (1933). Stage productions touched upon include *Poppy,* the Ziegfeld Follies, and the Carroll *Vanities.* The review is most valuable today in noting some stage material (now largely lost) which Fields incorporated directly into his films, such as the observation, "It's the old army game!"[57]—which turns up in several later Fields films, as well as being the title of one (1926).

The best analyses of comedy are naturally those that also maintain a sense of humor, and just as Ferguson and Sennwald donated to the cause as they examined it, so did ARGUS. For example, the comedian's classic *It's a Gift* is said to provide "a Field-day," while a scene from *You're Telling Me* sketches him as "hilarious when walking silently down the street, slightly under the influence of alcoholic liquor and swaying a little in the breeze."[58] And the "romping insanity" of *Poppy*

> is about as mysterious as a cobblestone and just about as old-fashioned. No one will resent it for that. It is good antique hokum trussed up for a Fields vehicle. All that matters is that *Professor Eustace McGargle* is back in perfect form . . . a lovable old reprobate grifting . . . a possibly dishonest quarter into a definitely dishonest half-dollar.[59]

Unfortunately, at the same time the comedian was having severe health problems, so was *The Literary Digest.* In 1937 an ailing Fields was unable to make any films, and the magazine tried a new format simply entitled *The Digest.* But while the comedian made his film comeback in *The Big Broadcast of 1938,* the magazine ceased publication early that same year.

Ferguson, Sennwald, and ARGUS are Fields's keynote contemporary reviewers, though quality criticism is hardly limited to their work. For example, Mordaunt Hall's reviews of Fields (like Sennwald, he wrote for *The New York Times*) have aged very little, being most insightful when they note the inclusion of stage material in his films. (See especially his reviews of *It's the Old Army Game* and *You're Telling Me.*)[60]

Hall's review of *Running Wild* (1927), in fact, is quite possibly the basis of Fields friend and sometimes director Gregory LaCava's celebrated observation that the comedian most needed restraint to be effective—to play straight man to the world.[61] *Running Wild,* written and directed by LaCava, had Fields going from being an extreme case of milquetoast to the posture of a lion. Hall, while not panning the film, felt:

> Quite often Mr. Fields overdoes the fun, with the result that it falls somewhat flat. He was . . . far more comic in the screen

version of *The Potters* [his previous picture, and often considered his greatest silent film]. . . . There was a marked restraint about *The Potters,* while in this current subject [*Running Wild*], the authorship of which is credited to its director, Gregory LaCava, Mr. Fields manifests a fondness for returning to his extravagant actions and plausibility is flung to the four winds.[62]

One more contemporary Fields reviewer worth noting is James Agee, film critic for both *The Nation* (1942-1948) and *Time* (1941-1948). However, unlike Hall, who was an important early commentator on the comedian's films, Agee does not begin to critique until the close of Fields's career. Thus some of Agee's best insights on the comedian appear as asides in reviews of other films. For example, his 1943 review of Alfred Hitchcock's *Shadow of a Doubt* praises its "clever observation of rabbity white-collar life which, in spite of a specious sweetness, is the best since W.C. Fields's *It's a Gift.*"[63] His 1946 review of the Jerome Kern biographic film, *Till the Clouds Roll By,* finds fault with the "misplaced reverence" accorded the musical numbers: "This I realize is called *feeling* the music; for that kind of feeling I prefer W.C. Fields's cadenza on the zither, which was rendered in sparring-gloves."[64]

Agee's writing style and general views on Fields seem indebted to the work of Otis Ferguson. This is best exemplified by Agee's 1941 review of *Never Give a Sucker an Even Break,* which quickly proceeds to a Ferguson scenario: an amusing but perceptive short overview of Fields's career— including both high praise ("Fields is one of the funniest men on earth") and constructive criticism ("His unique talent needs intelligent direction. It does not need all the props that its owner thinks are a necessity for his performance.")[65] Yet Agee's wit is not quite so biting as Ferguson's, and he is more apt to pass on a comic line, such as Fields's cure for insomnia— "Get plenty of sleep"—rather than comically sparring with the target at hand. Furthermore, Agee's sense of romanticism allows him to be more indulgent than Ferguson over flaws in his favorites—"*Sucker* has no plot and needs none."[66] (Still, with Ferguson's World War II death, in 1943, much of his style would continue in Agee's writing.)

Interestingly enough, the close of Agee's *Sucker* review—"The great comedian can play straight better and more firmly than anyone in the business"[67]—comes full circle to Mordaunt Hall's 1927 suggestion of restraint. Thus while Ferguson, Sennwald, and ARGUS have received the key focus, Hall and Agee are good bookend representatives (Fields's early film career and its conclusion) of the numerous reviews inspired by the man with the potato nose.

Other mainstream publications worth consulting for contemporary Fields film reviews are *Variety, Time* magazine, and *Newsweek.* Most of these reviews are unsigned and not of the quality of the previously highlighted work. But they do represent additional influential observations on Fields's films made at the time of release.

As might be expected of a publication which focuses on entertainment for those actively involved in entertainment, *Variety*'s reviews of Fields are more critically demanding (often to *Variety*'s detriment) and more conscious of the film business than any other source dealt with in this section. While generally praising the comedian, *Variety* frequently belabors the rest of the production. This approach is hardly new—Ferguson, among others, also did this—but *Variety* generally does not provide the insightful overview which was also a regular inclusion of a Ferguson review. For example, *Variety* says of *The Man on the Flying Trapeze:*

> Whatever business this picture drags into theatres will be entirely due to W.C. Fields' name on the marquee. Picture itself is light-weight, a misnomer and a weakie. Comic's drawing power may built it up to moderate rating in the nabes [neighborhood theaters], which is the best it can hope for.[68]

Although Ferguson was bothered by this film's production, his review also happened to be a platform for his most eloquent seminar on Fields, which included labeling him both a "national treasure" and an American Falstaff.[69] Sennwald's review, however, was the most prophetic of all: "It is possible that the final bibliography of Mr. Fields's works will list his new picture . . . as one of his most important screen triumphs."[70]

Variety's reviews of Fields are most valuable for their direct, though not always pleasing, business appraisals of the comedian. The review of *You Can't Cheat An Honest Man* matter-of-factly weighs the chances for the film's success on the drawing power not of Fields but of his costars: "Picture is due for spotty biz in the keys, with [Edgar] Bergen-[Charlie] McCarthy's radio following to pull it through."[71] *Variety*'s critique of *Never Give a Sucker an Even Break* qualifies its praise by placing the work in the B-movie category: "with sufficient laugh content for the comedian's fans to get across as an acceptable B supporter where ridiculous comedy and wild slapstick catches audience attention."[72] And the opening focus of *Variety*'s *My Little Chickadee* review is not Fields but rather the comeback story of costar Mae West, who had been off the screen for two years.[73]

Time magazine's reviews of Fields films before Agee, while generally positive, tend to be shorter and more tied to plot rehashes than the critical analyses already showcased here. They are occasionally valuable, however, for the inclusion of production background and/or still-fresh comic details about the comedian. An example of the former occurs in *Time*'s review of *You Can't Cheat an Honest Man:*

Most Hollywood producers harass themselves and Mr. Fields by trying to chivy him into playing the part written for him, instead of letting him alone in his own classic interpretation of W.C. Fields. . . . Producer Lester Cowan shrewdly devised a new technique. Instead of paying his stars a salary, he persuaded them to work on a profit-sharing basis, had Fields write his own story and let matters take their course. The result was that the shooting . . . completed for a mere $400,000—amounted practically to a miniature Hollywood revolution.[74]

Time's comic detail on Fields is best demonstrated by the tongue-in-cheek understatement of a biographical overview tacked onto the review of *You're Telling Me,* part of which follows: "Proud possessor of a Phi Beta Kappa key, which he found, Fields is mildly eccentric, wears snakeskin shoes, sleeps in silk underwear, dislikes people who ask if his nose is made of putty."[75]

Time often was more critically perceptive of Fields, or at least more direct, in articles about other comedians. In a 1944 cover story on Jimmy Durante, *Time* declared:

The fact that Jimmy's nose is big is no more important *per se* than the fact that W.C. Fields's nose is red. Jimmy, like Fields, is no gagster, however appealing. . . . Jimmy, like Fields, is a high comedian, who can convulse both children and sophisticates.[76]

And a 1940 *Time* review of the Marx Brothers' *Go West* baldly stated: "Like W.C. Fields, Groucho, Harpo and Chico Marx are screamingly funny to their admirers, idiotic to others."[77]

Newsweek was less established in the 1930s than *Time* (founded in 1933 versus *Time*'s 1923 beginnings) and more diffused in its coverage of the performing arts (*Newsweek* film reviews were found under an "Entertainment" umbrella versus Time's "Cinema" section). With reviews of a shorter overall length, *Newsweek* on Fields was not the equal of *Time*.

Newsweek's and *Time*'s strengths and weaknesses are the same, however. They both tend to rehash the film rather than analyze it, yet often balance this with production background. Thus *Newsweek*'s review of *David Copperfield* discusses Hollywood's mid-1930s fascination with England's great nineteenth-century novels, while the review of *Poppy* concentrates more on the comeback nature of Fields, who was in poor health before, during, and after the completion of the project.[78] *Newsweek*'s analysis and background of Fields are probably best combined in its short review of *My Little Chickadee*. Simply entitled "Mae and Bill Out West," it briefly sketches the fireworks anticipated with their teaming and compares their comedy techniques.[79]

Before examining more recent film criticism on Fields, it would seem appropriate to discuss those articles that attempted a general overview of the comedian (as opposed to a film review) during his lifetime. Many essays that might normally have appeared here were included in the earlier "Fields on Fields" section because of the propensity of many authors to lace their work with numerous, lengthy quotations by the comedian. However, several other articles are worth consideration here.

An appropriate starting point for more ambitious essays on Fields is Harold Cary's 1925 *Colliers* article, "The Loneliest Man in the Movies." This was reprinted in part (with credit) the following year in *The Literary Digest* as "How the Films Fought Shy of 'Bill' Fields" and included additional material not found in the *Colliers* piece.[80] It is an appropriate beginning because Fields's starring feature film career had only just been established (1925) with the critical and commercial success of *Sally of the Sawdust* (from the play *Poppy*, in which he also starred).

Much of the article, in fact, focuses on the difficulty the comedian had in becoming established in film—a "man who has been trying by every known means for fifteen years to get into movies."[81] (Fields had appeared in three earlier films, but it was the success of *Poppy* and its screen adaptation which finally made a movie career accessible.) And the comedian notes the catch-22 irony that movies initially "wouldn't have me because I was a [juggling] pantomimist. I couldn't get a straight offer for the silent drama until I got a speaking part on the stage."[82] Consequently, Fields is "The Loneliest Man in the Movies" because "he has never forgotten the years on end when he trouped up and down this country and every other country where there is a theatre."[83]

The essay examines those troupe years and then explores the nature of his comedy. Cary is most insightful when he posits Fields "is funny because you and I, and our relatives, the rest of the human race, are funny. He slightly caricatures us . . . sees through our bluff and calls it."[84] Cary suggests the affinity Fields's character *sometimes* has with the "main street" satire of a Sinclair Lewis, an analogy seldom made.

Writer and friend Alva Johnston did an excellent though often neglected three-part series (February 2, 9, and 16, 1935) in *The New Yorker*. The first article is at its best in analyzing the comedian's work along sociological lines. For example, Fields's extremely difficult childhood "gave him the nonchalance [a key comedy trait for Johnston] of the man who has endured everything and who is used to catastrophes."[85]

Unfortunately, Johnston soon stops being a sociological critic and becomes an anecdotal biographer. Yet there is importance in this. While not all the stories were new even in 1935,[86] the comedian's Thurberish life and hard times had seldom if ever been dealt with in such affectionate detail and insightful commentary. This *New Yorker* series and Johnston's 1938 Fields piece, "Who Knows What Is Funny?"[87] would seem to have had a major influence on Robert Lewis Taylor's *W.C. Fields: His Follies and Fortunes.*

Johnston's occasional straight biographical observations can also serve a critical purpose: "Living by petty larceny and petty fraud, he frequently found himself in embarrassing situations, and he met them by acting the part of an upright imbecile."[88] Comedy theory simply calls this type of character the wise fool, and it is certainly a posture Fields's screen personae have assumed on numerous occasions. Fields's wise fool situations frequently were tied to screen events of "petty larceny and petty fraud" which resulted in "embarrassing situations."

Johnston's second article in the series continues in the anecdotal style but includes some analytical criticism. For example, the classic tale of how Fields whacked an intruding Ed Wynn with a pool cue during Fields's solo billiard act (Wynn, having hidden himself under the table, was disrupting Fields's elaborately choreographed routine) is given new life by the author's comparison of the two comedians' styles. Thus while Fields was a prop comedian, Wynn was a "fly-catcher," a comedian who "gets his laughs mainly by grimaces and by quick movements of the hands, as in catching insects."[89] Besides expanding further on the differences between the prop comedian and the fly-catcher, Johnston makes important comments on Fields and improvisation, adding biographical insights that can be tied directly to the comedian's films.

Johnston's third and final article in the series opens strongly with a perceptive look at Fields's comedy in terms of physical presence—a neglected subject for this comedian and most others. The article's beginning also analyzes Fields's propensity to attack the stuffed shirt. And though this installment, too, soon returns to the anecdotal approach, there are still some fresh insights. These include a description of the period's "thirty-third-degree Fields fans" and a brief but fascinating clue to the "why" behind the comedian's eccentricities (lodged in an earlier era's conception of the artist).[90]

It is logical that this three-part series is important, both because of the author's friendship with Fields and because of the comedian's fondness for *The New Yorker*—"one of his special delights."[91] However, because back issues of the magazine are more readily available than many other cited Fields sources (such as *Photoplay* and *Motion Picture Classic*), it remains a mystery why Johnston's series is often left out of Fields bibliographies.

Johnston's August 1938 *Saturday Evening Post* essay, "Who Knows What Is Funny?" begins where his *New Yorker* (February 1935) series ended. Whereas the earlier work is a biographical overview from childhood, "Who Knows" focuses on Fields the film star during the 1930s. However, Johnston still draws upon the comedian's youth to underline points. For example, the young Fields survived "because he seized everything he could get away with," a habit the comedian more than continued in his adult life.[92]

The article is at its most revealing when it examines Fields's relationship with his writers because the comedian's collaborators are seldom acknowledged, let alone written about. The title of the piece is even drawn from this subject—"Who knows what is funny?" was Fields's way of closing an argument with a writer if the suggested material did not meet the comedian's standards.

The *Post* article repeats some of the material in the *New Yorker* series, such as the billiard cue rivalry with Ed Wynn or Fields's ongoing problems with inefficient property men (dull razors being sharp razors, and so on). Yet Johnston's later piece is still quite capable of standing on its own and, when in tandem with the *New Yorker* series, is one of the best single-author texts on the comedian prior to the appearance of Robert Lewis Taylor's biography.

The year 1935 was a good one for critical essays on Fields. Besides Johnston's *New Yorker* material, Ed Sullivan wrote a valuable article for *Silver Screen* entitled "That Lovable Liar: An Appreciation of W.C. Fields and His Gift for Picturesque Exaggeration." And if among thirties film reviewers Andre Sennwald best realized the appropriateness of equating Fields's screen personae with classic figures from literature, Sullivan had comparable credentials among the general essayists of the period. Sullivan initially mentions several characters, but Mark Twain's Jim Smiley, of the famous short story, "The Notorious Jumping Frog of Calaveras County," receives the key focus. Yet Sullivan best dissects Fields's art when he draws general parallels with the world of Twain:

> The homely, earthy characters created by Twain had much in common with Fields, for he is down to earth and earthy, too. . . . Twain's gentle, drawling humor occupied itself time and again with the creation of fabulous liars and windbags, and here again is a definite point of resemblance. Fields is at his very peak when he is a fabulous liar.[93]

The rediscovery of Fields during the antiestablishment 1960s, probably because of the propensity with which he parodied "Main Street" America, still frequently obscures the fact that Fields often turned that parody on his own "creation of fabulous liars and windbags." That is, he often parodied his own personifications. Although Otis Ferguson still provides the best overview of the comedian as both victim *or* victimizer, Sullivan provides an important examination of a frequently neglected vantage point in Fields study.

Sullivan also investigates the significance of Fields's ad-libbing, his early years, the comedy traditions of Philadelphia, his lack of appeal to women, and his comparability to Charlie Chaplin. All in all Sullivan addresses several Fields topics which now seem remarkably contemporary.

Fields's ill health in 1936 and 1937 and his comeback (first in radio and then in films) generated interest in a number of articles on the comedian. But the best of these rapidly turned into interviews with the comedian such as those in Chapter 3. Until his death in 1946, the key Fields pieces continued to be largely his doing. This is best exemplified by his book *Fields for President* (1940) which was serialized in several journals.

The important post-1946 critical literature on the comedian begins with James Agee's celebrated cover story for *Life* on September 3, 1949, "Comedy's Greatest Era." Though the frequently anthologized essay focuses on silent comedy, establishing the still accepted pantheon of Charlie Chaplin, Buster Keaton, Harold Lloyd and Harry Langdon, it provides a unique showcase for a short but insightful commemoration of Fields:

> The talkies brought one great comedian, the late, majestically lethargic W.C. Fields, who could not possibly have worked as well in silence [though he had a modestly successful silent film career]; he was the toughest and the most warmly human of all screen comedians, and *It's a Gift* and *The Bank Dick,* fiendishly funny and incisive white-collar comedies, rank high among the best comedies (and best movies) ever made.[94]

Agee's September 1949 article followed shortly after the publication of Taylor's *W.C. Fields: His Follies and Fortunes,* which generated a number of reviews—sometimes in a critical-essay style. Ken Tynan's 1951 *Sight and Sound* piece, "Toby Jug and Bottle," later anthologized in his *Curtains* (1961), is the best such review.[95]

Tynan's comments, frequently as anecdotal as the book it praises, manage to address a wide assortment of critical subjects, from director Gregory LaCava's suggestions to Fields on comedy restraint to the significance of actress Kathleen Howard in the Fields milieu. Also included are observations on the comedian's visual and verbal gifts (including a provocative linking of Fields to James Boswell's biographical portrait of Samuel Johnson), further analysis of the male nature of Fields's comedy, another look at *It's a Gift* (then being revived in England), and the comedian's general "deafness" to direction.

Undoubtedly the renewal of Fields interest generated by the Taylor book helped lead to a 1950 revival of his films. In fact, the August 26, 1950, *Saturday Review* movie column, "The Film Forum," is largely a review of Taylor's biography. The column was devoted to the 16-mm availability, for purchase or rental, of four Fields films: *You Can't Cheat an Honest Man, The Bank Dick, My Little Chickadee,* and *Never Give a Sucker an Even Break.*

The 1954 publication of Gene Fowler's *Minutes of the Last Meeting,* the composite biography of Fields's inner circle during his final years, also generated a number of reviews, but there is nothing comparable to Tynan's lengthy examination of Taylor's biography. This is no doubt partly due to Fields being only one of several characters showcased in the text.[96] However, it also reflects the general decline of interest in Fields as a topic of critical interest during much of the 1950s.

The best review of the Fowler text for the student of Fields was *Time* magazine's "Eccentric's Eccentric," which devoted the most space to the comedian.[97] Yet while it recycles the anecdotal nature of the book under review, the metaphorical richness of the original text is lost when presented in mere snippets.

The year 1954 also saw the appearance of John Montgomery's *Comedy Films: 1894-1954,* one of the first attempts at a historical overview of the subject. And, as if taking a cue from "Eccentric's Eccentric," Montgomery places Fields at the head of his chapter "The Eccentrics," stating that: "Of all the strange characters of the screen, W.C. Fields stood head, shoulders, and stomach above the rest."[98]

Despite stating in his foreword that "THIS IS A FACTUAL and not a critical account of the history and traditions of the comic film,"[99] Montgomery frequently does play critic. And while he generally praises Fields the comedian, Montgomery is so put off by the private Fields that his displeasure begins to color his criticism, making it occasionally difficult to differentiate between which of these Fieldses he is addressing:

> His life was completely anti-social. . . . Although many of his films contained brilliantly funny moments, there was often a vicious twist in the humour. His wit was cruel, his language sometimes obscene, and having built up a reputation for being a rebel, he took care to be an outside one.[100]

Although this strikes a contemporary reader as rather moralistically biased criticism, it possibly demonstrates another reason why Fields seems largely forgotten in the 1950s: his antiestablishment base was out of keeping with the return-to-normalcy nature of the period. After all, this was a period when Harold Lloyd (whose comedy persona is best remembered as the boy-next-door go-getter) was to be honored with a special Academy Award in 1952 for being a "master comedian and good citizen."[101]

The best Fields material in *Comedy Films: 1894-1954* is when the comedian or other critics are cited. For example, there are some insightful Fields quotes on screen comedy from early in his film career. Though

Montgomery does not cite a source in the text and his book is without footnotes, a key reference would seem to have been Sara Redway's interview/article "W.C. FIELDS Pleads for Rough HUMOR" from the September 1925 issue of *Motion Picture Classic* (as excerpted in Chapter 3).

After Montgomery's Fields section, 1950s criticism on the comedian is relatively rare. Arthur Knight's brief but perceptive observations in *The Liveliest Art* (1957) stand out as he links the "inspired mayhem" of the Marx Brothers with that of Fields.[102] (This tie might have been inspired by celebrated film historian Lewis Jacobs's one-sentence aside in *The Rise of the American Film: A Critical History,* 1939, on "out-and-out crazy" comedians like Fields and the Marx Brothers.)[103]

The year 1957 also saw the publication of William Cohn's *The Laugh Makers: A Pictorial History of American Comedians.* Despite the "Pictorial" subtitle, a healthy text accompanies the artwork. Yet because of its survey nature, no one comedian receives an extended examination. The Fields section is short but occasionally thought provoking, including a comparison between the comedian and Mark Twain's Colonel Sellers.[104] And there are Fields anecdotes by Mack Sennett and Ziegfeld comedian Walter Catlett.

It was not until well into the antiestablishment 1960s that critical attention on Fields mushroomed, a phenomenon that continues today. The starting point for the review of these more recent studies would seem to be Raymond Durgnat's December 1965 *Films and Filming* article, "Subversion in the Fields." This essay was part of a much longer philosophy-of-comedy thesis made possible by a grant from the Department of Film at the Slade School of Fine Art, University College (England), in 1960-1961. Later it was serialized in *Films and Filming* between July 1965 and January 1966. The thesis would eventually be expanded and published in book form as *The Crazy Mirror: Hollywood Comedy and the American Image* (1969). A revised, longer "Subversion in the Fields" would resurface in the text as Chapter 24, "Suckers and Soaks."

The original piece begins with a comparison of Fields and the Marx Brothers. But unlike the comments of Arthur Knight and Lewis Jacobs, Durgnat's work also provides insightful differences, such as "the people [Fields] satirised were more recognisable as 'average Americans' than the butts of the Marx Brothers."[105] The essay, like the later book, is always critically provocative, but the material is often rather eclectic, as the author attempts to touch bases with a large number of comedians. But before leaving Fields behind, Durgnat is at his best when examining the comedian's use of fantasy: "these 'absurd' realms have, in Fields' films, a function of 'derisive liberation' that anticipates goonery ["The Goon Show" radio program that would launch Peter Sellers, among others] and its indefinable but pervasive affinities with satire."[106]

After Durgnat's influential philosophy of comedy, with its high ratings for Fields, Bosley Crowther's March 3, 1966, *New York Times* review of the *W.C. Fields Comedy Festival* continues and chronicles this sixties rebirth of interest in the comedian. The festival, merely the first of several major Fields screenings in the second half of the decade, was a compilation from the sound era, containing clips from 1931 (*Her Majesty Love*) to 1944 (*Sensations of 1945*).

Besides an opening salute to the die-hard Fields fan, Crowther spends the meat of his review on two short subjects—*The Fatal Glass of Beer* and *The Dentist*—which he considers "superior Fields."[107] Further evidence of the Fields revival is apparent in the close of the review, as Crowther notes that the comedian's son, W. Claude Fields, Jr., had recently been appearing at screenings of the film.

The month after Crowther's review, Wallace Markfield's ambitious "The Dark Geography of W.C. Fields" appeared in the *New York Times Magazine*. Markfield's opening remarks address both the Fields revival and his long neglect by historians and critics. What then follows is a refreshing look at the film world of Fields, frequently punctuated with comparisons to the opposing values of Charles Chaplin's screen persona, Charlie.

Markfield also takes a general look at the nature of Fields's humor, especially his voice, which he describes as something "an ancient heathen idol might have used against a missionary."[108] Comments on his slowness of speech and his long pauses underline for Markfield Fields's ability to make his comedy seem effortless, in contrast to many contemporary (mid-1960s) comedians. Markfield's concluding thoughts come in the form of a striking metaphor—"Fields did all his work from way inside the dark geography of his mind"—from which the article title is paraphrased.[109]

Markfield's piece also contains two mini articles by Guy Flatley: "Who Was He?" (a short biographical overview of Fields) and "A Fields-Eye View of Things" (a list of memorable observations by Fields, arranged by subject).

After these 1966 new critical beginnings for Fields (Donald Deschner's book, *The Films of W.C. Fields*, also appeared that year), serious studies of the comedian continued to grow. In 1967 *Newsweek* ran a comically insightful overview on Fields and the renewal of interest in his work entitled "The Great Debunker":

> Fields fans are especially popular with the generation he would have cooked back in the 1940s. Today's young people, alienated from an impersonal, bureaucratic world they never made, rally to the standard of the orotund, nay-saying Fields who threw bricks at the establishment, only to have those bricks invariably ricochet and crown him.[110]

This article, which interesting enough appears in a *Newsweek* issue also containing a review of Chaplin's last film (*A Countess from Hong Kong*), mentions Fields movie revivals then taking place at both Great Britain's National Film Theater and New York's Gallery of Modern Art. The former festival would inspire two excellent British articles on the comedian.

The first and more ambitious of the two is film historian (frequently comedy film historian) David Robinson's "Dukinfield Meets McGargle: Creation of a Character" in the Summer 1967 *Sight and Sound*. This article is argumentatively the best single critical essay on Fields. As the title suggests, Robinson analyzes both the private and the public man. But whereas this scenario had frequently been used before, Robinson manages to bring new perceptiveness to what is often established Fields material, from thoughts on the comedian's ties with the Victorian Era to the career-catalyst role of Professor Eustace P. McGargle in *Poppy*. Robinson can also be touchingly reflective; he observes near the article's close, "What is extraordinary is the manner in which he [Fields] was able to transmute his present mental torments and bitter memories into rapturous comedy . . . [such as] those hilariously awful [film] families."[111] (Any semblance of the 1950s moralizing is gone.)

The second critical Fields article inspired by the National Film Theater Festival is Douglas McVay's "Elysian Fields" essay in the 1967 Winter issue of *Film*. Neither as inspired nor as detailed as Robinson's essay, it is still a valuable work largely because of the brief closing comments on two possible Fields influences—the Charles Coburn cardshark in *The Lady Eve* (1941) and Walter Matthau's shyster lawyer in *Meet Whiplash Willie* (the British title for *The Fortune Cookie*, 1966, which earned Matthau a Best Supporting Actor Oscar).

The publication of Everson's aforementioned *The Art of W.C. Fields* and the reissue of Taylor's *W.C. Fields: His Follies and Fortunes* also were in 1967. As with the earlier publication of books on Fields, Everson's work generated a number of reviews, the best of which was Hugh Kenner's "The Confidence Man" in the April 23, 1968, issue of the *National Review*.[112]

Better than any of these reviews, however, is Judith Crist's 1967 overview on the rediscovery of Fields entitled "The Anti-Establishment Man." It begins in the best tradition of sociological criticism, especially the use of the pop-poster photo of Fields the gambler (from *My Little Chickadee*) as a metaphor for the values or lack of values in the comedian's world:

> All the pomposity of the poker ritual, all the fraudulent cogency
> to disguise the cheat, all of the "con" and all the mistrust of a
> mistrustful world lie in the frown, the jowl, the shifty eye.[113]

Crist then moves to a brief but interesting comparison with Chaplin's tramp figure, closing the segment in a manner reminiscent of critic Robert Warshow's celebrated defense for the evolution of Chaplin's screen character from Charlie to Monsieur Verdoux (one must emulate the murderous tendencies of society, if one is to survive.)[114] In like manner,

Crist states that Fields "is put upon by society, and he's out to get his by fraudulence, because society is a fraud."[115]

"The Anti-Establishment Man" is a short essay, but Crist manages consistent insight, displaying a descriptive flair that borders on the Fieldsian "poetry" of some of the thirties critics. One of her closing lines observes that Fields's style was "a black brand of comedy, an amoral one tinted by the paranoia that is only suggested by Durante's image of being 'surrounded by assassins.'"[116]

If Crist at times reaches the rarefied air of Fields champions like Ferguson and Sennwald, her contemporary, Penelope Gilliatt, is a regular soul mate of these thirties critics. Gilliatt's June 21, 1969, *New Yorker* piece, "To W.C. Fields, Dyspeptic Mumbler, Who Invented His Own Way Out," is the best of her writing on the comedian and is reproduced in her outstanding critical comedy anthology *Unholy Fools: Wits, Comics, Disturbers of the Peace: Film & Theater* (1973).

Like Fields's own comic asides, Gilliatt peppers this essay with penetrating barbs of truth and titilation. For example, she describes his voice inflection when uttering "Godfrey Daniel!" as "the quiet caw he used for homemade curses, flummoxing [certainly a word Fields might have savored] the Hays Office."[117] On the asides themselves she observes, "Fields doesn't so much speak as amuse himself with self-addressed soliloquies. The to-and-fro of less doughty men is not for him. He is only the fro. . . . [and drawing from the LaCava comment] He plays the muttering straight man to Life."[118] Fields was certainly, as Gilliatt says, "the author of his own life."[119] And if one word (or, for the sake of Fields's ambitious verbal shenanigans, one hyphenated word) could describe him, it would have to be Gilliatt's choice of "fifth-columnist."[120]

Gilliatt's aphoristic abilities in this Fields essay were not hurt by the fact that references to him frequently appear in her other reviews. A generous sprinkling of his name appears throughout *Unholy Fools,* a collection covering 1960 to 1973. For instance, her 1969 review of *Goodbye, Columbus* states that the funniest actors have intelligent screen personae, which she exemplifies by "W.C. Fields applying his mind to running rings around spiteful toddlers, or Keaton alertly solving the problem of boiling two eggs in the kitchen of a luxury liner equipped to deal only with hundreds."[121] Regardless of the reference, however, Gilliatt genuinely likes the Fields personae—"I would say he was one of the four or five funniest men we have lately had in the world"—and uses her Fields references both to better understand the comedian and to further define the comedic.[122]

A third contemporary feminist critic with a propensity for referring to Fields is Pauline Kael. For the student of Fields her best anthology is *Kiss Kiss Bang Bang*. Appearing in 1968, it is sandwiched chronologically between Crist's "The Anti-Establishment Man" and Gilliatt's "To W.C. Fields." While *Kiss Kiss Bang Bang* has only one essay entirely devoted to the comedian (a review of *My Little Chickadee*), Fields remains a frequent point of reference throughout the text, as was the case with Gilliatt's *Unholy Fools.* Yet Kael is not the critical Fields fan that Gilliatt is. While Gilliatt places the comedian in a select pantheon of four or five members, Kael hedges on her feelings: "For women, he [Fields] is an acquired taste—like sour-mash bourbon. But then, you can't go on sipping daiquiris forever."[123] Consequently, her views on Fields's dual personae accent the chiseler rather than the underdog and not always in the most complimentary light: "Fields was shifty, weasling, mean-spirited, put-upon. . . . His film effusions form one big snarl of contempt for abstinence, truth, honest endeavor, respectability, and human and animal offspring."[124]

Kael's *My Little Chickadee* review is in a capsulized "Notes on 280 Movies" section of *Kiss Kiss Bang Bang.* The best other Fields-related Kael book, *5001 Nights at the Movies: A Guide from A to Z* (1982), is entirely in the capsulized-review form. Eleven short Fields reviews are contained, including an abbreviated version of her *My Little Chickadee* piece (down from approximately 800 words in *Kiss Kiss* to 150 in *5001 Nights*). The other ten capsule reviews are *If I Had a Million* (1932), *Million Dollar Legs* (1932), *The Fatal Glass of Beer* (1933), *Alice in Wonderland* (1933), *The Man on the Flying Trapeze* (1935), *Poppy (1936), The Big Broadcast of 1938* (1938), *Never Give a Sucker an Even Break* (1941), *Tales of Manhattan* (1942, Fields's twenty-minute segment was removed before it was released to reduce running time), and *Follow the Boys* (1944). Though the self-imposed space limitations of *5001 Nights* do not allow for any detailed analysis, Kael's work still manages to include perceptive and often provocative lines, with touches of her cynical sense of humor:

> The movie Fields wants to make [the film within the film in *Never Give a Sucker an Even Break*] is set in a Ruritania in the clouds that is native American surrealism—comic-strip foolishness and then some. Up there, he encounters the greatbosomed comic divinity, Margaret Dumont. The film also has its horror: an erstwhile ingenue named Gloria Jean. You can't just shut your eyes because she *sings.*[125]

Easily Kael's favorite Fields film is *Million Dollar Legs,* though her capsule review is especially brief. However, she had expanded on this preference earlier when she compared the film to the Marx Brothers' *Duck Soup* (1933) in her controversial essay "Raising Kane" (an antiauteur look at *Citizen Kane*).[126]

Since women are so frequently under attack in Fields's films, it is ironic that some of the most perceptive contemporary writing on Fields has been done by female critics like Crist, Gilliatt, and Kael. Although there are no easy answers as to why this has occurred, possibly Fields's even closer association with antiestablishment values has proven increasingly attractive to a more active feminist movement.

The same year of Kael's *Kiss Kiss*, Andrew Sarris published his *The American Cinema: Directors and Directions, 1929-1968,* which might be further subtitled an Auteur Bible. (And Kael and Sarris would soon begin their feud on the merits of auteurism.) However, *The American Cinema* contains an excellent section on cinema clowns who were largely "nondirectorial auteurs."[127] The short essay on Fields attempts both to address the 1960s vogue for the comedian and to compare his silent and verbal humor.

Two historical overviews on film comedy appeared in 1969; Raymond Durgnat's *The Crazy Mirror* and David Robinson's *The Great Funnies: A History of Film Comedy*. Durgnat's chapter on Fields is a reworking of his previously examined *Films and Filming* article, "Subversion in the Fields." Robinson's book, which consists of more pictures than commentary, does not dwell on any one comedian. Thus the references to Fields in *The Great Funnies* cannot approach the detailed excellence of Robinson's earlier essay "Dukinfield Meets McGargle: Creation of a Character."

In March of 1970, *Cue* magazine featured an article on Fields by Willard Van Dyke, director of the Department of Films of the Museum of Modern Art. Entitled "Cue Salutes," it is more an attempt to explain the "survivability of W.C. Fields."[128] Black-comedy parallels are drawn between Fields and Buster Keaton, a characteristic which now makes their films seem more timely than when they originally appeared. Other Fields contemporaries discussed include Charlie Chaplin, Harold Lloyd, and the Marx Brothers.

Liberal use is also made of Everson's *The Art of W.C. Fields*, though in one case the quoted material does not mesh with an earlier observation by Van Dyke. That is, Van Dyke stated, "W.C. Fields—and Buster Keaton, too . . . were out of step with then-current standards of comedy."[129] Yet Van Dyke later uses the Everson quote—"they [depression audiences] certainly could recognize and relate to Fields on their own level."[130]

In 1971 Gerald Mast's *A Short History of the Movies* (now in its third edition) first appeared. While little space was dedicated to Fields, Mast's observations on the comedian are the most insightful to appear in a general film history text. The cornerstone statement is the "neglected fact that Fields's funniness, like that of all the great American screen comics, is fundamentally physical."[131] And not only did Fields's physical comedy match his visual comedy personae (almost a cartoon caricature), there was also reinforcement from his verbal wit. Mast, in *A Short History,* is the first to sketch the verbal ties, but they are best articulated six years later in his *Film/Cinema/Movie: A Theory of Experience* (1977): "W.C. Fields also used his voice as camouflage, like his fancy euphemisms and fancy costumes, an apparently complacent and honey-combed voice makes a fine adornment for artfully crooked or nasty intentions."[132]

In 1973 Mast wrote the best historical overview of film comedy yet available—*The Comic Mind: Comedy and the Movies* (now in its second edition). Its Fields material is superb in three key ways. First, Mast goes beyond the general parallels other authors make, at best, between Fields and competing 1930s personality comedians like Mae West and the Marx Brothers. Second, Mast enriches the reader's sense of historical continuity, from his frequent comparisons of Fields and John Bunny (America's first great film comedian) to his statements on the enduringly iconoclastic nature of American screen humor.

Third, Mast combines a career overview with perceptive though sometimes provocative views of several pivotal Fields films. Mast's reflections are frequently revisionist, such as how the often-celebrated *Million Dollar Legs* is atypical Fields or why *Never Give a Sucker an Even Break* "was intended to be the worst movie ever made."[133] Like David Robinson's aforementioned "Dukinfield Meets McGargle: Creation of a Character," Mast's *Comic Mind* thoughts on Fields are not to be overlooked.

In 1971 Andrew Bergman's *We're in the Money: Depression America and Its Films* was published. Originally a doctoral dissertation at the University of Wisconsin, it is a sociological look at American films of the 1930s. While not without controversy, such as his chapter on screwball comedy, it remains a pivotal work on the films of depression America.[134]

Bergman's Chapter 3, "Some Anarcho-Nihilist Laff Riots," focuses on the Marx Brothers and Fields. While the Marxes receive the lion's share of the chapter (an analysis of Fields's *Million Dollar Legs* categorizes it more in the Marx camp), descriptions of their comedy are often equally true of Fields's art: "The Depression did not create their comedy; that craft had been mastered by years on the road, playing vaudeville stages and Broadway. But the Depression endorsed it and made it a national pastime."[135]

Bergman devotes the Fields section to the comedian's *The Fatal Glass of Beer,* a 1933 short subject which attacks two of America's most celebrated institutions—the family and the frontier. Like the Marxes' *Duck Soup,* the focus film early in the chapter, *The Fatal Glass of Beer* represents a now-celebrated work which did poorly upon its initial release. Bergman's point, however, is that Fields and the Marx Brothers not only utilized black comedy ahead of their time, their "freewheeling nihilism . . . has not been approached since."[136] Sociologically for Bergman, this meant that "the most desperate years of our national experience produced our most desperate comedy."[137]

In the winter of 1971-1972, a short article entitled "Out of the Past: Harold Lloyd & W.C. Fields" appeared in the film journal *The Velvet Light Trap.* Author Tom Flinn writes a double review of Fields's *It's the Old Army Game* and Harold Lloyd's *For Heaven's Sake,* which had first appeared within a month of each other in 1926.

Flinn uses his praise of *It's the Old Army Game* to encourage others to discover Fields's silent films. In fact, he is so impressed with this film that he prefers it to the sound remake, *It's a Gift*—generally considered Fields's greatest film. Flinn focuses on two classic routines from *It's the Old Army Game*—the back-porch attempt at sleep and the family picnic. (These routines, however, were not exactly repeated in *It's a Gift*, which is what Flinn implies.)

The importance of this article is its recognition of W.C. Fields as *silent comedian*. It was followed in 1972 by the *Mise-en-scène* journal essay "The Sounds of Silence: Comedy of the 1920s," which is sometimes included in Fields bibliographies. But what would seem, by title, to be an extension of Flinn's "Out of the Past" spends little time on Fields, and even when it does, the concentration is on the comedian's sound, not silent, career. A more detailed look at Fields as silent comedian must wait until Walter Kerr's *The Silent Clowns,* 1975.

While the major Fields news of 1973 was the already-examined *W.C. Fields by Himself,* the year's best critical piece on the comedian was "The Latter-Day Falstaff," Chapter 9 of Donald W. McCaffrey's *The Golden Age of Sound Comedy: Comic Films and Comedians of the Thirties.* Film comedy historian McCaffrey provides an excellent overview of Fields's 1930s career. He examines both sides of the comedian's comedy personae— the antiheroic husband/father and the carnival con man. Close attention is paid to four Fields films: *The Old-Fashioned Way, It's a Gift, The Man on the Flying Trapeze,* and *The Bank Dick.*

McCaffrey considers the latter three films to be Fields's masterpieces. The first production receives special attention because "uneven as *The Old-Fashioned Way* is, it remains Fields's first solid creation."[138] All four works are drawn from stories authored or coauthored by the comedian.

McCaffrey's case for his pantheon three is strong, but he does not pursue the most fascinating repercussion of his grouping. That is, he notes, "All three films feature him [Fields] in the role of nagged, bumbling, little man living in a small town."[139] But McCaffrey does not address the irony that while Fields's greatest films find him in a submissive position, the continuing most popular stereotype is of the comedian as con man.

McCaffrey's essay is frequently provocative, whether he is selecting a pantheon of Fields films or deciding which works are most flawed. For instance, he dismisses Fields's silent films as merely "mediocre."[140] While few would suggest that his silent career surpassed Fields's sound works, several critics have expressed a preference for specific silent films over the sound remakes. Moreover, many of the celebrated scenes from his sound work had already been recorded (sometimes with variations) in his silent films. As a result, the term "mediocre" seems rather a misnomer.

McCaffrey also has little time for *You Can't Cheat an Honest Man* (1939), *My Little Chickadee* (1940), and *Never Give a Sucker an Even Break* (1941), because they "have other comedians whose talents are not as brilliant as Fields's so that the total film meanders in quality of humour and plot."[141] While some critics and historians have noted flaws in these works, McCaffrey's dismissal is one of the quickest on record, though he later attributes any ongoing popularity of *Chickadee* to its "'camp' qualitites."[142]

The essay is to be recommended for two reasons. One, it provides a thirties overview of Fields in a volume that attempts to examine all elements of American film comedy during the decade. Two, the pantheon selection, regardless of one's views, is both insightful (especially with *It's a Gift*) and intellectually provocative.

In 1975 McCaffrey's critical overview of thirties American film comedy was followed by Walter Kerr's examination of an earlier era in *The Silent Film Clowns.* Kerr's Chapter 30, "The Demiclowns," is partly dedicated to Fields. He defines demiclowns as "silent comedians who might have functioned equally well with sound, or on stage. Their work is not distinctively indelibly *silent.*"[143] Some 1920s examples include Douglas MacLean, Reginald Denny, and William Haines. Such performers did not have a specific physical comedy persona of "telltale idiosyncrasies, habits of eye, hand, and spine that might recur in any situation and be funny because they were inappropriate to all."[144]

The student of Fields would naturally contest a statement that denied the comedian a physical shtick, from his eleven-gallon hat to his potato nose. But Kerr acknowledges this and legitimizes Fields's inclusion here by virtue of his being "a major comedian under wraps."[145]

Kerr then focuses almost entirely on *It's the Old Army Game,* especially the comedian's back-porch attempt at sleep. The other Fields films discussed are *Janice Meredith* (also known today as *The Beautiful Rebel*) and *Sally of the Sawdust.*

Kerr deserves credit for acknowledging the presence of humorist J.P. McEvoy in the Fields world. But Kerr is rather vague on the influence of McEvoy, and he mistakenly credits the humorist with several Fields film scripts from the 1920s. Only two Fields films were drawn from earlier McEvoy material—*The Comic Supplement* revue for *It's the Old Army Game* and the play *The Potters* for the film of the same name. But still, McEvoy has all but been forgotten, and Kerr performs an important task by drawing attention to this popular humorist from the 1920s and 1930s.

In 1976 Edward Edelson's film comedy survey *Funny Men of the Movies* appeared, with Chapter 8, "Uncle Bill," devoted to Fields. As the informal chapter title suggests, this is a modest overview of the comedian, often addressed to the Fields fan. Its most important service is underlining today's great popularity among Fields fans of *You Can't Cheat an Honest Man, My Little Chickadee, The Bank Dick,* and *Never Give a Sucker an Even Break.* With the exception of *The Bank Dick,* the majority of critics (both of yesterday and today) have expressed some reservations about these films.

In 1977 another survey of film comedy appeared, but one uniquely different from those already examined. *The National Society of Film Critics on Movie Comedy,* edited by Stuart Byron and Elisabeth Weis, is an anthology. Unlike *American Film Criticism: From the Beginnings to Citizen Kane* (edited by Stanley Kauffmann, with Bruce Henstell), *Movie Comedy* contains contemporary essays, often in film revival format, of a wide spectrum of comedy subjects, from Mack Sennett to Luis Buñuel.

Movie Comedy contains two Fields essays—the already examined Judith Crist piece which served as the introduction to Richard J. Anobile's *A Flask of Fields* and Pulitzer Prize-winning film critic Roger Ebert's "Fields vs. Chaplin." Ebert relies too much on the stereotype of Chaplin's tramp as a loser,[146] yet his contrasting of Fields as *comedian* and Chaplin as *clown* is provocative. Ebert hypothesizes that "comedians live in imaginary worlds that look just like our own. . . . Clowns, on the other hand, live in real worlds which consist of a few props."[147] For *comedian* Fields, even though his film world seems realistic, unusual things happen—"Bass fiddles have babies, Mae West is replaced by a goat on a wedding night, and golf carts become airplanes."[148]

Leonard Maltin's *The Great Movie Comedians: From Charlie Chaplin to Woody Allen* appeared in 1978. A much more scholarly text than Edelson's *Funny Men of the Movies*, it is probably the best film comedy handbook available, with the exception of Gerald Mast's *The Comic Mind*. (Maltin has authored numerous books, from the mediocre *Movie Comedy Teams*, 1970, to the truly outstanding *Of Mice and Magic: A History of American Animated Cartoons*, 1980. *The Great Movie Comedians* falls in the latter category.)

Chapter 14 of *The Great Movie Comedians*, simply titled "W.C. Fields," is a superb balancing of a film comedy artist and an off-screen puzzle. The enigmatic nature of the latter Fields is nicely suggested by Maltin's references to the conflicting reports of friends, family, and mistress. In addition, Maltin notes the "powerful godfather" Fields had at Paramount for a number of years in producer William LeBaron, something few sources expand on quite so fully.[149] LeBaron had much to do with the creative freedom Fields enjoyed on some of his best films.

Maltin realizes Fields is the "ultimate American underdog." He reminds the reader that "people love to recall Fields' meanness, but they rarely remember that he would seldom act unless provoked. In fact, his tolerance is enormous."[150]

Maltin's attention to detail, always a characteristic of his writing, is much in evidence in *The Great Movie Comedians*, from references to original routines included in *W.C. Fields by Himself* to an informative description of the production level of Fields's films (as in an A versus a B picture).

In 1970 the first series of reference books appeared in *Magill's Survey of Cinema: English Language Films*. Each volume is composed of contemporary reviews of significant English language films. The reviews, written specifically for the project, are approximately three pages in length, contain principal cast and credits, and are arranged alphabetically.

The Fields films reviewed in the first series are *Million Dollar Legs, You Can't Cheat an Honest Man, The Bank Dick,* and *Never Give a Sucker an Even Break.* In 1981 a second series of volumes was published in *Magill's Survey of Cinema.* Three additional Fields films are critiqued: *It's a Gift, David Copperfield,* and *My Little Chickadee.*

For a generally excellent capsulized look at a specific Fields film, or that of another favorite, the Magill series is a good starting point. Besides cast and credits, the volumes include story synopses, comments on the central player's career at the time of the film's release, and critical analyses drawing upon both the film's initial response and its reputation today.

Fields on Fields

The "Fields on Fields" book section of this chapter has already examined the pivotal "W.C. Fields Papers" housed in the Library of Congress (copyrighted sketches from the 1910s and 1920s), *Fields for President* (1940), *W.C. Fields by Himself: His Intended Autobiography* (edited by grandson Ronald J. Fields, 1973), and the numerous W.C. Fields joke book anthologies which have been assembled. All of these works might be described as Fields anthologies—collections of shorter works—now conveniently gathered together, thanks largely to the efforts of the Library of Congress and his family. (*Fields for President* was the only book by the comedian published in his lifetime.)

This section focuses on some significant shorter works which generally have not been reproduced in the above or other books. Exceptions are limited to a few essays whose unique status necessitates special attention. Several articles are largely interview in nature, though their original titles seldom suggested this. Lengthy quotations are avoided because a number of the pieces have been reproduced partially, or in total, in Chapter 3.

The essays are grouped into two categories: (1) Fields's thoughts on the nature of comedy, and (2) Fields's application of these humor axioms in his comedy prose. Within each category the essays are arranged chronologically.

The comedian's thoughts on comedy pervade the "Fields on Fields" category. As early as 1901, two essays by Fields appeared in Percy Thomas Tibbles's prestigious but now rare British volume, *The Magician's Handbook: A Complete Encyclopedia of the Magic Art for Professional and Amateur Entertainers.* Fields's essays, which explain the mechanics of two comic juggling tricks, are entitled "A New Hat and Cigar Effect" and "The Great Cigar-Box Trick." The former routine involved flipping a top hat, with a cigar balanced upon it, upward from his foot, with the hat landing on his head and the cigar in his mouth. The only "trick" involved is Fields's suggestion to use a *wooden* cigar as it is easier to handle.

"The Great Cigar-Box Trick" has more subterfuge. Fields throws five cigar boxes into the air and "catches the whole five balanced upon each other's end, making quite a tall pile as they steady down."[151] However, just as the applause reaches its zenith, the balance of the boxes is "accidently" destroyed and they fall. Actually, they almost fall, making it obvious to the viewer that the boxes are attached by a cord.

In each essay Fields meticulously explains the mechanics of the routine as well as the fine tuning involved in milking it for laughs. The deliberate comedy style described anticipates the screen heritage Fields would eventually give the world, even though he does not talk general comedy theory in Tibbles's book.

An excellent starting point for Fields on comedy comes in a brief excerpt from an untitled 1914 interview which was included in *W.C. Fields by Himself*. The comedian suggests humor is the result of real-world "types being overdrawn."[152] In eight key interview-articles, done between 1925 and 1937, Fields elaborates on the foundation.

The initial piece is from 1925, the year of his first starring feature. Credited to Sara Redway and entitled "W.C. FIELDS Pleads for Rough HUMOR," it apeared in the September issue of *Motion Picture Classic*. Part interview, part essay, the majority of Fields's observations are directed at comedy. In terms of comedy theory, Redway capsulizes the comedian's views nicely—"Mr. Fields believes in the lowest-common-denominator theory."[153]

The comedian's advice is to draw from real life the things which people truly know. For instance, Fields believes his then-current Ziegfeld Follies routine with a flivver (Ford) is more popular than an earlier pool-table act because more people are familiar with a flivver. Keeping things basic also means never forgetting slapstick, says Fields. A fall is always funny because life is slapstick, and comedy audiences are in search of laughter, not lessons. Be afraid, moreover, of "nice humor," not "vulgar" comedy, warns Fields, for "Chaplin, the greatest of all comedians, is vulgar."[154] Fields even suggests that there are times when the real world needs no exaggeration to qualify as comedy.

Fields's desire for slice-of-life comedy, which honors slapstick and periodic absurdities, both natural and comedian-made, probably was best articulated earlier that year in the Harold Cary article "The Loneliest Man in the Movies." The comedian observes: "In pantomime or in speaking parts, what gets the laughs is this: A bit of real, homely truth, action or words, developed to a surprise ending."[155] Fields then draws an unacknowledged example from *Sally of the Sawdust*:

> My daughter wants to throw a stone at a bad man. I stop her from throwing, shaking my head and giving her a little slap. My disapproval is complete. You think: "That's right, she shouldn't throw a stone even at the villain." Then I hand her a brick to

throw. The bit of truth is that if you are going to strike better hit hard.[156]

Ruth Waterbury's interview-article with the comedian, "The Old Army Game" from the October 1925 issue of *Photoplay*, further articulates Fields's Redway article statements, from the dangers of film comedy becoming "too nice" to an "ambition . . . to bring back slapstick two dollared up."[157]

Fields's goal for his then yet-to-be-established screen character is, in fact, closely tied to slapstick. As noted in Chapter 1, Fields wanted to be the "pathetic" husband of the newspaper cartoons.[158] And his future screen persona would have much in common with cartoon characters, such as Jiggs in George McManus's "Bringing Up Father" (1913), probably the most celebrated antiheroic husband in the history of newspaper cartoons.

Waterbury's article also finds the comedian stating his preference for pantomime over verbal comedy. Though the Fields voice would soon become famous, the cornerstone of his character would always be tied to the visual slapstick humor of both the early newspaper cartoons and the film comedy two-reelers. Fields never seemed to lose sight of that.

In Helen Hanemann's interview-article with Fields, "He Hated Alarm-Clocks" from the August 1926 issue of *Motion Picture*, the comedian underlines a point from each of the two earlier articles. First, while the Hanemann piece suggests that Fields is a walking encyclopedia on comedy routines, the comedian again asserts the importance of drawing from real life: "little things I've watched on the street . . . I've always had the best luck with gags I've actually seen take place."[159] Second, he is thankful for the lengthy pantomime apprenticeship he served on stage before his mid-1920s success in film.

The following month, September 1926, Dunham Thorp capsulized many of these points in the title of his *Motion Picture Classic* interview-article: "The Up-To-Date Old Timer." As Fields had observed earlier, slapstick needed to be "two dollared up," and this piece found him reiterating his demand for updated treatment of basic comic ideas.

"The Up-To-Date Old Timer" also allows Fields to flesh out further his fundamental comedy values. For example, in praising pantomime he speaks of its universality, drawing upon his earlier European stage experiences as an international artist. (His comments are reminiscent of a 1922 article by Charlie Chaplin, where the creator of The Tramp describes performing for non-English speaking audiences in the Channel Islands.)[160]

Fields likewise gives a qualified yes to the need for consistency of character. While he does not want to "continue making pictures in the make-up of Eustace McGargle," he acknowledges that all his future "characters will probably be more or less related types."[161]

In September 1934 *American Magazine* published "Anything for a

Laugh,'' an article by Fields entirely devoted to the nature of comedy. Though it has been suggested this piece was ghosted for Fields, the article's views are consistent with his earlier comedy opinions. In fact, he opens with another reference to the need to draw comedy from real life: ''The biggest laugh on the stage I ever got was an almost exact reproduction of an occurrence one evening when I was visiting a friend.''[162]

Fields then lists a number of rules on what is funny, from specific place names to *bending,* not *breaking,* comedy props. And while the comedian frequently suggests he knows the what of comedy and not the why, he closes with several observations based in comic superiority: ''I know we laugh at the troubles of others, provided those troubles are not too serious. . . . I like, in an audience, the fellow who roars continuously at the troubles of the character I am portraying on the stage.''[163] Fields had first hinted at this in passing in the Redway article when he observed that his audiences did not come for a message—''They come to laugh at me.''[164]

Fields emphasizes the importance of audience superiority when he describes his then most recent film character as ''a stupid and self-important inventor''—Sam Bisbee of *You're Telling Me* (who has been compared to Sinclair Lewis's George Babbitt). Interestingly enough, while the comedian continues to support the importance of comic surprise, his statement on the stupidity of Bisbee is drawn from a scene in which the laughter is dependent on audience awareness.

The interview segments of Jack Grant's 1935 *Movie Classic* article, ''THAT NOSE of W.C. Fields,'' focus on the use of comic character names. Fields credits Dickens's work as the best example of this technique and as his own catalyst. But even here, the real world acted as his main supplier: ''Nearly all of the names I have used on the screen are real people I have met in traveling around the crazy world.''[165]

The most all-inclusive shorter work concerning Fields's thoughts on the nature of comedy is Maude Cheatham's interview-article, ''Juggler of Laughs,'' from the April 1935 *Silver Screen*. The piece examines at length a number of the comedy issues touched upon in the earlier publications. For example, Fields expands upon three of his longtime comedy fundamentals (draw from reality, keep it basic, and exaggerate—if necessary) when he states:

> I never go out for a gag. I base my comedy on humanness, so I just watch people. We're all very funny only we don't know it. No one is original, and we all do about the same things, so I take the simplest, every day incidents, exaggerate them and turn them into an act.[166]

''Juggler of Laughs'' also finds Fields addressing comic superiority, pantomime, and the when and why of his decision to play a definite comedy type—as a youngster he had overheard and been impressed by a man praising another individual's consistency. (In the nearly nine years between Cheatham's interview and Dunham Thorp's "The Up-To-Date Old Timer," Fields's qualified "yes" to a definite comedy type has lost all restraints.)

The final interview-article of the highlighted eight is Jack Reid's "Nobody's Dummy" from the October 1937 *Motion Picture*. Unfortunately, the piece is anticlimactic after "Juggler of Laughs." While the latter work often provides detailed Fields summaries on comedy, "Nobody's Dummy," appearing shortly after Fields's series of mid-1930s illnesses, is more a happy-to-be-alive cross-section of several subjects. Comedy still merits special attention, but exacting analysis does not. For example, the comedian provides an all-too-brief comparison of stage and radio comedy. (His ill health had led to first an interest, and then a participation, in radio. And of course, the article's title is a reference to Fields's radio rivalry with Edgar Bergen's dummy, Charlie McCarthy.) There is even a fleeting reference to the possibility of a Fields career in television.

Fields minimizes a conscious construction of his brand of comedy yet cannot resist an insightful look at the sometimes aggressive nature of his comedy personae: "I'm the most belligerent guy on the screen. . . . But at the same time, I'm afraid of everybody. Just a great big frightened bully. There's a lot of that in human nature."[167] The comedian also comments on the uniqueness of (and the initial recommendations against) playing a comedy character opposed to dogs and children alike.

"Nobody's Dummy" is a fleeting look at Fields before his last hurrah in films. While it does not expand on comedy in the desired detail, a passing remark by the comedian offers the answer to the success of his sometimes comic aggressor character: "People seem to think there's no real harm in me."[168]

Many of these points, as well as the comic importance of ill-fitting clothing, are examined by Fields in a monologue on humor which Carlotta Monti included in *W.C. Fields & Me*. Though often without the detail of the articles, Fields's statements in the Monti book are informatively direct: "Always bear in mind that everyone has a percentage of the sadist in him, even though infinitesimal."[169]

Category two of "Fields on Fields," the shorter works, focuses on two essays done entirely for comic effect. Granted that Fields invariably peppered all his writing with comedy, but in the following two selections he maintains a comic antihero persona throughout, á la the writings of Robert Benchley and James Thurber, with more than a touch of the nineteenth-century tall tale. It is Fields's screen and radio personae maintained in prose, as he embraces his two favorite comedy subjects—alcohol and the battle of the sexes.

"Alcohol and Me," from the October 13, 1942, issue of *PIC*, is a delightful argument on why drink, rather than the dog, should be considered man's best friend. Precipitated in part by the real news that

Fields was on the wagon, the comedian justifies the essay by claiming, with tongue firmly in cheek, a "vicious rumor" has begun to circulate, that "having given up alcohol, I am about to acquire a dog. This is a scoundrelly lie."[170]

As one might assume of a comedy character so closely associated with drinking, the Fields personae approach his defense of alcohol in mock religious terms:

> The responsibility for this crusade has weighed heavily upon my shoulders. Many times I have felt I was a lone voice crying in the wilderness. . . . Then I would let my voice really cry out in all its power and glory. I would cry, "Set 'em up again!"[171]

Like Benchley, who was often very methodical in delineating comic truth, Fields then proceeds to an orderly comparison of dogs and drink.

He first approaches the subject from a semantic position, observing there are more epithets associated with dogs than alcohol. For every "demon rum" there exists " 'you dirty dog,' 'yellow dog,' 'I wouldn't do that to a dog,' 'a dog's life,' 'he dogged it,' 'it shouldn't happen to a dog,' 'doggone it,' etc."[172]

Second, he corrects historical misconceptions. For example, once when Fields was stranded in a snowstorm, he was approached by a rescue dog and the proverbial bottle of brandy. But when Fields reached for the brandy, the dog "bit my hand, grabbed the bottle and drank the contents himself. He turned out to be a lap dog."[173]

He then appeals to the reader's common sense: "When two kindred souls get together for a friendly session, do they sit there and pet dogs?"[174]

Fourth, Fields cites a number of uncontested facts on why alcohol (in this case, whiskey) is preferable to the pooch: "Whiskey does not need to be periodically wormed, it does not need to be fed, it never requires a special kennel, it has no toenails to be clipped. . . . Whiskey sits quietly in its special nook."[175]

Finally, Fields draws from his own filmmaking experience for one last bit of testimony on the special merits of alcohol. He relates a variation of his well-known story on spiking Baby LeRoy's bottle. Only this time, in recognition of the subject at hand (the celebration of alcohol), LeRoy gets through a scene *because* of alcohol, instead of the more traditional ending of the story, which finds the little trouper too dizzy to continue.

While "Alcohol and Me" is hardly a Thurber celebration of the dog, like Thurber, Fields ties man's antiheroic nature into his relationship with canines. That is, Thurber saw dogs as poor antiheroic victims—reflections of their antiheroic masters. Fields saw the dog as

> simply an antidote for an inferiority complex. We order him around, tell him to sit up, lie down, roll over, and all manner of

other useless maneuvers, simply to show bystanders that we can boss something. No man is boss in his own home, but he can make up for it, he thinks, by making a dog play dead.[176]

The second focus essay is "My Views on Marriage," which originally appeared as Chapter 2 of *Fields for President* (1940). Discussion of the essay follows that of the 1942 "Alcohol and Me" in this section because, as Robert Lewis Taylor first observed, "My Views on Marriage" was frequently anthologized in ensuing years.[177] It was probably best showcased in editor Ed Fitzgerald's *Tales for Males* (1945), where Fields shared covers with the likes of Mark Twain, Benjamin Franklin, James Thurber, and others. Consequently, its reputation as a solo piece actually follows "Alcohol and Me."

Despite anthology inclusion, "My Views on Marriage," like all of Fields's comedy prose, has not received adequate recognition. Taylor, for instance, complained that the essay has "a long, wheezy passage about how he [Fields] had once tried to impress a woman named Abigail Twirlbaffing (by playing 'The Whistler and Dog' backward on a cornet)."[178] (Fields's own view on prose versus film comedy was that laughs were easier to get from live action than from words on a page.)[179]

A reading of the Twirlbaffing section today does not produce the same review. Granted, there are more effective moments of comic absurdity in the piece, but just as it is difficult to read Taylor's description of the Twirlbaffing segment without a smile, this portion remains funny today. In fact, the segment exists as an explanation for a comic axiom later utilized by Woody Allen in *Play It Again, Sam* (1972). Beginning with "Never try to impress a woman!"[180] Fields, and later Allen, comically extrapolate from the devastating expectations this can produce in the woman.

The high point of "My Views on Marriage" is the work schedule Fields has devised for wives. Entitled "The Fields Formula for Fretting Females," it is impossible to read without thinking of Thurber's battle of the sexes. A typical Fields entry reads as follows: "2:15-5:30: Spade garden, darn socks, wash Rover, put up jelly, polish car, burn rubbish, wash woodwork, paint garage, clean side walls of tires."[181] Fields maintains this comedy overstatement throughout the schedule, closing with the topper: "7:00-12:00: Keep busy—keep smiling—for, as every man knows, the husband is tired."[182]

Fields's comedy prose, as best demonstrated by "Alcohol and Me" and "My Views on Marriage," generally follows the humor standards he endorsed when considering comedy theory. He remained true to his type—an alcoholic misogynist. He utilized largely true or possible facts from life, such as the obvious differences between dogs and drink. He then somewhat exaggerated the reality, as demonstrated in the female chores chart. And he encouraged the reader to assume a position of comic superiority (though not without sympathy) to Fields's antihero.

A further examination of Fields's comedy essays should include the *This Week* Sunday supplement of the *New York Herald Tribune* for both December 4, 1938, and March 10, 1940. The former includes what will become the income tax chapter in *Fields for President;* the latter presents a slightly edited version of the book's chapter on etiquette. The *Herald Tribune* showcases each essay beautifully, including large comic photographs of Fields. Surprisingly, neither piece seems to have ever made a Fields bibliography.

Fields's World View

Fields, as with most people, never fully articulated his philosophy of life. Nevertheless, there are numerous pertinent statements scattered throughout the Fields literature, as well as more ambitious interpretations by friends, family, and followers. But before beginning an analysis of key materials, special attention should be given the essay "Life Begins at 20—Says W.C. Fields" from the September 1935 issue of Motion Picture.

This piece, written as if the then fifty-five-year-old comedian had just turned twenty, might have been included among Fields's comedy prose. (Actually, little Fields wrote or said was without some semblance of comedy.) Yet "Life Begins at 20," presented in part as a parody of the philosophical essay, frequently drifts into statements that demand more than comic enjoyment:

> Life is really one long headache the morning after the night before. It is a mirror moved all around town by a one-eyed truckman. . . . By the time he finally gets it into the hands of the fellow who knows what to do with it, the thing's worn out, and he's got to go back to the warehouse for another mirror.[183]

Certainly, this Sisyphus-like statement is a world view consistent with Fields's antiheroic screen personae. But as this chapter section will demonstrate, it is also applicable to the comedian's real life.

Fields's world view would probably best begin with biographer Taylor's observation: "It was not hard for Fields to take on 'persecution complexes.'"[184] Without belaboring the examples already noted, all Fields reference material is inundated with this *them against me* phenomenon.

Because his comedy personae are based in persecution (the henpecked husband and the on-the-lam carnival huckster), it is tempting to assume the personal life persecution stories (distrust of friends, servants, animals; cheating at every activity; and so on) were just so much publicity. But the evidence has become too substantial to minimize it in that manner.

Fields's sense of persecution must be tied to the difficulties of his childhood and career beginnings. As Fields friend and author Alva

Johnston notes: "In his early years he lived only because he seized everything he could get away with, and he still operates that way."[185] It is difficult to obtain material by or about the comedian which does not draw attention to this attitude. Author Harold Cary noted that the later loneliness of the early trouping years was not only still with Fields (in 1925), he also feared "in the back of his mind that the day would come when he would have to go back to his trouping again."[186] Filtered through these fears, his comically celebrated habit of starting bank accounts throughout the world, under a host of eccentric names, loses much of its strangeness.

Fields grew up at a time when Charles Darwin's theory of evolution was a major topic of discussion, and no principle of Darwin's work was more celebrated than his survival of the fittest. Thus, given Fields's own personal struggle—first for mere existence and then to establish an entertainment career (his time spent training to be a juggler is often likened to a battle, with resultant physical and mental scars)—plus the Darwinian tenor of the times, it is not surprising that a sense of persecution assumes such a prominent role in his life. And appropriately enough, in "Life Begins at 20" Fields even puns an offshoot axiom of the survival of the fittest: "during all my twenty years, I have learned that life is really a juggle."[187]

Fields's recovery from serious health problems during 1936 and 1937 added yet another chapter to the comedian's saga of personal struggle to success. A series of late 1937 articles heralded his comeback tenacity: *Photoplay*'s "That Man's Here Again" (August 1937), *Motion Picture*'s "Nobody's Dummy" (October 1937), and *Screen Book Magazine*'s "Mr. Fields Wins by a NOSE!" (November 1937).[188]

The first of these articles describes his comeback best: "Bill Fields [for months] forgotten and alone, through his own courage, became the topnotch man of the hour. It is the sensation of Hollywood."[189] However, the author of those words, Sara Hamilton, was one who had not forgotten him (see her July 1936 *Photoplay* article, "Dangerous Days for Bill Fields").[190]

If a dog-eat-dog premise is at the base of Fields's philosophy, it also goes a long way toward explaining a number of the comedian's other idiosyncrasies, such as his on- and off-screen iconoclasm. Starting with Fields's boyhood break with his father, examples can be found throughout the Fields literature. But Dunham Thorp, in "The Up-To-Date Old Timer," probably captured Fields's most pathological defense of doing things his way, however unorthodox, when he recorded the comedian saying, "Even if the actor is wrong [in how he plays a character] it's almost worth letting him have his way so that he'll keep his peace of mind."[191]

In time there would not even be any admission of error. Friend Alva Johnston observed in 1938 that "Fields claims that he has never been wrong and never had a bad idea."[192] And while Johnston comically went on to demonstrate how false this was (he explains how different film directors negated poor ideas by Fields), the comedian's battle against establishment and authority figures remained front and center.

Another idiosyncrasy with survival-of-the-fittest roots is what Carlotta Monti described as Fields's enjoyment at playing "director of organized confusion."[193] As if expanding upon the brainchild of Louis XIV, who created the competition of the court system to prevent unified opposition from followers, Fields constantly kept his servants bickering among themselves by planting false stories. No king better implemented the strategy of divide and conquer.

The tally of these and most other discussions of Fields closely equates the real man with the philosophy of the screen personae.[194] After all, as *Life* magazine's obituary of the comedian reads, "His rasping advice, 'Never give a sucker an even break,' summed up the harsh philosophy of all men who live by their wits."[195] More simply still, from Fields's own "Life Begins at 20": "A fellow doesn't happen to be a clown—he just is."[196]

What about, however, those periodic reports of another, softer Fields? There have always been a few examples in the literature on the comedian (besides the previously examined revisionism of his family in *W.C. Fields by Himself: His Intended Autobiography*). The most conspicuous occur in the recovery articles of 1937. Like the interviews with Richard Pryor after his nearly fatal accident, Fields was moved by the concerns of his fans: "I became aware that I had more friends than I'd ever dreamed of having."[197] (See also Hamilton's 1936 "Dangerous Days for Bill Fields.")

Yet probably the most fascinating piece exposing the vulnerability of Fields while he was alive came from his friend and fellow Ziegfeld Follies comedian Will Rogers. Entitled "Radio Fairy Tales of Real Life Behind Scenes," it was originally published June 22, 1924, in the *New York Times*. Rogers, in a style not unlike that currently employed by Paul Harvey in his "The Rest of Story" radio series, told true tales about three unnamed performers: Fred Stone, Eddie Cantor, and Fields. Rogers's story on Fields simply relates how, coming in on the comedian unexpectedly, he had found him looking at a picture of a horse-drawn vegetable cart, the place his youthful juggling career began. "Respect and sentiment were written on every line of his face as he gazed at this picture."[198]

More recently, Louise Brooks's "The Other Face of W.C. Fields," which first appeared in the Spring 1971 issue of *Sight and Sound* (later to be anthologized in Brooks's *Lulu in Hollywood*, 1982), has generated the most interest. Brooks, the now-celebrated film actress of G.W. Pabst's *Pandora's Box* (1929), had appeared with Fields in the Ziegfeld Follies and played his daughter in *It's the Old Army Game* (1926).

Unfortunately, the promise of the title is not fulfilled in the essay. While there is no questioning her basic premise, "the history of no life is a jest"[199] (a reference to the distortions so often attached to Fields's life), Brooks does not provide the reader with *another* Fields. In fact, her final anecdote, about how the comedian broke off his relationship with mistress Bessie Poole, is not a different Fields, it is vintage Fields, right down to his parting line: "Goodbye Bessie, goodbye my dear—my little rosebud."[200]

Brooks correctly notes examples of how film history has been fabricated and falsified. Yet she seems to imply all film history is this way. And it is apparent she has not kept up with the literature on Fields. She shows no apparent awareness of any significant post-1971 texts, and there is one glaring omission which should have been addressed when the essay was later anthologized. That is, she states Fields "seems to have left no diaries, no letters, no serious autobiographical material. Most of his life will remain unknown."[201] Maybe she felt acknowledgement of *W.C. Fields by Himself*, with its diarylike letters, serious autobiographical material, and more would have negated the very purpose of her essay. It would not have. As previously observed, there are inconsistencies in *W.C. Fields by Himself* most importantly, the contradiction between Fields's writing and the family's interpretation of it. Brooks could have addressed this; she at least should have acknowledged the source. Its neglect merely undercuts her creditability.

Her Fields essay is still recommended reading. There is some new information and several rich observations on his art, especially her thoughts on the realistic versus the fantasy elements in Fields's comedy. And while the latter perspective does not present "the other face of W.C. Fields," it is still insightful reading from one of the few Fields costars also to become celebrated—which is possibly an indirect Fields lesson all its own.

Without trying to flip-flop back and forth in time, the next two most revealing essays on Fields's world view also balance themselves between his lifetime and after. The first is Sara Hamilton's "A Red-Nosed Romeo" from the December 1934 issue of *Photoplay*. Hamilton, as this section's frequent references to her Fields essays have demonstrated, has both a special interest in and rapport with the comedian.

"A Red-Nosed Romeo" is not about midnight romances and dancing until dawn. Instead it simply addresses the most basic of Fields attributes— his yarn-telling abilities. Yet that ability is such a given, rare is the piece which directly considers it. Hamilton showcases, in her own nicely comic style, the attraction tall tale-telling Fields held for both sexes. The comedian still seems to prefer the company of males, but then, 1934 was not the time to discuss Fields's live-in mistress Carlotta Monti. However, it does help to explain the fascination a number of women held for Fields through the years.

The comedian certainly must have felt comfortable with author Hamilton, for he completely opened up to her. Most explicitly, this refers to his yarn telling. Any student of comedy knows Fields has a tendency to exaggerate, but little Fields energy has ever been directed at examining the phenomenon. Yet Hamilton has him saying:

> I'm not nearly as good at it [telling tales] as I used to be. They [his circle of friends and colleagues] ketch me up. Yes, sir, they ketch me up. Someone will say, "Bill, tell so-and-so about you and the one-eyed acrobat." And I'll think, "Oh, oh, they got me." For the life of me I can't remember what I made up about that one."[202]

Like Konrad Bercovici's interview-article with Chaplin in *Colliers* (August 15, 1925), which also documented the yarn-telling ability of that comedian (see my *Charlie Chaplin: A Bio-Bibliography*, 1983), the admission Hamilton drew from Fields proves he was well aware his personality could be equally "creative" outside the professional spotlight. But unlike the creator of The Tramp, whose little fabrications frequently had specific purposes, Fields's joy was generally in the telling. Thus Fields was a comsummate storyteller both on and off the screen.

Fields's foundation for many of these tales was based on very real entertainment tours of the world. And while Hamilton's essay addressed his storytelling traits in general, the more recent piece being teamed with it focuses on some specific Fields dialogue which occurred both on and off the screen.

Moody E. Prior's "In Search of the Grampian Hills with W.C. Fields," from the Winter 1978-1979 *American Scholar* (frequently mistakenly listed in bibliographies as appearing in *American Scholastic*), is a moving look at the closest the comedian ever came to acknowledging a life after death. Certainly it is a veiled statement, and the comedian has committed no compromise on his goal not to succumb to religion at life's close. Yet Prior poses a thought-provoking look at Fields's Grampian Hills to which he referred at the close of two late films, as well as in private conversation. Prior painstakingly explores both the real and literary roots of this location. And he convincingly posits the view that the Grampian Hills represent a Fieldsian Utopia somewhere beyond the struggle of day-to-day existence. But while Prior chooses to focus on the added richness which knowledge of the Grampian Hills gives to a literary reading of the Fields films, it is even more meaningful as a real-life insight into the supposedly most cynical of comedians.

Fieldsian philosophy represents the last section in this bibliographical chapter. Because the very nature of much of the writing on the comedian is so often filled with Fieldsian axioms and the stuff of legends— he was a world-class performer thirty years before the coming of sound films—it creates an added temptation to include everything in this section—or at least make note of specific philosophical passages in aforementioned texts. Students of Fields must recognize the ambiguous ground upon which any "philosophy of Fields" section must stand. Thus some final legitimate pieces for further consideration would include: J.P. McEvoy's "W.C. Fields' Best Friend" from the *This Week* Sunday supplement to the July 26, 1942, issue of the *New York Herald Tribune*; *Life* magazine's January 6, 1947, obituary of the comedian; Will Fowler's "Why W.C. Fields Hated Christmas: A Holiday Fable," *Show Business Illustrated,* January 2, 1962 (later appearing with slight variations as "A Holiday Visit with W.C. Fields" in *Life* magazine's December 15, 1972, edition); Corey Ford's "The One and Only W.C. Fields" from the October 1967 issue of *Harper's* magazine (later appearing in a slightly altered form in Ford's 1967 book—*The Time of Laughter*); Raymond Lee's "The Brabbling Boozer Returns" from the Summer 1969 copy of *Classic Film Collector;* Don Marlowe's "Fieldsiana" in the Fall 1970 *Classic Film Collector;* and Peter W. Kaplan's delightfully fabricated interview with the comedian on Fields's one hundredth birthday, in the March-April 1979 *Film Comment.*

A good deal of what appears in these pieces is not so much new as it is enriched in the telling—not unlike Fields's comedy. But bits and pieces of his philosophy seem to appear in every Fields source. And of course, the booklength texts must not be ignored, especially those by Taylor, Monti, and Ronald Fields.

Monti's book, in fact, merits additional attention because it has a preoccupation with the comedian's philosophy. Thus it chronicles everything from "The Gospel According to Woody" to his "own commandments."[203] And Fields's thoughts on religion, while never without comic irony, reveal a character not unlike Mark Twain in his later years—a cross between an atheist and a professor of religion.[204]

Fields's knowledge of the Bible would seem to tell much about himself. Like many talented people with little formal education, the comedian was forever a student, and the Bible somehow became one of his texts. However, his difficulty in embracing its teachings underscores the self-made man who needs proof of a concrete nature. His familiarity with the source also demonstrates the added complexity of the individual behind the often simplistic comic personae.

FIELDS ARCHIVES AND FILM SOURCES

There is no one library with an inclusive collection of writings by and about Fields. The Library of Congress in Washington, D.C., comes the closest, with invaluable Fields holdings catalogued in several departments. Most important are the comedian's copyrighted sketches, which are housed in the Library's Manuscript Division (Madison Building) as the "W.C. Fields Papers" (see Chapter 5 for a complete listing). Sadly, they appear to be all but unknown to students of Fields. No previous texts on the comedian seem even to have mentioned them.

The Library Reading Room (Jefferson Building) offers access to all major texts on the comedian. The Reading Room also provides availability to both a large collection of Fields material preserved on long-playing records and a wide cross-section of periodicals, from which the obscure Fields piece frequently can be located. The Harry Houdini Collection (Jefferson Building) includes the only United States copy known to exist of Percy Thomas Tibbles's *The Magician's Handbook,* which includes two early Fields essays.[205]

The Library's Motion Picture, Broadcasting, and Recorded Sound division (Madison Building) contains a large number of the comedian's films. The United States Copyright Office (Madison Building, and the original location of the "W.C. Fields Papers" when they were catalogued separately as individual copyrighted sketches) also contains other materials of interest to Fields researchers, such as J.P. McEvoy's *The Comic Supplement* of 1924.

After the Library of Congress, the most important research center for Fields is the New York Public Library system, particularly the Lincoln Center branch, which houses the Billy Rose Theatre Collection. No other library in the country, including the Library of Congress, can match its theater collection of such now-obscure cinema journals as *Movie Classic, Motion Picture, Screen Book Magazine,* and *Silver Screen*—all of which are imperative for a serious study of Fields.

The Billy Rose Theatre Collection also contains several all-important clipping and program files on the comedian, besides numerous other files on people of special interest to the Fields scholar (such as J.P. McEvoy) and productions in which the comedian appeared. (See also the clipping files at both the Academy of Motion Picture Arts and Sciences Library and the Louis B. Mayer Library at the American Film Institute Campus—Los Angeles.) Of special interest to this book is the Billy Rose Collection's copy of McEvoy's 1925 version of *The Comic Supplement,* which shows the influence of Fields.

The New York Public Library has an excellent collection of former New York City-based newspapers on microfilm; these were instrumental in tracing a number of nearly forgotten Fields articles. (While the files in the Billy Rose Theatre Collection are invaluable, many articles have only partial reference citations and/or are in a deteriorating or incomplete state. The Fields scholar must therefore become even more of a detective than the traditional researcher and utilize the New York newspaper microfilms.) The New York Public Library also has an excellent collection of Fields material on long-playing records.

The pivotal Fields material held by his family has been collected by his grandson Ronald J. Fields in *W.C. Fields by Himself: His Intended Auto-*

biography. Though the reader may not agree with the family's interpretation of the material, it is an important collection of Fields's writing (public and private), and it certainly is the most accessible of the comedian's "archives."

Though Fields has never been a subject innundated with scholarly work, much has been written about the comedian in a wide assortment of non-trade publications (journals not focusing on film or stage work). Thus any library with a strong general periodical collection, particularly one with stacks open to the researcher, can be of assistance to the Fields scholar. In the author's case, the University of Iowa's (Iowa City) main library, with its outstanding periodical collection, provided a large number of the Fields articles herein examined.

The majority of his short subjects (and excerpts from his features marketed as short subjects) have long been available for purchase in 8-mm, super-8, and 16-mm film stock (see especially Blackhawk Films, Davenport, Iowa). Following the renewal of interest in the comedian shortly after his death, the 16-mm film rental trade has provided easy access to such pivotal Fields features as *You Can't Cheat an Honest Man, My Little Chickadee, The Bank Dick,* and *Never Give a Sucker an Even Break.*[206]

All of Fields's sound features have appeared and continue to appear on American television, where the author originally viewed most of them.[207] While Fields's silent films were once thought to be largely lost, most have now been accounted for, although only *Sally of the Sawdust* and *Running Wild* seem to be easily accessible through traditional film rental channels. In recent years, Fields's films are slowly becoming available on low-cost video tape and disc—a development that promises to revolutionize the study of Fields, as well as of film in general.

NOTES

1. Ronald J. Fields, ed., *W.C. Fields by Himself: His Intended Autobiography* (Englewood Cliffs, N.J.: Prentice-Hall, 1973), p. 18.

2. "Self-Made Curmudgeon," *Time*, October 17, 1949, p. 113.

3. William K. Everson, *The Art of W.C. Fields* (1967; rpt. New York: Bonanza Books, 1972), pp. 8, 27, 69, 79.

4. Ibid., p. 8.

5. Robert Lewis Taylor, *W.C. Fields: His Follies and Fortunes* (Garden City, N.Y.: Doubleday and Company, 1949), p. 161. The book was originally serialized May 21-July 9, 1949, in *The Saturday Evening Post* as "W.C. Fields: Rowdy King of Comedy." See the following 1949 *Post* issues: May 21, p. 19; May 28, p. 24; June 4, p. 26; June 11, p. 37; June 18, p. 30; June 25, p. 30; July 2, p. 34; July 9, p. 30.

6. Taylor, *W.C. Fields: His Follies and Fortunes,* p. 27.

7. Gene Fowler, *Minutes of the Last Meeting* (New York: Viking Press, 1954), pp. 6, 7.

8. Ibid., p. 9.

9. Ibid., pp. 39, 9ɔ.

10. "Eccentric's Eccentric," *Time,* April 5, 1954, p. 108.

11. Fowler, *Minutes of the Last Meeting,* p. 4. (A variation of the phrase occurs on p. 245.)

12. Ibid., pp. 103-104.

13. Carlotta Monti (with Cy Rice), *W.C. Fields & Me* (1971; rpt. New York: Warner Books, 1973), p. 12.

14. Ibid., pp. 48-52. See also Jack Grant, "THAT NOSE of W.C. Fields," *Movie Classic,* February 1935, p. 60.

15. Monti, *W.C. Fields & Me,* p. 49.

16. Arthur Cooper, "His Last Chickadee," *Newsweek,* June 21, 1971, pp. 92-92b.

17. Monti, *W.C. Fields & Me,* pp. 72-78.

18. Ibid., p. 227.

19. Taylor, *W.C. Fields: His Follies and Fortunes,* p. 279.

20. W.C. Fields, *Fields for President* (1940; rpt. New York: Dodd, Mead and Company, 1971), p. 43.

21. Robert Benchley, "An Interview with Mussolini," in *The Early Worm* (1927; rpt. Garden City, N.Y.: Blue Ribbon Books, 1946), pp. 29-31.

22. W.C. Fields, *Fields for President,* pp. 68-69.

23. Ibid., p. 152.

24. Michael M. Taylor, Introduction to *Fields for President,* by W.C. Fields, p. xxii.

25. R.J. Fields, *W.C. Fields by Himself,* p. xi.

26. Ibid., p. xii.

27. Ibid., p. 65.

28. "W.C. Fields Files" (James Smart's *Philadelphia Evening Bulletin* 1973 column on Ronald J. Fields), Billy Rose Theatre Collection, New York Public Library at Lincoln Center.

29. R.J. Fields, *W.C. Fields by Himself,* p. 59.

30. Most sources touch upon this, but see especially Taylor, *W.C. Fields: His Follies and Fortunes,* pp. 338-340; and Monti, *W.C. Fields & Me,* pp. 228-230.

31. Martin Lewis, ed., *The Quotations of W.C. Fields* (New York: Drake Publishers, 1976), p. 100.

32. Everson, *Art of W.C. Fields,* pp. 3-6.

33. Ibid., pp. 3-5.

34. Ibid., p. 4.

35. Ibid.

36. Philip Rosen, "The Chaplin World-View," *The Cinema Journal,* Fall 1969, p. 3.

37. Everson, *Art of W.C. Fields,* pp. 1-2.

38. Louise Brooks, "The Other Face of W.C. Fields," *Sight and Sound* (Spring 1971), pp. 92-96. This later appeared in a somewhat different form as Chapter 5, "The Other Face of W.C. Fields," in Brooks's *Lulu in Hollywood* (New York: Alfred A. Knopf, 1982), pp. 71-84.

39. *W.C. Fields in Never Give a Sucker an Even Break and Tillie and Gus* (New York: Simon and Schuster, 1973), pp. 96, 32.

40. Otis Ferguson, "The Great McGonigle" (also listed as "A Minor Falstaff"), *New Republic,* August 21, 1935, p. 48. For a more recent commentary on why some

excellent contemporary critics of Fields (who liked his comedy) had trouble with some of his films, see Vincent Canby, "W.C. Fields and Elaine May—Two of a Kind?" *New York Times,* March 14, 1971, pp. 1, 9.

41. Otis Ferguson, "The Old-Fashioned Way," *New Republic*, December 30, 1940, p. 900. The review was reprinted in Donald Deschner, ed., *The Films of W.C. Fields* (1966; rpt. Secaucus, N.J.: Citadel Press, 1974), pp. 180-183; Stanley Kauffmann, ed., with Bruce Henstell, *American Film Criticism: From the Beginnings to Citizen Kane* (New York: Liveright, 1972; Greenwood Press, 1979), pp. 406-408: and Robert Wilson, ed., with a foreword by Andrew Sarris, *The Film Criticism of Otis Ferguson* (Philadelphia: Temple University Press, 1971), pp. 326-327.

· 42. Ferguson, "Old-Fashioned Way," p. 900.

43. Ibid.

44. Otis Ferguson, "Happy Endings," *New Republic*, November 10, 1941, p. 622.

45. Ferguson, "The Great McGonigle," p. 48.

46. Andre Sennwald, "W.C. Fields, Buffoon," *New York Times,* January 13, 1935, sect. 9, p. 5.

47. André Bazin, "Charlie Chaplin," in *What Is Cinema?*, vol. 1, selected and trans. by Hugh Gray (1958; rpt. Los Angeles: University of California Press, 1967), p. 144.

48. Andre Sennwald, *David Copperfield* review, January 18, 1935, in *New York Times Film Reviews, 1932-1938,* vol. 2, project manager Abraham Abramson (New York: New York Times and Arno Press, 1970), pp. 1137-1138.

49. Andre Sennwald, *It's a Gift* review, January 2, 1935, in *New York Times Film Reviews, 1932-1938,* vol. 2, p. 1132.

50. Ferguson, "Great McGonigle," p. 48.

51. Sennwald, *It's a Gift* review, p. 1132.

52. Ibid.

53. Heywood Broun, "W.C. Fields and the Cosmos," January 7, 1931, pp. 24-25.

54. Andre Sennwald, *The Old-Fashioned Way* review, July 14, 1934, in *New York Times Film Reviews, 1932-1938*, vol. 2, p. 1078.

55. ARGUS, *You're Telling Me* review, *Literary Digest,* April 21, 1934, p. 40.

56. ARGUS, *Six of a Kind* review, *Literary Digest,* March 24, 1934, p. 45.

57. Ibid.

58. ARGUS, *It's a Gift* review, *Literary Digest,* April 21, 1934, p. 30, and the *You're Telling Me* review, p. 40.

59. ARGUS, *Poppy* review and article, "W.C. Fields in a Robin Hood Spirit: Comedian in New Screen Role after Winning Back His Health," *Literary Digest,* June 20, 1936, p. 19.

60. Mordaunt Hall, *It's the Old Army Game* review, July 5, 1926, in *New York Times Film Reviews, 1913-1931,* vol. 1, project manager Abraham Abramson (New York: New York Times and Arno Press, 1970), p. 318; *You're Telling Me* review, April 7, 1934, in *New York Times Film Reviews, 1932-1938,* vol. 2, p. 1048.

61. Taylor, *W.C. Fields: His Follies and Fortunes,* p. 199.

62. Mordaunt Hall, *Running Wild* review, June 13, 1927, in *New York Times Film Reviews, 1913-1931,* vol. 1, p. 370.

63. James Agee, *Shadow of a Doubt* review from *Nation,* January 23, 1943, in *Agee on Film,* vol. 1 (New York: Grosset and Dunlap, 1969), p. 26.

64. James Agee, *Till the Clouds Roll By* review from *Nation,* December 28, 1946, in *Agee on Film,* vol. 1, p. 235.

65. James Agee, *Never Give a Sucker An Even Break* review from *Time,* November 24, 1941, in *Agee on Film,* vol. 1, pp. 334, 335.

66. Agee, *Never Give a Sucker an Even Break* review, p. 334.

67. Ibid., p. 335.

68. *The Man on the Flying Trapeze* review, *Variety,* August 7, 1935, p. 21.

69. Ferguson, "The Great McGonigle," p. 48.

70. Andre Sennwald, *The Man on the Flying Trapeze* review, August 3, 1935, in *New York Times Film Reviews, 1932-1938,* vol. 2, p. 1196.

71. *You Can't Cheat an Honest Man* review, *Variety,* February 22, 1939, p. 12.

72. *Never Give a Sucker an Even Break* review, *Variety,* October 10, 1941, p. 9.

73. *My Little Chickadee* review, *Variety,* February 14, 1940, p. 18.

74. *You Can't Cheat an Honest Man* review, *Time,* February 27, 1939, p. 30.

75. *You're Telling Me* review, *Time,* April 16, 1934, p. 48.

76. "Jimmy [Durante], That Well-Dressed Man" (cover story), *Time,* January 24, 1944, p. 71.

77. *Go West* review, *Time,* December 23, 1940, p. 46.

78. "Laughter and Tears in MGM's *David Copperfield*" (review), *Newsweek,* January 26, 1935, p. 27; "W.C. Fields Returns for the Third Time in *Poppy*" (review), *Newsweek,* June 20, 1936, p. 24.

79. "Mae and Bill Out West" (*My Little Chickadee* review), *Newsweek,* February 26, 1940, p. 30.

80. Harold Cary, "The Loneliest Man in the Movies," *Colliers,* November 28, 1925, p. 26; "How the Films Fought Shy of 'Bill' Fields," *Literary Digest,* February 20, 1926, pp. 52, 54.

81. Cary, "Loneliest Man in the Movies," p. 26.

82. Ibid. For a fascinating period look at Fields the stage star, see "Fred Stone and W.C. Fields," in *Vanity Fair, Selections from America's Most Memorable Magazine: A Cavalcade of the 1920s and 1930s,* ed. by Cleveland Amory and Frederic Bradlee (New York: Viking Press, 1960), pp. 81-82.

83. Cary, "Loneliest Man in the Movies," p. 26.

84. Ibid.

85. Alva Johnston, "Profiles: Legitimate Nonchalance—I," *The New Yorker,* February 2, 1935, p. 23.

86. See the "Fields on Fields" shorter works section or Jim Tully, "The Clown Who Juggled Apples," *Photoplay,* January 1934, pp. 60, 108-109.

87. Alva Johnston, "Who Knows What Is Funny?" *Saturday Evening Post,* August 6, 1938, pp. 10-11, 43, 45-46. An abridged and slightly revised version of the essay would appear under the same title in the December 1975 issue of the *Saturday Evening Post.*

88. Johnston, "Profiles: I," p. 23.

89. Alva Johnston, "Profiles: Legitimate Nonchalance—II," *New Yorker,* February 9, 1935, p. 26.

90. Alva Johnston, "Profiles: Legitimate Nonchalance—III," *New Yorker,* February 16, 1935, p. 22.

91. Taylor, *W.C. Fields: His Follies and Fortunes,* p. 278.

92. Johnston, "Who Knows What Is Funny?" p. 45.

93. Ed Sullivan, "That Lovable Liar: An Appreciation of W.C. Fields and His Gift for Picturesque Exaggeration," *Silver Screen,* September 1935, p. 58.

94. James Agee, "Comedy's Greatest Era," essay from *Life,* September 3, 1949, in *Agee on Film,* vol. 1, pp. 17-18.

95. Ken Tynan, "Toby Jug and Bottle," *Sight and Sound,* February 1951, pp. 395-398. Anthologized as "W.C. Fields" in Tynan's *Curtains* (New York: Atheneum, 1961), pp. 352-358.

96. *Newsweek* and *Saturday Review* both ran a delightful group caricature of the circle. "With Wit and Love," *Newsweek,* April 5, 1954, pp. 96-97; Lee Rogow, "High Priests of Martini," *Saturday Review,* April 24, 1954, p. 19.

97. "Eccentrics's Eccentric." *Time* (April 5, 1954), pp. 108, 110.

98. John Montgomery, Chapter 16, "The Eccentrics," in *Comedy Films: 1894-1954,* 2d ed., by John Montgomery (1954; rpt. London: George Allen & Unwin, 1968), p. 221.

99. Montgomery, author's foreword to *Comedy Films: 1894-1954,* p. 11.

100. Montgomery, Chapter 16, "The Eccentrics," in *Comedy Films: 1894-1954,* p. 224.

101. *The New Hollywood and the Academy Awards* (Beverly Hills: Hollywood Awards Publications, 1971), p. 141.

102. Arthur Knight, Chapter 4, "The Movies Learn to Talk," in his *Liveliest Art: A Panoramic History of the Movies,* 2d ed. (1957; rpt. New York: New American Library, 1979), p. 171.

103. Lewis Jacobs, Chapter 25, "Significant Contemporary Film Content," in his *The Rise of the American Film: A Critical History,* 2d ed. (1939; rpt New York: Teachers College Press, 1971), p. 536.

104. William Cahn, Chapter 6, "From Follies to Flickers," in his *The Laugh Makers: A Pictorial History of American Comedians* (New York: G.P. Putnam's Sons, 1957), p. 77.

105. Raymond Durgnat, "Subversion in the Fields," *Films and Filming,* December 1965, p. 42.

106. Ibid., p. 43.

107. Bosley Crowther, *W.C. Fields Comedy Festival* review, March 3, 1966, in *New York Times Film Reviews, 1959-1968,* vol. 5, project manager Abraham Abramson (New York: New York Times and Arno Press, 1970), p. 3599.

108. Wallace Markfield, "The Dark Geography of W.C. Fields," *New York Times Magazine,* April 24, 1966, p. 116.

109. Ibid.

110. Paul D. Zimmerman, "The Great Debunker," *Newsweek,* April 3, 1967, p. 88.

111. David Robinson, "Dukinfield Meets McGargle: Creation of a Character," *Sight and Sound,* Summer 1967, p. 129.

112. Hugh Kenner, "The Confidence Man." *National Review,* April 23, 1968, pp. 399-400. See also reviews in: Oscar Handlin, "Reader's Choice: Fear and Laughter," *Atlantic Monthly,* January 1968, pp. 116, 118; Jay Jacobs, "Days of Wine and Legends," *The Reporter: The Magazine of Facts and Ideas,* January 25, 1968, pp. 49-50.

113. Judith Crist, "The Anti-Establishment Man," in her *The Private Eye, the*

Cowboy, and the Very Naked Girl: Movies from Cleo to Clyde (Chicago: Holt, Rinehart and Winston, 1968), p. 226. (The essay originally appeared in the February 26, 1967, *New York Herald Tribune,* pp. 16-17.)

114. Robert Warshow, "Monsieur Verdoux," in his *The Immediate Experience: Movies, Comics, Theatre & Other Aspects of Popular Culture* (1962; rpt. New York: Atheneum, 1972), pp. 207-221. (The essay originally appeared in 1947.)

115. Crist, "Anti-Establishment Man," p. 227.

116. Ibid., p. 228.

117. Penelope Gilliatt, "To W.C. Fields, Dyspeptic Mumbler, Who Invented His Own Way Out," *New Yorker,* June 21, 1969, p. 86; See also the same title in *Unholy Fools: Wits, Comics, Disturbers of the Peace: Film & Theater* (New York: Viking Press, 1973), p. 257.

118. Gilliatt, "To W.C. Fields, Dyspeptic Mumbler," p. 86.

119. Ibid., p. 90.

120. Gilliatt's reference to "fifth-columnist" does not appear in the original 1969 "To W.C. Fields" essay but rather in a two-page extension (pp. 262-263, drawn from a 1967 Gilliatt article) of the anthologized piece in *Unholy Fools.*

121. Penelope Gilliatt, "Feeling in the Wrong Is Wrong," in *Unholy Fools,* p. 255.

122. Gilliatt, "To W.C. Fields, Dyspeptic Mumbler," p. 86.

123. Pauline Kael, "My Little Chickadee" (review), in *Kiss Kiss Bang Bang* (Boston: Little, Brown and Company, 1968), p. 314.

124. Ibid., p. 313.

125. Pauline Kael, "Never Give a Sucker An Even Break" (review), in her *5001 Nights at the Movies: A Guide from A to Z* (New York: Holt, Rinehart and Winston, 1982), p. 408.

126. Pauline Kael, "Raising Kane," in her *The Citizen Kane Book* (Boston: Little, Brown and Company, 1971), p. 15.

127. Andrew Sarris, "Make Way for the Clowns," in his *The American Cinema: Directors and Directions, 1929-1968* (New York: E.P. Dutton and Company, 1968), p. 237.

128. Willard Van Dyke, "Cue Salutes: [W.C. Fields]," *Cue,* March 28, 1970, p. 54.

129. Ibid.

130. Everson, *Art of W.C. Fields* as quoted in Van Dyke, "Cue Salutes," p. 55.

131. Gerald Mast, Chapter 11, "The American Studio Years: 1930-1945," in his *A Short History of the Movies,* 3d ed. (1971; rpt. Indianapolis: Bobbs-Merrill Educational, 1981), p. 234.

132. Gerald Mast, *Film/Cinema/Movie: A Theory of Experience* (New York: Harper and Row, 1977), p. 226.

133. Gerald Mast, Chapter 17, "The Clown Tradition," in his *The Comic Mind: Comedy and the Movies* (1973; rpt. Chicago: University of Chicago Press, 1979), p. 291.

134. Screwball comedy and Bergman are discussed more fully in Wes D. Gehring, *Screwball Comedy: Defining a Film Genre* (Muncie, Ind.: Ball State University Press, Monograph Series, 1983).

135. Andrew Bergman, Chapter 3, "Some Anarcho-Nihilist Laff Riots," in his *We're in the Money: Depression America and Its Films* (1971; rpt. New York: New York University Press, 1972), p. 31.

136. Ibid., p. 41.

137. Ibid.

138. Donald W. McCaffrey, Chapter 9, "The Latter-Day Falstaff," in his *The Golden Age of Sound Comedy: Comic Films and Comedians of the Thirties* (New York: A.S. Barnes and Company, 1973), p. 168.

139. Ibid., p. 171.

140. Ibid., p. 165.

141. Ibid., p. 171.

142. Ibid., p. 172.

143. Walter Kerr, Chapter 30, "The Demiclowns," in his *The Silent Clowns* (New York: Alfred A. Knopf, 1975), p. 289.

144. Ibid., p. 292.

145. Ibid., p. 295. See also Tom Shales, "W.C. Fields," in *The American Film Heritage: Impressions from the American Film Institute Archives,* ed. by Kathleen Karr (Washington, D.C.: Acropolis, 1972), pp. 168-171.

146. See Wes Gehring, *Charlie Chaplin: A Bio-Bibliography* (Westport, Conn.: Greenwood Press, 1983), pp. 63-73.

147. Roger Ebert, "Fields vs. Chaplin," in *The National Society of Film Critics on Movie Comedy,* ed. by Stuart Byron and Elisabeth Weis (New York: Penguin Books, 1977), p. 53.

148. Ibid.

149. Leonard Maltin, Chapter 14, "W.C. Fields," in his *The Great Movie Comedians: From Charlie Chaplin to Woody Allen* (New York: Crown Publishers, 1978), p. 149.

150. Ibid.

151. W.C. Fields, "The Great Cigar-Box Trick," in *The Magician's Handbook: A Complete Encyclopedia of the Magic Art for Professional and Amateur Entertainers,* ed. by Percy Thomas Tibbles (London: Dawbarn and Ward, 1901), p. 125.

152. R.J. Fields, *W.C. Fields by Himself,* p. 53.

153. Sara Redway, "W.C. FIELDS Pleads for Rough HUMOR," *Motion Picture Classic*, September 1925, p. 73.

154. Ibid., p. 33.

155. Cary, "Loneliest Man in the Movies," p. 26.

156. Ibid.

157. Ruth Waterbury, "The Old Army Game," *Photoplay,* October 1925, p. 68.

158. Ibid., p. 102.

159. Helen Hanemann, "He Hated Alarm-Clocks: And Proves That Old Saying about the Early Worm Is Not to Be Taken Too Seriously," *Motion Picture,* August 1926, p. 98.

160. Charles Chaplin, "In Defense of Myself," *Colliers,* November 11, 1922, p. 8.

161. Dunham Thorp, "The Up-To-Date Old Timer," *Motion Picture Classic,* September 1926, p. 88.

162. W.C. Fields, "Anything for a Laugh," *American Magazine,* September 1934, p. 73.

163. Ibid., p. 130.

164. Redway, "W.C. FIELDS Pleads for Rough HUMOR," p. 73. For other Fields laws, see Johnston, "Who Knows What Is Funny?"

165. Grant, "THAT NOSE of W.C. Fields," p. 60.

166. Maude Cheatham, "Juggler of Laughs," *Silver Screen,* p. 30.

167. James Reid, "Nobody's Dummy," *Motion Picture,* October 1937, p. 86.

168. Ibid.

169. Monti, *W.C. Fields & Me,* p. 73.

170. W.C. Fields, "Alcohol and Me," *PIC,* October 13, 1942, p. 32.

171. Ibid.

172. Ibid.

173. Ibid., p. 34.

174. Ibid.

175. Ibid.

176. Ibid., p. 32.

177. Taylor, *W.C. Fields: His Follies and Fortunes,* p. 279.

178. Ibid.

179. Monti, *W.C. Fields & Me,* p. 72.

180. W.C. Fields, "My Views on Marriage," in *Tales for Males*, ed. by Ed Fitzgerald (New York: Cadillac Publishing Co., 1945), p. 218.

181. Ibid., p. 222.

182. Ibid.

183. W.C. Fields, "Life Begins at 20—Says W.C. Fields," *Motion Picture,* September 1935, p. 49.

184. Taylor, *W.C. Fields, His Follies and Fortunes,* p. 161.

185. Johnston, "Who Knows What Is Funny?" p. 45.

186. Cary, "Loneliest Man in the Movies," p. 26.

187. W.C. Fields, "Life Begins at 20," p. 70.

188. Sara Hamilton, "That Man's Here Again," *Photoplay,* August 1937, pp. 16 + ; James Reid, "Nobody's Dummy," *Motion Picture,* October 1937, pp. 37 + ; Charles Darnton, "Mr. Fields Wins by a NOSE!" *Screen Book Magazine,* November 1937, pp. 34 + .

189. Hamilton, "That Man's Here Again," p. 103.

190. Sara Hamilton, "Dangerous Days for Bill Fields," *Photoplay*, July 1936, pp. 30-31, 108-109.

191. Thorp, "The Up-To-Date Old Timer," p. 39.

192. Johnston, "Who Knows What Is Funny?" p. 46.

193. Monti, *W.C. Fields & Me,* p. 46.

194. The best such article-length equation during his lifetime is Johnston's aforementioned "Who Knows What Is Funny?" while Jan Kindler performs that task in the years since Fields's death in "Elysian Fields," *Playboy,* March 1969, pp. 116-118, 187-188, 190-192, 194, 196-199.

195. "W.C. Fields," *Life,* January 6, 1947, p. 63.

196. W.C. Fields, "Life Begins at 20," p. 70.

197. Darnton, "Mr. Fields Wins by a NOSE!" p. 35.

198. Will Rogers, "Radio Fairy Tales of Real Life Behind Scenes" (May 18, 1924, syndicated weekly newspaper article), in *Will Rogers' Weekly Articles,* vol. 1, *The Harding/Coolidge Years: 1922-1925,* ed. by James M. Smallwood (Stillwater: Oklahoma State University Press, 1980), p. 254.

199. Louise Brooks, "The Other Face of W.C. Fields," *Sight and Sound,* Spring 1971, p. 93.

200. Ibid., p. 96.

201. Ibid. p. 93. The statement is not changed when the essay is anthologized: Brooks, "The Other Face of W.C. Fields," in *Lulu in Hollywood* (New York: Alfred A. Knopf, 1982), p. 74.

202. Sara Hamilton, "A Red-Nosed Romeo," *Photoplay,* December 1934, p. 33.

203. Monti, *W.C. Fields & Me,* pp. 61, 69.

204. This is a Twain years removed from *Tom Sawyer* and *The Adventures of Huckleberry Finn.* It is the embittered author of *The Mysterious Stranger* and "The Man that Corrupted Hadleyburg," a description sometimes applicable to the late years of Fields.

205. According to the two key national reference sources (*The National Union Catalog* and the OCLC Bibliographic Data Base) of library holdings throughout this country, the only United States copy of the Tibbles book is in the Houdini Collection.

206. "The Film Forum," *The Saturday Review,* August 26, 1950, p. 28.

207. All Fields's sound features are also listed in Leonard Maltin, ed., *TV Movies: Everything You Want to Know and More about 15,000 Movies Now Being Shown on Regular and Cable TV,* 1983-1984 rev. ed. (1969; rpt. New York: A Signet Book, 1982).

5.

BIBLIOGRAPHICAL CHECKLIST OF KEY FIELDS SOURCES

BOOKS ABOUT OR BY FIELDS

Anobile, Richard J., ed. *DRAT! Being the Encapsulated View of Life by W.C. Fields in His Own Words*. 1968; rpt. New York: World Publishing Company 1969.

>*Contents:* "Notes on 'Drat!'" (Richard J. Anobile); "Ah, But It's Great to Be Alive" (an introduction by Ed McMahon); "I Never Met Fields Except in the Dark" (Richard F. Shepard); "The Encapsulated View of Life of W.C. Fields" (W.C. Fields); and "From Boy Juggler to Star Comedian" (W.C. Fields).

_____. *A Flask of Fields: Verbal and Visual Gems from the Films of W.C. Fields*. New York: Darien House, 1972.

_____. *Godfrey Daniels: Verbal and Visual Gems from the Short Films of W.C. Fields*. New York: Darien House, 1975.

Deschner, Donald. *The Films of W.C. Fields*. 1966; rpt. Secaucus, N.J.: Citadel Press, 1974.

>*Contents:* "Introduction" (Arthur Knight); "Biography" (uncredited); "Speaking of Benefits" (W.C. Fields); "Anything for a Laugh" (W.C. Fields); "The Films" (credits, synopses, and review excerpts); "The Old-Fashioned Way" (Otis Ferguson); and "W.C. Fields and the Cosmos" (Heywood Broun).

Everson, William K. *The Art of W.C. Fields*. Indianapolis: Bobbs-Merrill Co., 1967; rpt. New York: Bonanza Books, 1972.

Fields' Day: The Best of W.C. Fields. Kansas City, Mo.: Hallmark Cards, 1972.

Fields, Ronald J., ed. *W.C. Fields by Himself: His Intended Autobiography*. Englewood Cliffs, N.J.: Prentice-Hall, 1973.

Fields, W.C. *Fields for President*. 1940; rpt. New York: Dodd, Mead, and Company, 1971.

_____. *W.C. Fields in the Bank Dick*. New York: Simon and Schuster (Classic Film Scripts Series), 1973.

Fowler, Gene. *Minutes of the Last Meeting*. New York: Viking Press, 1954.

Lewis, Martin, ed. *The Quotations of W.C. Fields.* New York: Drake, 1976.

McEvoy, J.P. "The Comic Supplement" (unpublished musical comedy revue—the January 1925 dress rehearsal copy). Billy Rose Theatre Collection, New York Public Library at Lincoln Center. (This shows the influence of Fields, especially when compared to McEvoy's 1924 copyright version of "The Comic Supplement," Library of Congress, Madison Building, Washington, D.C.)

Mason, Paul, ed. *I Never Met a Kid I Liked.* Los Angeles: Stanyan Books, 1970.

_____. *Never Trust a Man Who Doesn't Drink.* Los Angeles: Stanyan Books, 1971.

Monti, Carlotta, with Cy Rice. *W.C. Fields & Me.* New York: Prentice-Hall, 1971; rpt. New York: Warner Books, 1973.

Taylor, Robert Lewis. *W.C. Fields: His Follies and Fortunes.* Garden City, N.Y.: Doubleday and Company, 1949.

W.C. Fields in Never Give a Sucker an Even Break and Tillie and Gus. New York: Simon and Schuster (Classic Film Scripts Series), 1973.

W.C. Fields Speaks. Los Angeles: Price/Stern/Sloan Publishers, 1981.

Yanni, Nicholas. *W.C. Fields.* 1974; rpt. New York: Pyramid Publications, 1975.

SHORTER WORKS ABOUT AND/OR BY FIELDS

Articles, Interviews, Book Chapters, and Monographs

Agee, James. *Never Give a Sucker an Even Break* review (from *Time,* November 24, 1941); *Shadow of a Doubt* review (from *Nation,* January 23, 1943); *Till the Clouds Roll By* review (from *Nation,* December 28, 1946); and "Comedy's Greatest Era" (from *Life,* September 3, 1949). In James Agee, *Agee on Film,* vol. 1. New York: Grosset and Dunlap, 1969.

ARGUS. *It's a Gift* review, *Literary Digest.* April 21, 1934, p. 30.

_____. *Poppy* review/article: "W.C. Fields in a Robin Hood Spirit: Comedian in New Screen Role after Winning Back His Health," *Literary Digest,* June 20, 1936, p. 19.

_____. *Six of a Kind* review, *Literary Digest,* March 24, 1934, p. 45.

_____. *You're Telling Me* review, *Literary Digest,* April 21, 1934, p. 40.

Bergman, Andrew. "Some Anarcho-Nihilist Laff Riots." In *We're in the Money: Depression America and It's Films.* New York: New York University Press, 1971; rpt. New York: Harper and Row, 1972.

Brooks, Louise. "The Other Face of W.C. Fields," *Sight and Sound,* Spring 1971, pp. 92-96. (Later appeared slightly altered as Chapter 5, "The Other Face of W.C. Fields," in Brooks's *Lulu in Hollywood.* New York: Alfred A. Knopf, 1982, pp. 71-84.)

Broun, Heywood. "W.C. Fields and the Cosmos," *Nation,* January 7, 1931, pp. 24-25.

Byron, Stuart, and Elisabeth Weis, eds. *The National Society of Film Critics on Movie Comedy.* New York: Penguin Books, 1977.
    Fields Contents: "W.C. Fields" (Judith Crist) and "Fields vs. Chaplin" (Roger Ebert).

Canby, Vincent. "W.C. Fields and Elaine May—Two of a Kind?" *New York Times,* March 14, 1971, pp. 1, 9.

Capsule reviews of all Fields's sound features. In *TV Movies: Everything You Want to Know and More about 15,000 Movies Now Being Shown on Regular and Cable TV,* 1983-1984 rev. ed. 1969; rpt. New York: A Signet Book, 1982.

Cary, Harold. "The Loneliest Man in the Movies," *Colliers: The National Weekly,* November 28, 1925, p. 26.

Cheatham, Maude. "Juggler of Laughs," *Silver Screen,* April 1935, pp. 30, 31, 62.

Cooper, Arthur. "His Last Chickadee," *Newsweek,* June 21, 1971, pp. 92-92b.

Crist, Judith. "The Anti-Establishment Man," *New York Herald Tribune,* February 26, 1967, pp. 16-17. (Later appeared in Crist's *The Private Eye, the Cowboy, and the Very Naked Girl: Movies from Cleo to Clyde.* Chicago: Holt, Rinehart and Winston, 1968, pp. 225-228.)

Crowther, Bosley. *W.C. Fields Comedy Festival* (March 3, 1966) review. In *New York Times Film Reviews, 1959-1968,* vol. 5. Project manager Abraham Abramson. New York: New York Times and Arno Press, 1970.

Darnton, Charles. "Mr. Fields Wins by a NOSE!" *Screen Book Magazine,* November 1937, pp. 34, 35, 105.

Durgnat, Raymond. "Subversion in the Fields," *Films and Filming,* December 1965, pp. 42-43. (Later appeared in expanded form as: Chapter 24, "Suckers and Soaks," in Durgnat's *The Crazy Mirror: Hollywood Comedy and the American Image.* 1969; rpt. New York: Dell, 1972, pp. 142-149.)

Ebert, Roger. "Fields vs. Chaplin," in *The National Society of Film Critics on Movie Comedy.* Edited by Stuart Byron and Elisabeth Weis. New York: Penguin Books, 1977, pp. 53-54.

"Eccentric's Eccentric," *Time,* April 5, 1954, pp. 108, 110.

Edelson, Edward. Chapter 8, "Uncle Bill." In *Funny Men of the Movies.* 1976; rpt. New York: Pocket Books, 1980, pp. 73-83.

Evans, Carol. "The Sounds of Silence: Comedy of the 1920s," *Mise-en-scène,* vol. 1, 1972, pp. 23-27.

Ferguson, Otis. "The Great McGonigle" (also listed as "A Minor Falstaff"), *New Republic,* August 21, 1935, p. 48.

_____. "The Great McGonigle," "The Old-Fashioned Way," "Happy Endings," "While We Were Laughing," "Credit for Comedy," and "Best Neglected Film." In *The Film Criticism of Otis Ferguson.* Edited by Robert Wilson. Philadelphia: Temple University Press, 1971.

_____. "Happy Endings," *New Republic,* November 10, 1941, p. 622.

_____. "The Old-Fashioned Way," *New Republic,* December 30, 1940, p. 900. (Note 41 in Chapter 4 gives several sources in which it has been reprinted).

Fields, W.C. "Alcohol and Me," *PIC,* October 13, 1942, pp. 32-34.

_____. "Anything for a Laugh," *American Magazine,* September 1934, pp. 73, 129-130.

_____. "From Boy Comedian to Star Comedian," *Theatre Magazine,* October 1928, pp. 44, 76.

_____. "How to Figure Your Income Tax," *This Week, New York Herald Tribune* Sunday magazine supplement, March 10, 1940, pp. 9, 22.

_____. "Life Begins at 20—Says W.C. Fields," *Motion Picture,* September 1935, pp. 49, 70-71.

_____. "My Rules of Etiquette," *This Week, New York Herald Tribune* Sunday magazine supplement, December 4, 1938, pp. 12-13.

_____. "My Views on Marriage," In *Tales for Males.* Edited by Ed Fitzgerald. New York: Cadillac Publishing Co., 1945, pp. 216-222.

_____. "A New Hat and Cigar Effect" and "The Great Cigar-Box Trick." In *The Magician's Handbook: A Complete Encyclopedia of the Magic Art for Professional and Amateur Entertainers.* Edited by Percy Thomas Tibbles. London: Dawbarn and Ward, 1901, pp. 122-127.

"The Film Forum," *Saturday Review,* August 26, 1950, p. 28.

Flinn, Tom, "Out of the Past," *Velvet Light Trap,* Winter 1971-1972, pp. 6-7.

Ford, Corey. "The One and Only W.C. Fields," *Harper's,* October 1967, pp. 65-68. (Later appeared in slightly altered form as Chapter 10 in Ford's *The Time of Laughter.* Boston: Little, Brown and Company, 1967, pp. 171-195.)

Fowler, Will. "Why W.C. Fields Hated Christmas: A Holiday Fable," *Show Business Illustrated,* January 2, 1962, pp. 115-116. (Appeared with slight variation as "A Holiday Visit with W.C. Fields: 'Sleigh Bells Give Me Double Nausea,'" in *Life,* December 15, 1972, p. 42.)

"Fred Stone and W.C. Fields." In *Vanity Fair, Selections from America's Most Memorable Magazine: A Calvalcade of the 1920s and 1930s.* Edited by Cleveland Amory and Frederic Bradlee. New York: Viking Press, 1960, pp. 81-82.

Gilliatt, Penelope. "Feeling in the Wrong Is Wrong." In *Unholy Fools: Wits, Comics, Disturbers of the Peace: Film & Theater.* New York: Viking Press, 1973, pp. 253-256.

_____. "To W.C. Fields, Dyspeptic Mumbler, Who Invented His Own Way Out," *New Yorker,* June 21, 1969, pp. 86, 89-90. (Later appeared in expanded form in Gilliatt's *Unholy Fools, Wits, Comics, Disturbers of the Peace: Film & Theater.* New York: Viking Press, 1973, pp. 257-261.)

Grant, Jack. "THAT NOSE of W.C. Fields," *Movie Classic,* February 1935, pp. 56, 60.

Hall, Mordaunt. *It's the Old Army Game* review, July 5, 1926, and *Running Wild* review, June 13, 1927. In *New York Times Film Reviews, 1913-1931,* vol. 1. Project manager Abraham Abramson. New York: New York Times and Arno Press, 1970.

_____. *You're Telling Me* review, April 7, 1934. In *New York Times Film Review, 1913-1931,* vol. 2. Project manager Abraham Abramson. New York: New York Times and Arno Press, 1970.

Hamilton, Sara. "Dangerous Days for Bill Fields," *Photoplay,* July 1936, pp. 30-31, 108-109.

_____. "A Red-Nosed Romeo," *Photoplay,* December 1934, pp. 32-33, 113.

_____. "That Man's Here Again," *Photoplay,* August 1937, pp. 16, 103-104.

Handlin, Oscar. "Reader's Choice: Fear and Laughter," *Atlantic Monthly,* January 1968, pp. 116, 118.

Hanemann, Helen. "He Hated Alarm-Clocks: And Proves That Old Saying about the Early Worm Is Not to Be Taken Too Seriously," *Motion Picture,* August 1926, pp. 39, 98.

"How the Films Fought Shy of Bill Fields," *Literary Digest,* February 20, 1926, pp. 52, 54.

Jacobs, Jay. "Days of Wine and Legends," *Reporter: The Magazine of Facts and Ideas,* January 25, 1968, pp. 49-50.

Jacobs, Lewis. Chapter 25, "Significant Contemporary Film Content." In *The Rise of the American Film: A Critical History,* 2d ed. New York: Harcourt Brace, 1939; rpt. New York: Teachers College Press, 1971, p. 536.

Johnston, Alva. "Profiles: Legitimate Nonchalance," *New Yorker,* February 2, February 9, and February 16, 1935, pp. 23-26, 25-28, 22-26 respectively.

_____. "Who Knows What Is Funny?" *Saturday Evening Post,* August 6, 1938, pp. 10-11, 43, 45-46. (An abridged and slightly revised version with the same title appeared in the December 1975 issue of the *Post,* pp. 42-43, 85.)

Kael, Pauline. *5001 Nights at the Movies: A Guide from A to Z.* New York: Holt, Rinehart and Winston, 1982.

Fields contents (capsule reviews): "If I Had a Million," "Million Dollar Legs," "The Fatal Glass of Beer," "Alice in Wonderland," "The Man on the Flying Trapeze," Poppy," "The Big Broadcast of 1938," "My Little Chickadee," "Never Give a Sucker an Even Break," and "Tales of Manhattan."

_____. *My Little Chickadee* review. In *Kiss Kiss Bang Bang.* Boston: Little, Brown and Company, 1968, pp. 313-314.

Kaplan, Peter W. "W.C. Fields at 100," March-April, 1979, pp. 57-59.

Kauffmann, Stanley, ed., with Bruce Henstell. *American Film Criticism: From the Beginnings to Citizen Kane.* New York: Liveright, 1972; rpt. Westport, Conn: Greenwood Press, 1979.

Fields contents: "It's a Gift" (Andre Sennwald); "The Man on the Flying Trapeze" (Andre Sennwald); and "The Bank Dick" (Otis Ferguson).

Kenner, Hugh. "The Confidence Man," *National Review,* April 23, 1968, pp.399-400.

Kerr, Walter. Chapter 30, "The Demiclowns." In *The Silent Clowns.* New York: Alfred A. Knopf, 1975, pp. 295-297.

Kindler, Jan. "Elysian Fields," *Playboy,* March 1969, pp. 116-118, 187-88, 190-192, 194, 196-199.

Kingsley, Grace. "Hobnobbing in Hollywood," *Los Angeles Times,* December 8, 1933, sect. 1, p. 7.

Knight, Arthur. Chapter 4, "The Movies Learn to Talk." In his *The Liveliest Art: A Panoramic History of the Movies,* 2d ed. 1957; rpt. New York: New American Library (Macmillan), 1979, pp. 171, 173-174.

"Laughter and Tears in MGM's *David Copperfield,*" *Newsweek,* January 26, 1935, p. 27.

Lee, Raymond, "The Brabbling Boozer Returns," *Classic Film Collector,* Summer 1969, pp. 46-47.

McCaffrey, Donald W. Chapter 9, "The Latter-Day Falstaff." In *The Golden Age of Sound Comedy: Comic Films and Comedians of the Thirties.* New York: A.S. Barnes and Company, 1973, pp. 165-182.

McEvoy, J.P. "W.C. Fields' Best Friend," *This Week, New York Herald Tribune* Sunday magazine supplement, July 26, 1942, pp. 15-16.

McVay, Douglas. "Elysian Fields," *Film,* Winter 1967, pp. 22-23.

"Mae and Bill Out West," *Newsweek,* February 26, 1940, p. 30.

Magill, Frank N., ed. *Magill's Survey of Cinema: English Language Films* (first series), 4 vols. Englewood Cliffs, N.J.: Salem Press, 1970.

Fields contents: "The Bank Dick" (Rob Edelman, vol. 1); "Million Dollar

Legs" (Daniel Einstein, vol. 3); "Never Give a Sucker an Even Break" (Robert Mitchell, vol. 3); and "You Can't Cheat an Honest Man" (Robert Mitchell, vol. 4).

_____. *Magill's Survey of Cinema: English Language Films* (second series). 4 vols. Englewood Cliffs, N.J.: Salem Press, 1981.

Fields contents: "David Copperfield" (Robert Mitchell, vol. 2); "It's a Gift" (Howard H. Prouty, vol. 3); and "My Little Chickadee" (Robert Mitchell, vol. 4).

Maltin, Leonard. Chapter 14, "W.C. Fields." In *The Great Movie Comedians: From Charlie Chaplin to Woody Allen.* New York: Crown Publishers, 1978, pp. 142-151.

Man on the Flying Trapeze review, *Variety,* August 7, 1935, p. 21.

Markfield, Wallace. "The Dark Geography of W.C. Fields," *New York Times Magazine,* April 24, 1966, pp. 32-33, 110, 112, 114, 116, 117, 119-120.

Marlowe, Don. "Fieldsiana," *Classic Film Collector,* Fall 1970, p. 48.

Mast, Gerald. Chapter 11, "The American Studio Years: 1930-1945." In *A Short History of the Movies,* 3d ed. 1971; rpt. Indianapolis: Bobbs-Merrill Educational, 1981, pp. 234-235.

_____. Chapter 17, "The Clown Tradition." In *The Comic Mind: Comedy and the Movies.* 1973; rpt. Chicago: University of Chicago Press, 1979, pp. 288-293.

Montgomery, John. Chapter 16, "The Eccentrics." In *Comedy Films: 1894-1954,* 2d ed. 1954; rpt. London: George Allen & Unwin, 1968, pp. 221-225.

Mullett, Mary B. "Bill Fields Disliked His Label, So He Laughed It Off," *American Magazine,* January 1926, pp. 19, 143-147.

My Little Chickadee, review, *Variety,* February 14, 1940, p. 18.

Never Give a Sucker An Even Break review, *Variety,* October 10, 1941, p. 9.

Prior, Moody E. "In Search of the Grampion Hills with W.C. Fields," *American Scholar,* Winter 1978-1979, pp. 101-105.

Redway, Sara. "W.C. FIELDS Pleads for Rough HUMOR," *Motion Picture Classic,* September 1925, pp. 32-33, 73.

Reid, James. "Nobody's Dummy," *Motion Picture,* October 1937, pp. 37, 84-86.

Robinson, David. "Dukinfield Meets McGargle: Creation of a Character," *Sight and Sound,* Summer 1967, pp. 125-129.

Rogers, Will. "Radio Fairy Tales of Real Life Behind Scenes" (May 18, 1924 syndicated newspaper article). In *Will Rogers' Weekly Articles,* vol. 1, *The Harding/Coolidge Years: 1922-1925.* Edited by James M. Smallwood. Stillwater: Oklahoma State University Press, 1980, pp. 250-254.

Rogow, Lee. "High Priests of Martini," *Saturday Review,* April 24, 1954, p. 19.

Sarris, Andrew. "Make Way for the Clowns." In *The American Cinema: Directors and Directions, 1929-1968.* New York: E.P. Dutton and Co., 1968, pp. 238-239.

"Self-Made Curmudgeon," *Time,* October 17. 1949, p. 113.

Sennwald, Andre. *The Old-Fashioned Way* review (July 14, 1934), *It's a Gift* review (January 2, 1935), *David Copperfield* review (January 18, 1935), and *Man on the Flying Trapeze* review (August 3, 1935). In *New York Times Film Reviews, 1932-1938,* vol. 2. Project manager Abraham Abramson. New York: New York Times and Arno Press, 1970.

_____. "W.C. Fields, Buffoon,' *New York Times,* January 13, 1935, sect. 9, p. 5.

Shales, Tom. "W.C. Fields." In *The American Film Heritage: Impressions from the American Film Institute Archives.* Edited by Kathleen Karr. Washington, D.C.: Acropolis, 1972, pp. 168-171.

Sullivan, Ed. "That Lovable Liar: An Appreciation of W.C. Fields and His Gift for Picturesque Exaggeration," *Silver Screen,* September 1935, pp. 14-15, 57-58.

Thorp, Dunham. "The Up-To-Date Old Timer," *Motion Picture Classic,* September 1926, pp. 38-39, 88-89.

Tully, Jim. "The Clown Who Juggled Apples," *Photoplay,* January 1934, pp. 60, 108-109.

Tynan, Ken. "Toby Jug and Bottle," *Sight and Sound,* February 1951, pp. 395-398. Anthologized as "W.C. Fields" in Tynan's *Curtains.* New York: Atheneun, 1961, pp. 352-358.

You Can't Cheat An Honest Man review, *Time,* February 27, 1939, p. 30.

You Can't Cheat An Honest Man review, *Variety,* February 22, 1939, p. 12.

Van Dyke, Willard. "Cue Salutes: [W.C. Fields]," *Cue,* March 28, 1970, pp. 54-55.

Waterbury, Ruth. "The Old Army Game," *Photoplay*, October 1925, pp. 68, 101-102.

"W.C. Fields Returns for the Third Time in *Poppy,*" *Newsweek,* June 20, 1936, p. 24.

"W.C. Fields," *Life,* January 6, 1947, p. 63.

"With Wit and Love," *Newsweek*, April 5, 1954, pp. 96-97.

You're Telling Me review, *Time,* April 16, 1934, pp. 47-48.

Zimmerman, Paul D. "The Great Debunker," *Newsweek,* April 3, 1967, p. 88.

W.C. FIELDS FILES AND PAPERS

"W.C. Fields Files," Billy Rose Theatre Collection, New York Public Library at Lincoln Center.

"W.C. Fields Papers," Library of Congress, Washington, D.C. Unpublished copyrighted material by Fields, though some sketches, or variations of them, appeared in *W.C. Fields by Himself: His Intended Autobiography.*

Between 1918 and late 1930 Fields copyrighted twenty-three separate comedy documents on sixteen subjects (some sketches were copyrighted more than once when changes were made). The vast majority of the writing represented material he used on stage, and later in films—such classic Fields comedy frustrations as golf and back porch sleeping patterns. The writing is arranged chronologically, though later copyrighted revision dates of the same routine follow the titles. Also, short descriptions are added to material without a self-explanatory title. Though once housed individually by title in the Copyright Division of the Library of Congress, the documents are now available as one collection, the "W.C. Fields Papers," in the Manuscript Division of the Library (Madison Building).

Aug. 30, 1918   "An Episode of Lawn Tennis"—D 50680

Oct. 28, 1918   "An Episode of Lawn Tennis"—D 50680

Feb. 1919   "An Episode at the Dentist's"—D 51214 (July 12, 1928—84613; November 2, 1928—86848)

Mar. 21, 1919   "The Mountain Sweep Stakes"—D 51508 (A film script parodying movies, Fields describes it as "A Moving, Talking, Eastern, Western, Society, Dramatic, Spectacular Comedy Motion Stage Picture")

Apr. 7, 1919   "Just Before the Dawn"—D 51558 (coauthored with Mortimer M. Newfield; a three-act military farce)

Oct. 16, 1919   "The Family Ford"—D 52882 (September 3, 1920—D55401; October 9, 1920—D55748)

Feb. 26, 1921   "The Pullman Sleeper"—D 56911

May 25, 1921   "Off to the Country"—D 57748 (June 29, 1921—D 58027; April 3, 1922—D 60419)

May 25, 1921   "What a Night"—D 57747 (A parody of the detective-mystery genre, with frequent surreal action)

May 22, 1922   "The Sport Model"—D 60861

May 29, 1922   "10,000 People Killed"—D 60900 (October 10, 1922—D 62425; concerns a radio broadcast misunderstanding)

July 31, 1922   "The Caledonian Express"—D 61555 (subtitled heading "Or An American Abroad")

Feb. 6, 1925   "The Sleeping Porch"—D 70336

July 12, 1928   "Stolen Bonds"—D 84614 (Better known under the film title for which it was adapted: *The Fatal Glass of Beer,* 1933)

July 12, 1928   "My School Days Are Over"—D 84612

Nov. 25, 1930   "The Midget Car"—D 8113

APPENDIXES

CHRONOLOGICAL
BIOGRAPHY

Jan. 29, 1880   Born William Claude Dukenfield to James and Kate Dukenfield in Philadelphia. James sold vegetables from a cart and Kate was a housewife.

1891   Fields runs away from home. Just when he returned is open to debate, but at eleven he begins a difficult apprenticeship in survival. At the same time he practices juggling with an obsession.

1895   Fields obtains a pivotal early booking as a juggler at Fortescue's Pier, an Atlantic City amusement park. His other duties include "drowning" several times a day in order to draw crowds for the food concession business.

Apr. 8, 1900   Already an established star, he marries Harriet Hughes, a chorus girl from one of the acts appearing with him in San Francisco. For a time she travels with him as an assistant in his act.

1901   Two Fields essays on juggling appear in Percy Thomas Tibbles's authoritative British publication, *The Magician's Handbook: A Complete Encyclopedia*, which describes the contributing authors as "magicians who have made their names famous during the past and present centuries."

1903   A Fields advertisement from this year states his last European tour included the Winter Garden (Berlin) twice, Folies Bergères (Paris), Palace (London), Hippodrome (London), Orpheum (Vienna), Victoria Salon (Dresden), Theatre Varite (Prague), and Palace (Manchester).

July 28, 1904   A son, William Claude Fields, Jr., is born. Harriet's pregnancy, and then the birth of William, resulted in her retirement from show business. Though the marriage was never officially dissolved, and Fields supported her for the rest of his life, the relationship became a permanent and frequently hostile separation.

Oct. 11, 1913   Fields gives a command performance at Buckingham Palace before King Edward VII. Appearing with him is the great Sarah Bernhardt.

1914   He signs with the *Ziegfeld Follies.* Starting in 1915, Fields will be with the next seven editions of the *Follies,* enabling him to showcase his talents among the greatest comedians of the day: Will Rogers, Ed Wynn, Fanny Brice, Bert Williams, and Eddie Cantor.

1915   *Pool Sharks,* his first film, is made. A one-reeler, it records his even then famous pool routine from the stage. Though quickly followed by another one-reeler, *His Lordship's Dilemma,* his film career would not be established for ten years.

1917   Fields's mistress, Bessie Poole, a *Ziegfeld Follies* dancer, gives birth to a son, William Rexford Fields Morris.

Aug. 30, 1918   Fields copyrights the stage routine "An Episode on the Links," which, like his pool routine, is a classic Fields sketch. In the next twelve years he will copyright twenty-three separate documents on sixteen subjects (some sketches were copyrighted more than once when changes were made).

Feb. 1919   The first of three versions of "An Episode at the Dentist's" is copyrighted.

Oct. 16, 1919   The first of three versions of "The Family Ford" is copyrighted.

May 25, 1921   The first of three versions of "Off to the Country" is copyrighted.

1922   Sinclair Lewis's novel *Babbitt* is published. It would seem to have had an important, though unacknowledged, creative influence on Fields.

Sept. 3, 1923   *Poppy,* Dorothy Donnelly's musical comedy, opens on Broadway. Fields is a major hit as Professor Eustace McGargle.

1924   J.P. McEvoy copyrights *The Comic Supplement,* a musical comedy revue, which Fields both later appears in (1925) and seemingly assists in revising (though this is not acknowledged).

While never given the prominence of *Poppy* in Fields studies, it is of equal importance to his career.

Aug. 11, 1924   *Janice Meredith,* a film epic on the American Revolution, has a gala opening in New York City. Fields has a small but memorable role as a drunken British sergeant.

Feb. 6, 1925   Fields copyrights "The Sleeping Porch."

Sept. 3, 1925   D.W. Griffith's film adaptation of *Poppy,* retitled *Sally of the Sawdust,* has a special New York City opening. Griffith and *Sally* stars Fields and Carol Dempster make a personal appearance on stage. Fields again is a major hit as Professor McGargle. It marks the real beginning of his silent film career.

1926   Fields stars in the feature films *That Royle Girl, It's the Old Army Game* (drawn from *The Comic Supplement*), and *So's Your Old Man.*

1927   The following Fields features appear: *The Potters* (from J.P. McEvoy's 1923 play of the same name), *Running Wild,* and *Two Flaming Youths* (released late in the year and sometimes carrying a 1928 date).

Jan. 3, 1928   *Poppy* author Dorothy Donnelly (born one day before Fields on January 28, 1880) dies of nephritis-pneumonia at her New York City home. Donnelly, a noted actress turned playwright, had been in ill health for five years.

1928   Fields's features *Tillie's Punctured Romance* and *Fools for Luck* open to poor reviews, and his film career is temporarily on hold.

July 12, 1928   Fields copyrights "Stolen Bonds."

Aug. 7, 1928   He opens in Earl Carroll's *Vanities*; his material includes "Stolen Bonds."

Oct. 8, 1928   Former mistress Bessie Poole dies of myocarditis and complications a few days after a nightclub fight.

Mar. 1930   Fields plays the Palace (New York City), performing "Stolen Bonds" and his golf routine.

1930   Fields appears in his first sound film, the short subject *A Golf Specialist.*

Nov. 25, 1930   He files his last copyright, for "The Midget Car."

Dec. 22, 1930   The musical comedy *Ballyhoo* opens on Broadway with Fields in the starring role. Because of a number of problems, it has a relatively short run.

1931   Fields decides to go west permanently. He had established California residency in 1927, but stage commitments kept him in the East for much of the interim.

Nov. 1931   Fields has a comically pivotal role in *Her Majesty Love,* his first sound feature.

1932   Fields is a featured star in *Million Dollar Legs* and *If I Had a Million*, as well as being the creative force behind the Mack Sennett-produced *The Dentist*. Fields also meets and begins a lifetime relationship with his last mistress, film starlet Carlotta Monti.

1933   He writes and stars in three additional short subjects for Sennett and appears in a now obscure one-reeler entitled *Hip Action*. There are also the following features: *International House, Tillie and Gus,* and *Alice in Wonderland*.

1934   There are five features: *Six of a Kind, You're Telling Me, The Old-Fashioned Way, Mrs. Wiggs of the Cabbage Patch,* and *It's a Gift* (probably his greatest film).

1935   Fields stars in *David Copperfield* (playing his beloved Micawber), *Mississippi*, and *The Man on the Flying Trapeze*.

June 1936   *Poppy*, the second film adaptation of the play, appears. Fields, who was in poor health before, during, and after shooting the film, is in serious condition at the time it is released.

1937   Though microphones must be brought to his sickbed, Fields is a hit when he takes part in a special radio show honoring Adolph Zukor.

May 9, 1937   Fields is part of a new hit radio program, NBC's "The Chase & Sanborn Hour," with Edgar Bergen and Charlie McCarthy.

Nov. 1937   In Charles Darnton's *Screen Book Magazine* article, "Mr. Fields Wins By a NOSE!." Fields reveals how moved he was by the outpouring of concern by fans during his long illness. And he feels like this is a new life, a fresh beginning: "It's all borrowed time . . . but I'm certainly enjoying it." (For a long time he is even on the wagon.)

Mar. 7, 1938	Fields stars in a "Lux Radio Theatre" presentation of *Poppy*. Program producer and master of ceremonies is Cecil B. De Mille.
1938	*The Big Broadcast of 1938* is released.
Oct. 1938	Fields becomes a regular on CBS's "Your Hit Parade," a forty-five-minute radio program which combined the fifteen top songs of the week with a quarter-hour of comedy.
1939	*You Can't Cheat an Honest Man* is released, his first Universal film, after a lengthy association with Paramount.
1940	*W.C. Fields for President* appears in book form. The films *My Little Chickadee* (much attention is focused on his teaming with Mae West) and *The Bank Dick* (one of his greatest films) are released.
Oct. 1941	*Never Give a Sucker an Even Break,* his last starring feature, appears.
May 29, 1942	Close Fields friend John Barrymore dies. He had suffered from a number of ailments, especially cirrhosis of the liver, but pneumonia was the final cause of death. (Fields's own health is frequently poor in the 1940s.)
1942	*Tales of Manhattan* appears, but the Fields segment is removed in order to shorten the film's running time.
1944	Fields performs short sketches in the following features: *Follow the Boys, Song of the Open Road,* and *Sensations of 1945.*
Dec. 25, 1946	Fields dies in a California sanitarium. He had suffered from a number of health problems, the most serious being cirrhosis of the liver. He leaves a sizable estate ($771,448, the majority of which is to establish an orphanage), but his estranged wife and son successfully fight the will. Though it takes years, they become its chief recipients.
1949	Robert Lewis Taylor's celebrated biography of the comedian is published—*W.C. Fields: His Follies and Fortunes.*
1951	Edith Williams (Chicago) claims to be Fields's real widow and sues to receive her share of the comedian's estate. Although individual settlements are made through the years, the legal fight over the will continues.
Apr. 4, 1954	The estate is finally 100 percent settled. Harriet Fields has successfully fought the claims of Edith Williams.

1954   Gene Fowler's *Minutes of the Last Meeting,* a group biography of his friends—W.C. Fields, John Decker, and Sadakichi Hartmann—is published.

Aug. 8, 1958   Author J.P. McEvoy (born 1894) dies of a stroke at his New York City home. He had been in poor health for several months.

1960s   The antiestablishment sixties take the antiestablishment Fields to heart. His films are frequently revived; a recording of some Fields observations makes the record charts; Fields posters and numerous other items on which his likeness is reproduced begin to appear everywhere; writing about his life and career increases; and it becomes very popular to do Fields imitations.

July 1971   Mickey Rooney begins touring as Fields in the musical *Just W.C.*

1971   The comedian's *W.C. Fields for President* is reissued, and Carlotta Monti's book appears: *W.C. Fields & Me.*

1973   *W.C. Fields by Himself: His Intended Autobiography* is published. The comedian's grandson, Ronald J. Fields, acts as editor.

1976   The movie *W.C. Fields and Me* is released. Rod Steiger plays Fields and Valerie Perrine has the part of Monti. While Monti's biography is insightful, the movie is full of fiction not in her book. Steiger and Perrine do, however, give creditable performances.

Jan. 29, 1980   On the one hundredth anniversary of Fields's birth the United States government honors his memory with a postage stamp, something for which his fans had long campaigned. Somewhere the comedian is no doubt amused at the comic irony of the situation—an antiestablishment figure being honored by the establishment. But then, that is frequently the message of his art— the world is comically absurd. It is a fitting tribute.

FILMOGRAPHY

The following filmography was constructed from such key listings as Deschner's *The Films of W.C. Fields* (1966), Simon and Schuster's classic film scripts of *W.C. Fields in The Bank Dick* (1973) and *W.C. Fields in Never Give a Sucker an Even Break and Tillie and Gus* (1973), Yanni's *W.C. Fields* (1974), period film reviews, and—of course—the original film credits themselves, when available. Moreover, the majority of the Fields texts provided helpful assistance. Because the order of the films frequently varies from one source to another, review dates from both the *New York Times* and *Variety* have been consulted when contradictions existed. Titles with an asterisk (*) have had short subject extracts made available for rental; the names of these "new" one-reel films follow the credits of whichever feature they were drawn from.

GAUMONT

1915   *Pool Sharks* (1 reel—10-11 minutes).
        Director: Edwin Middleton. Story focus is Fields's pool stage routine.

MUTUAL (distributor, Gaumont produced)

        His Lordship's Dilemma (1 reel—10 to 11 minutes).
        Director: William Haddock. Now lost.

METRO-GOLDWYN (distributor, Cosmopolitan produced)

1924   *Janice Meredith* (153 minutes). Library of Congress print, which is well under this running time, is entitled *The Beautiful Rebel*.

Director: E. Mason Hopper. Based upon the Paul Leicester Ford novel. Screenplay: Lilly Hayward. Cast: Marion Davies (Janice Meredith), Harrison Ford (Charles Fownes), Macklyn Arbuckle (Squire Meredith), Joseph Kilgour (General Washington), George Nash (Lord Howe), Tyrone Power, Sr. (Lord Cornwallis), May Vokes (Susie), W.C. Fields (drunken British sergeant), Olin Howland (Philemon), Hattie Delaro (Mrs. Meredith), Spencer Charters (Squire Hennion), Douglas Stevenson (Captain Mowbray), Helen Lee Worthing (Mrs. Loring).

UNITED ARTISTS (distributor, Paramount produced)

1925   *Sally of the Sawdust* (104 minutes).
Director: D.W. Griffith. Based upon the Dorothy Donnelly stage play entitled *Poppy*. Screenplay: Forrest Haley. Cast: Carol Dempster (Sally), W.C. Fields (Professor Eustace McGargle), Alfred Lunt (Peyton Lennox), Erville Alderson (Judge Henry L. Foster), Effie Shannon (Mrs. Foster), Charles Hammond (Lennox, Sr.), Roy Applegate (detective), Florence Fair (Miss Vinton), Marie Shotwell (society leader), Glenn Anders (Leon, the acrobat).

PARAMOUNT (distributor, Famous Players—Lasky Corporation produced)

1926   *That Royle Girl* (114 minutes).
Director: D.W. Griffith. Based upon an Edwin Balmer story. Screenplay: Paul Scholfield. Cast: Carol Dempster (Joan Daisy Royle), W.C. Fields (her father), James Kirkwood (Calvin Clarke), Harrison Ford (Fred Ketlar), Paul Everton (George Baretta), Kathleen Chambers (Adele Ketlar), George Rigas (henchman), Florence Auer (Baretta's "girl"), Ida Waterman (Mrs. Clarke), Alice Laidley (Clarke's fiancée) Dorothea Love (Lola Nelson), Dore Davidson (Elman), Frank Allworth (Oliver), Bobby Watson (Hofer).

FAMOUS PLAYERS—LASKY CORPORATION (distributor, Adolph Zukor and Jessie Lasky produced)

1926   *It's the Old Army Game* (70 minutes).
Director: Edward Sutherland. Based upon the J.P. McEvoy musical comedy revue entitled *The Comic Supplement* (to which Fields contributed). Screenplay: Thomas J. Geraghty. Cast: W.C. Fields (Elmer Prettywillie), Louise Brooks (Mildred Marshall), Blanche Ring (Tessie Overholt), William Gaxton (George Parker), Mary Foy (Sarah Pancoast), Mickey Bennett (Mickey).

FAMOUS PLAYERS—LASKY CORPORATION

1926   *So's Your Old Man* (67 minutes).
Director: Gregory LaCava. Based upon the Julian Street story entitled

"Mr. Bisbee's Princess" (O. Henry Memorial Award Prize winner for 1925), by Howard Emmett Rogers. Screenplay: J. Clarkson Miller. Cast: W.C. Fields (Samuel Bisbee), Alice Joyce (Princess Lescaboura), Charles Rogers (Kenneth Murchison), Kittins Reichert (Alice Bisbee), Julia Ralph (Mrs. Murchison), Frank Montgomery (Jeff), Jerry Sinclair (Al).

PARAMOUNT (Famous Players—Lasky Corporation produced)

1927   *The Potters* (71 minutes). Now lost.
Director: Fred Newmeyer. Adapted by Sam Mintz and Ray Harris from the J.P. McEvoy play. Screenplay: J. Clarkson Miller. Cast: W.C. Fields (Pa Potter), Mary Alden (Ma Potter), Ivy Harris (Mamie), Jack Egan (Bill), "Skeets" Gallagher (Red Miller), Joseph Smiley (Rankin), Bradley Barker (Eagle).

PARAMOUNT

1927   *Running Wild* (68 minutes).
Director: Gregory LaCava. Adapation by Roy Briant from an original LaCava story. Screenplay: Roy Briant. Cast: W.C. Fields (Elmer Finch), Mary Brian (Elizabeth), Claud Buchanan (Jerry Harvey), Marie Shotwell (Mrs. Finch), Barney Raskle (Junior), Frederick Burton (Mr. Harvey), J. Moy Bennett (Mr. Johnson), Frank Evens (Amos Barker), Ed Roseman (Arvo, the hypnotist), Tom Madden (truck driver), Rex (himself).

Two Flaming Youths (55 minutes).
Director: John Waters. Based upon an original Percy Heath story. Screenplay: Percy Heath and Donald Davis. Cast: W.C. Fields (Gabby Gilfoil), Chester Conklin (Sheriff Ben Holden), Mary Brian (Mary Gilfoil), Jack Luden (Tony Holden), George Irving (Simeon Trott), Cissy Fitzgerald (Madge Malarkey), Jimmie Quinn (Slippery Sawtelle).

PARAMOUNT (distributor, Christie Studio produced)

1928   *Tillie's Punctured Romance* (57 minutes).
Director: Edward Sutherland. Based on characters from an earlier (1914) film of the same title. Screenplay: Monte Brice and Keene Thompson. Cast: W.C. Fields (ringmaster), Louise Fazenda (Tillie), Chester Conklin (circus owner), Mack Swain (Tillie's father), Doris Hill (heroine), Grant Withers (hero), Tom Kennedy (property man), Babe London (strong woman), Billy Platt (midget), and Kalla Pasha, Mickey Bennett, Mike Rafetto, Baron von Dobeneck.

PARAMOUNT

1928   *Fools for Luck* (60 minutes).
Director: Charles F. Reisner. Screenplay: J. Walter Ruben. Cast: W.C.

Fields (Richard Whitehead), Chester Conklin (Samuel Hunter), Sally Blane (Louise Hunter), Jack Luden (Ray Caldwell), Mary Alden (Mrs. Hunter), Arthur Housman (Charles Grogan), Robert Dudley (Jim Simpson), Martha Mattox (Mrs. Simpson).

RKO (distributor, a Radio Pictures Production)

1930   *The Golf Specialist* (2 reels).
Director: Monte Brice. Fields's first sound film, a short subject. Story focus is from Fields's copyrighted stage routine "An Episode on the Links."

WARNER BROTHERS

1931   *Her Majesty Love* (75 minutes).
Director: William Dieterle. Fields's first sound feature. Based upon an original story by R. Berbrauer and R. Oesterreicher. Screenplay: Robert Lord and Arthur Caesar. Dialogue: Henry Blanke and Joseph Jackson. Cast: Marilyn Miller (Lia Toerrek), Ben Lyon (Fred von Wellington), W.C. Fields (Lia's father), Ford Sterling (Otmar), Leon Errol (Baron von Schwarzdorf), Chester Conklin (Emil), Harry Stubbs (Hanneman), Maude Eburne (Aunt Harriette), Harry Holman (Reisenfold), Ruth Hall (factory secretary), William Irving ("Third" Man), Mae Madison (Fred's sister), and Clarence Wilson, Virginia Sale.

PARAMOUNT

1932   *Million Dollar Legs* (64 minutes).
Director: Edward Cline. Based upon a story by Joseph L. Mankiewicz. Screenplay: Henry Myers and Nick Barrows. Cast: Jack Oakie (Mig Tweeny), W.C. Fields (the president), Andy Clyde (major-domo), Lyda Roberti (Mata Machree), Susan Fleming (Angela), Ben Turpin (mysterious man), Hugh Herbert (sectretary of treasury), George Barbier (Mr. Baldwin), Dickie Moore (Willie, Angela's brother), Billy Gilbert (secretary of the interior), Vernon Dent (secretary of agriculture), Teddy Hart (secretary of war), John Sinclair (secretary of labor), Sam Adams (secretary of state), Irving Bacon (secretary of the navy), Ben Taggart (ship's captain), Hank Mann (customs inspector), Chick Collins (jumper), Sid Saylor (starter at the games).

*If I Had a Million** (88 minutes, many-segmented feature).
Director (Fields episode): Norman Taurog. Based upon a story by Robert D. Andrews. Allison Skipworth is also featured in the Fields episode. Other segment cast members include: Gary Cooper, George Raft, Charles Laughton, Jack Oakie, Charles Ruggles, Mary Boland. (The short subject: same title.)

PARAMOUNT (distributor, Mack Sennett produced)

1932   *The Dentist* (20 minutes).
Director: Leslie Pearce. Adapted from Fields's multicopyrighted "An Episode at the Dentist's." Screenplay: W.C. Fields. Cast includes: W.C. Fields (dentist), Babe Kane (daughter), Elise Cavanna (patient in controversial scene), Bud Jamison (golfing partner), Bobby Dunn (Fields's caddy). End-of-the-year release; *New York Times* and *Variety* reviews appear in January 1933.

1933   *The Fatal Glass of Beer* (21 minutes).
Director: Clyde Bruckman. Adapted from Fields's copyrighted screenplay "Stolen Bonds." Screenplay: W.C. Fields. Cast: W.C. Fields (northwoods trapper), Rosemary Theby (Fields's wife), George Chandler (their son), Richard Cramer (mountie).

The Pharmacist (20 minutes).
Director: Arthur Ripley. Adapted, in part, from the drugstore segment of J.P. McEvoy's *The Comic Supplement*. Screenplay: W.C. Fields. Cast includes: W.C. Fields (pharmacist), Babe Kane (youngest daughter), Elise Cavanna (his wife), Grady Sutton (Kane's boyfriend), Lorena Carr (oldest daughter).

WARNER BROTHERS

1933   *Hip Action* (1 reel, Number 3 in the Bobby Jones *How to Break 90* series).
Director: George Marshall. Cast: Bobby Jones, W.C. Fields, Warner Oland, William B. Davidson.

PARAMOUNT

1933   *International House* (70 minutes).
Director: Edward Sutherland. Based upon a story by Lou Heifetz and Neil Brant. Screenplay: Francis Martin and Walter DeLeon. Small-car comedy material draws, in part, from Fields's small-car stage material, such as the copyrighted "Midget Car." Cast: Peggy Hopkins Joyce (herself), W.C. Fields (Professor Quail), Stuart Erwin (Tommy Nash), Sari Maritza (Carol Fortescue), George Burns (Doctor Burns), Gracie Allen (Nurse Allen), Bela Lugosi (General Petronovich), Edmund Breese (Doctor Wong), Lumsden Hare (Sir Mortimer Fortescue), Franklin Pangborn (hotel manager), Harrison Greene (Herr von Baden), Henry Sedley (Serge Borsky), James Wong (Inspector Sun), and Sterling Holloway, Rudy Vallee, Colonel Stoopnagle and Budd, Cab Calloway and his orchestra, Baby Rose Marie, Ernest Wood, Edwin Stanley, Clem Beauchamp, Normal Ainslee, Louis Vincenot, Bo-Ling, Etta Lee, Bo-Ching, Lona Andre.

PARAMOUNT (distributor, Mack Sennett produced)

1933   *The Barber-Shop* (21 minutes).
Director: Arthur Ripley. Screenplay: W.C. Fields. Cast includes: W.C. Fields (Cornelius O'Hare, barber), Elise Cavanna (his wife).

PARAMOUNT

1933   *Tillie and Gus* (58 minutes).
Director: Francis Martin. Based upon an original story by Rupert Hughes.
Screenplay: Walter DeLeon and Francis Martin. Cast: W.C. Fields
(Augustus Winterbottom), Alison Skipworth (Tillie Winterbottom), Baby
LeRoy (the "king"), Jacqueline Wells (Mary Sheridan), Clifford Jones
(Tom Sheridan), Clarence Wilson (Phineas Pratt), George Barbier
(Captain Fogg), Barton MacLane (Commissioner McLennan), Edgar
Kennedy (judge), Robert McKenzie (defense attorney), Ivan Linow (the
Swede), Master Williams (High-Card Harrington).

Alice in Wonderland (90 minutes).
Director: Norman McLeod. Based upon original material by Lewis Carroll.
Screenplay: Joseph L. Mankiewicz and William Cameron Menzies. Cast:
Charlotte Henry (Alice), Richard Arlen (Cheshire Cat), Roscoe Ates (Fish),
William Austin (Gryphon), Gary Cooper (White Knight), Jack Duffy (Leg
of Mutton), Leon Errol (Uncle Gilbert), Louise Fazenda (White Queen),
W.C. Fields (Humpty Dumpty), Alec B. Francis (King of Hearts), Skeets
Gallagher (White Rabbit), Cary Grant (Mock Turtle), Lillian Harmer
(cook), Raymond Hatton (Mouse), Sterling Holloway (Frog), Edward
Everett Horton (Mad Hatter), Roscoe Karns (Tweedledee), Baby LeRoy
(Joker), Lucien Littlefield (Father William's son), Mae Marsh (Sheep),
Polly Moran (Dodo Bird), Jack Oakie (Tweedledum), Edna May Oliver
(Red Queen), George Ovey (Plum Pudding), Mae Robson (Queen of
Hearts), Charlie Ruggles (March Hare), Jackie Searle (Dormouse), Alison
Skipworth (Duchess), Ned Sparks (Caterpillar).

1934   *Six of a Kind* (65 minutes).
Director: Leo McCarey. Based upon an original story by Keene Thompson
and Douglas MacLean. Screenplay: Walter DeLeon and Harry Ruskin.
Cast: Charlie Ruggles (J. Pinkham Whinney), Mary Boland (Flora
Whinney), W.C. Fields (Sheriff John Hoxley), George Burns (George
Edward), Gracie Allen (Gracie DeVore), Alison Skipworth (Mrs. K.
Rumford), Bradley Page (Ferguson), Grace Bradley (Trixie), William J.
Kelly (Gillette), James Burke (Sparks), Dick Rush (Steele), Walter Long
(Butch), Leo Willis (Mike), Lew Kelly (Joe), Alp P. James (Doctor Busby).

1934   *You're Telling Me** (66 minutes, remake of *So's Your Old Man*).
Director: Earle Kenton. Based upon a Julian Street story. Screenplay:
Walter DeLeon and Paul M. Jones. Dialogue: J.P. McEvoy. Cast: W.C.
Fields (Sam Bisbee), Joan Marsh (Pauline Bisbee), Larry "Buster" Crabbe
(Bob Murchison), Adrienne Ames (Princess Lescaboura), Louise Carter
(Mrs. Bessie Bisbee), Kathleen Howard (Mrs. Murchison), James B.
"Pop" Kenton (Doc Beebe), Robert McKenzie (Charlie Bogle), George
Irving (president of tire company), Jerry Stewart (Frobisher), Dell
Henderson (mayor), Nora Cecil (Mrs. Price), George MacQuarrie
(Crabbe), John M. Sullivan (Gray), and others, including Vernon Dent,

Tammany Young, and Elise Cavanna. (The golf episode is available as a short subject entitled *Much Ado about Golf*.)

*The Old-Fashioned Way** (66 minutes, essentially loose remake of *Two Flaming Youths*).
Director: William Beaudine. Adapted from original story by Charles Bogle (W.C. Fields). Screenplay: Garnett Weston and Jack Cunningham. Cast: W.C. Fields (The Great McGonigle), Joe Morrison (Wally Livingston), Judith Allen (Betty McGonigle), Jan Duggan (Cleopatra Pepperday), Nora Cecil (Mrs. Wendelschaffer), Baby Leroy (Albert Wendelschaffer), Jack Mulhall (Dick Bronson), Joe Mills (Charles Lowell), Samuel Ethridge (Bartley Neuville), Emma Ray (Mother Mack), Ruth Marion, and others, including Tammany Young and Lew Kelly. (The short subject: *The Great McGonigle*, featuring Fields juggling.)

Mrs. Wiggs of the Cabbage Patch (80 minutes).
Director: Norman Taurog. Drawn from the frequently adapted novel and play by Alice Hegan Rice and Anne Crowford Flexner. Screenplay: William Slavens McNutt and Jane Storm. Cast: Pauline Lord (Mrs. Wiggs), W.C. Fields (Mr. Stubbins), Zasu Pitts (Miss Hazy), Evalyn Venable (Lucy Olcott), Kent Taylor (Bob Redding), Charles Middleton (Bagby), Donald Meek (Mr. Wiggs), Jimmy Butler (Bill Wiggs), Edith Fellows (Australia Wiggs), Carmencita Johnson (Asia Wiggs), Virginia Weidler (Europena Wiggs).

PARAMOUNT (distributor, William LeBaron produced)

*It's a Gift** (73 minutes, remake of *It's the Old Army Game*).
Director: Normal McLeod. Based upon an original story by Charles Bogle (W.C. Fields, see especially his copyrighted stage routine "The Steeping Porch" and the multicopyrighted "The Family Ford") and adapted from J.P. McEvoy's musical comedy revue *The Comic Supplement*. Cast: W.C. Fields (Harold Bissonette), Kathleen Howard (Amelia Bissonette), Jean Rouverol (Mildred Bissonette), Julian Madison (John Durston), Tom Bupp (Norman Bissonette), Baby LeRoy (Baby Dunk), Tammany Young (Everett Ricks) Morgan Wallace (Jasper Fitchmueller), Charles Sellon (Mr. Muckle), Josephine Whittell (Mrs. Dunk), Diana Lewis (Miss Dunk). (The short subjects: *The Big Thumb,* including encounters with both a blind man and Baby LeRoy, and *California Bound*.)

METRO-GOLDWYN-MAYER

1935   *David Copperfield* (133 minutes).
Director: George Cukor. Adapted by Hugh Walpole from the novel by Charles Dickens. Screenplay: Howard Estabrook. Cast: W.C. Fields (Micawber), Lionel Barrymore (Dan

Peggotty), Maureen O'Sullivan (Dora), Madge Evans (Agnes Wickfield), Edna May Oliver (Aunt Betsy), Lewis Stone (Mr. Wickfield), Frank Lawton (David, the man), Freddie Bartholomew (David, the boy), Elizabeth Allan (Mrs. Clara Copperfield), Roland Young (Uriah Heep), Basil Rathbone (Mr. Murdstone), Elsa Lanchester (Clickett), Jean Cadell (Mrs.' Micawber), Jessie Ralph (Nurse Peggotty), Lennox Pawle (Mr. Dick), Violet Kemple-Cooper (Jane Murdstone), Una O'Connor (Mrs. Gummidge), John Buckler (Ham), Hugh Williams (Steerforth), Ivan Simpson (Limmiter), Herbert Mundin (Barkis), Fay Chaldecott (Little Em'ly, the child), Marilyn Knowlden (Agnes, the child), Florine McKinney (Little Em'ly, the woman), Harry Beresford (Dr. Chillip), Mable Colcord (Mary Ann), Hugh Wapole (vicar).

PARAMOUNT

1935   *Mississippi* (75 minutes).
Director: Edward A. Sutherland. Adapted by Herbert Fields and Claude Binyon from a Booth Tarkington story. Screenplay: Francis Martin and Jack Cunningham. Cast: Bing Crosby (Tom Grayson), W.C. Fields (Commodore Jackson), Joan Bennett (Lucy Rumford), Gail Patrick (Elvira Rumford), Queenie Smith (Alabam'), Claude Gillingwater, Sr. (General Rumford), John Miljan (Major Patterson), Jan Duggan (an admirer of the commodore), Fred Kohler, Sr. (Captain Blackie), Edward Pawley (Joe Patterson), Paul Hurst (Hefty), Theresa Maxwell Conover (Miss Markham), Five Cabin Kids (Cabin Kids).

The Man on the Flying Trapeze (65 minutes, loose remake of *Running Wild*).
Director: Clyde Bruckman. Based on a story by Charles Bogle (W.C. Fields) and Sam Hardy. Screenplay: Ray Harris, Sam Hardy, Jack Cunningham, Bobby Vernon. Cast: W.C. Fields (Ambrose Wolfinger), Mary Brian (Hope Wolfinger), Kathleen Howard (Leona Wolfinger), Grady Sutton (Claude Bensinger), Vera Lewis (Mrs. Bensinger), Lucien Littlefield (Mr. Peabody), Oscar Apfel (President Malloy), Lew Kelly (Adolph Berg), Tammany Young ("Willie," the weasel), Walter Brennan ("Legs" Garnett), Edward Gargan (patrolman number one), James Burke (patrolman number two), and others, including Carlotta Monti (Ambrose's secretary), Harry Ekezian (a featured wrestler), and Tor Johnson (a featured wrestler).

1936   *Poppy* (75 minutes, loose remake of *Sally of the Sawdust,* but much closer to original Dorothy Donnelly play).
Director: A Edward Sutherland. Screenplay: Waldemar Young

and Virginia Van Upp. Cast: W.C. Fields (Professor Eustace McGargle), Rochelle Hudson (Poppy), Richard Cromwell (Billy Farnsworth), Catherine Doucet (Countess Maggie Tubbs DePuizzi), Lynne Overman (Attorney Whiffen), Granville Bates (Mayor Farnsworth), Maude Eburne (Sarah Tucker), Bill Wolfe (Egmont), Adrian Morris (Constable Bowman), Rosalind Keith (Frances Parker), and others, including Ralph M. Remley and Tammany Young.

1938   *The Big Broadcast of 1938* (97 minutes).
Director: Mitchell Leisen. Based on an original story by Frederick Hazlitt Brennan and adapted by Howard Lindsay and Russel Crouse. Screenplay: Walter DeLeon, Francis Martin, and Ken Englund. Cast: W.C. Fields (T. Frothingell Bellows/S.B. Bellows), Martha Raye (Martha Bellows), Dorothy Lamour (Dorothy Wyndham), Shirley Ross (Cleo Fielding), Lynne Overman (Scoop McPhail), Bob Hope (Buzz Fielding), Ben Blue (Mike), Lief Erikson (Bob Hayes), Grace Bradley (Grace Fielding), Rufe Davis (Turnkey), Patricia Wilder (Honey Chile), Lionel Pape (Lord Droopy), Dorothy Howe (Joan Fielding), Russell Hicks (Captain Stafford), and Billy Daniels, Michael Brooks, Jack Hubbard, Leonid Kinsky, Stanley King, Rex Moore, Bernard Punsley, Don Marion, Irving Bacon, Wally Maher, Rebecca Wassem, James Craig, Kristen Flagstad, Tito Guizar, and Shep Fields and his Rippling Rhythm Orchestra.

UNIVERSAL

1939   *You Can't Cheat an Honest Man** (76 minutes).
Director: George Marshall (officially, though an uncredited Edward Cline worked with Fields). Based on an original story by Charles Bogle (W.C. Fields). Screenplay: George Marion, Jr., Richard Mack, and Everett Freeman. Cast: W.C. Fields (Larson E. Whipsnade), Edgar Bergen (himself), Charlie McCarthy (himself), Constance Moore (Vicky Whipsnade), John Arledge (Phineas Whipsnade), James Bush (Roger Bel-Goodie), Thurston Hall (Mr. Bel-Goodie), Mary Forbes (Mrs. Bel-Goodie), Edward Brophy (Corbett), Arthur Hohl (Burr), Princess Baba (herself), Blacaman (himself), Eddie Anderson (Cheerful), and others, including Grady Suttom and an early appearance by Bergen's Mortimer Snerd. (The short subject: *Circus Slickers*.)

1940   *My Little Chickadee* (83 minutes).
Director: Edward Cline. Original screenplay: Mae West and W.C. Fields. (Recently, *Chickadee* Executive Producer Lester Cowan stated the plot was drawn from Ferenc Molnar's *The*

Guardsman.) Cast: W.C. Fields (Cuthbert J. Twillie), Mae West (Flower Belle Lee), Joseph Calleia (Jeff Badger/masked bandit), Dick Foran (Wayne Carter), Ruth Donnelly (Aunt Lou), Margaret Hamilton (Mrs. Gideon), Donald Meek (Budge), Fuzzy Knight (Cousin Zeb), Willard Robertson (Uncle John), George Moran (Clarence), Jackie Searle (boy), Fay Adler (Mrs. "Pygmy" Allen), with Gene Austin.

The Bank Dick* (74 minutes).
Director: Edward Cline. Original story and screenplay: W.C. Fields. Cast: W.C. Fields (Egbert Sousé), Cora Witherspoon (Agatha Sousé) Una Merkel (Myrtle Sousé), Evelyn Del Rio (Elsie Mae Adele Brunch Sousé) Jessie Ralph (Mrs. Hermisillo Brunch), Franklin Pangborn (J. Pinkerton Snoopington), Shemp Howard (Joe Guelpe), Richard Purcell (Mackley Q. Greene), Grady Sutton (Og Oggilby), Russell Hicks (J. Frothingham Waterbury), Pierre Watkins (Mr. Skinner), Al Hill (Filthy McNasty), George Moran (Cozy Cochran), Bill Wolfe (Otis), Jack Norton (A. Pismo Clam), Pat West (assistant director), Reed Hadley (François), Heather Wilde (Miss Plupp), Harlan Briggs (Doctor Stall), Bill Alston (Mr. Cheek). (The short subject: The Great Chase.)

1941   Never Give a Sucker an Even Break* (70 minutes).
Director: Edward Cline. Fields's last starring feature. Based on an original story by Otis Criblecoblis (W.C. Fields). Screenplay: John T. Neville and Prescott Chaplin. Cast: W.C. Fields (The Great Man), Gloria Jean (his niece), Leon Errol (his rival), Billy Lenhart (Butch), Kenneth Brown (Buddy), Margaret Dumont (Mrs. Hemogloben), Susan Miller (Ouliotta Hemogloben), Franklin Pangborn (the producer), Mona Barrie (the producer's wife), Charles Lang (Peter Carson, a young engineer), Anne Nagel (Madame Gorgeous), Nell O'Day (salesgirl), Irving Bacon (soda jerk), Jody Gilbert (waitress), Minerva Urecal (cleaning woman), Emmett Vogan (engineer), Carlotta Monti (receptionist). (The short subject: Hurry! Hurry!)

TWENTIETH CENTURY FOX (distributor, Boris Morros and S.P. Eagle—Sam Spiegel produced)

1942   Tales of Manhattan (118 minutes, many-segmented feature. In order to reduce running time the Fields episode was cut before the film was released).
The Fields segment had also featured Margaret Dumont.

UNIVERSAL (distributor, Charles K. Feldman Group Productions)

1944   *Follow the Boys** (118 minutes, Fields is one of many guest stars who perform for the in-film troops).
Director: Eddie Sutherland. Original screenplay: Lou Breslow and Gertrude Purcell. Fields does his classic pool routine, with Bill Wolf making an appearance during the action. Other guest stars include: Jeanette MacDonald, Orson Welles, Mercury Wonder Show, Marlene Dietrich, Dinah Shore, Donald O'Connor. (The short subject: *The Odd Ball.*)

UNITED ARTISTS (distributor, Charles R. Rogers produced)

1944   *Song of the Open Road* (93 minutes, Fields is one of several guest stars who perform).
Director: S. Sylvan Simon. Based on an unpublished story by Irving Phillips and Edward Verdier. Screenplay: Albert Mannheimer. (Fields was able to rekindle his feud with Edgar Bergen's Charlie McCarthy, who brought along his own dummy—Charlie McCarthy, Jr.)

UNITED ARTISTS (distributor, Andrew L. Stone produced)

1944   *Sensations of 1945** (87 minutes, Fields is one of several guests who perform).
Director: Andrew L. Stone. Based on an original story by Frederick Jackson and Andrew Stone. Screenplay: Dorothy Bennett. Fields does a railroad compartment sketch which includes an appearance by Bill Wolf. (The short subject: *One Too Many.*)

DISCOGRAPHY

The starting point for this section was the collections of the Library of Congress and the New York Public Library. It has been expanded with titles from the author's collection, as well as from collections of friends and colleagues. Because Fields material has been, and continues to be, released in a number of packaging arrangements, this alphabetized list does not purport to be complete and final; but with the Library of Congress-New York Public Library foundation, and with the other additions, the following discography effectively illustrates the ongoing interest in Fields.

The Best of W.C. Fields. 1976 (Columbia CG 34144, two discs).

Cecil B. De Mille Presents W.C. Fields in Poppy. 1973 (Mark 56 Records 595).

The Charlie McCarthy Show: How W.C. Got the Sheriff's Badge. 1976 (American Forces Radio and Television Service RU 11-76, 2B).

The Further Adventures of Larson E. Whipsnade and Other Taradiddles. 1974 (Columbia KC 33240).

The Great Radio Feuds. 1974 (Columbia KC 33241).

The Great Stars of Vaudeville. (Columbia Special Produces XSV 222901). Contains Fields's "Temperance Lecture."

Mae West & W.C. Fields: Side by Side. (Harmony, A Produce of Columbia Records HS 11405).

Poppy. 1974 (Columbia KC 33253).

Rich Little as W.C. Fields for President. 1972 (Caedmon TC 9101).

Salute to Edgar Bergen, Charlie McCarthy, and W.C. Fields. 1978 (American Forces Radio and Television Service RU 35-8, 58).

Salute to W.C. Fields. 1978 (American Forces Radio and Television Service RU 38-7, 2B).

Temperance Lecture: The Day I Drank a Glass of Water. 1950s (Jay Records 2001).

W.C. Fields. 1968 (Decca DL 79164).

W.C. Fields. 1973 (Mark 56 Records 571).

W.C. Fields, 1879 [*sic*]*-1946—Sound Recordings.* 1975 (Radiola MR 1049).

W.C. Fields on Radio: With Edgar Bergen & Charlie McCarthy. 1969 (Columbia CS 9890).

W.C. Fields: The Original Voice Tracks from His Greatest Movies. 1968 (Decca DL 79164).

FIELDS AND STREAM
by
Wes D. Gehring

W.C. Fields country is
Where all streams are
90 proof and double vision
Provides plenty for all.

W.C. Fields country is
Where folks like their
Children well done, if
They're done at all.

W.C. Fields country is
Where the national bird
Is the little chickadee and
The national "anthem" Godfrey Daniel.

W.C. Fields country is
Where the harvest is
Always hypocrites, and
Truth wears a potato nose.

INDEX

About the Author

WES D. GEHRING is Associate Professor of Film at Ball State University. He is the author of *Charlie Chaplin: A Bio-Bibliography* (Greenwood Press, 1983), *Leo McCarey and the Comic Anti-Hero in American Film* and monographs on screwball comedy and Charlie Chaplin. His articles have appeared in numerous periodicals.

Recent Titles in
Popular Culture Bio-Bibliographies: A Reference Series
Series Editor: M. Thomas Inge

Crockett: A Bio-Bibliography
Richard Boyd Hauck

Knute Rockne: A Bio-Bibliography
Michael R. Steele

John Henry: A Bio-Bibliography
Brett Williams

Charlie Chaplin: A Bio-Bibliography
Wes D. Gehring

Hank Williams: A Bio-Bibliography
George William Koon

Will Rogers: A Bio-Bibliography
Peter C. Rollins

Billy the Kid: A Bio-Bibliography
Jon Tuska

Errol Flynn: A Bio-Bibliography
Peter Valenti